D0031657

Presented to

**The County Free Library**

by

Dr. Hildebrand

# BUCK LEONARD
## The Black Lou Gehrig

# BUCK LEONARD
# The Black Lou Gehrig

*The Hall of Famer's Story in His Own Words*

## Buck Leonard with James A. Riley

Carroll & Graf Publishers, Inc.
New York

First Carroll & Graf edition 1995

Carroll & Graf Publishers, Inc.
260 Fifth Avenue
New York, NY 10001

Library of Congress Cataloging-in-Publication Data
Leonard, Buck, 1907–
    Buck Leonard : the black Lou Gehrig / Buck Leonard with James
A. Riley. — 1st Carroll & Graf ed.
        p.    cm.
    ISBN 0-7867-0119-6 : $20.00 ($28.00 Can.)
    1. Leonard, Buck, 1907–    . 2. Baseball players—United
States—Biography.   3. Afro-American baseball players—Biography.
I. Riley, James A.   II. Title.
GV863.L45A3   1995
796...357'092—dc20
[B]                                                              94-26563
                                                                    CIP

Manufactured in the United States of America

This book is dedicated to the leading ladies in our lives.

To  Sarah
—B.L.

To  Dottie
—J. R.

# CONTENTS

# INTRODUCTION

I first met Buck Leonard in 1981. Over the years, I have visited often in his Rocky Mount, North Carolina, home, and we have shared company, conversation, and experiences from St. Petersburg, Florida, to Cooperstown, New York, and numerous points in between. During the intervening years, I came to know him not only as a great ballplayer but also as a friend.

The word that best describes Buck Leonard is *class,* and the word that best describes my feelings toward him is *respect.* Not only as a great baseball player, but also as a man. His strong Christian beliefs are part of his life and are evident in his character. He lives by his own personal credo: "If I can't do something to help somebody, I won't do anything to hurt him."

His life is an example of the American Dream coming true. From a fatherless eleven-year-old boy shining shoes to help support his family, Buck persevered to become one of the greatest baseball players of his generation, and now enjoys the respect and admiration of the entire country.

Denied the opportunity to play in the major leagues because of his color, he was forced by social circumstance to spend his entire baseball career in the shadows of the Negro Leagues. But the relatively obscure baseball diamonds of black baseball served simultaneously as a field of dreams and as a proving ground. There, men like Buck Leonard dreamed of playing in the major leagues and proved their ability to perform at a major-league level, thus nudging the major leagues' door ajar and paving the way for Jackie Robinson to step through when change was in season.

People attempted to affect that change in different ways. Some tried to kick the door down. Others lived their life in such a way as to make people *want* to open the door. While the latter way may have taken longer, it had a more lasting influence. The changes in our national pastime and in our country were made possible and permanent by men like Buck Leonard. The world is a better place for him having passed through. Virtue has its own rewards, but sometimes the world presents additional rewards in recognition of this attribute. So it was with Buck Leonard.

During his seventeen seasons with the Homestead Grays, the team won nine consecutive pennants, and he paired with the legendary Josh Gibson to form a power tandem that earned them designation as the black Lou Gehrig and Babe Ruth. But even as he gained acclaim in the invisible sports world of black America, he never even dared dream that one day he would be enshrined alongside Ruth and Gehrig among the immortals in the Baseball Hall of Fame.

However, on the proudest day of his life, that is exactly what happened. A dream too remote from reality even to be dreamed did indeed come true. On August 7, 1972, Buck Leonard took his rightful place in the marbled halls when he was inducted into the National Baseball Hall of Fame at Cooperstown, New York.

Today Buck Leonard still makes his home in the town where he was born and reared, Rocky Mount, North Carolina, and as one of the last living legends of black baseball, he is a rare reservoir of baseball lore from the Negro Leagues. He personifies the image of a kindly grandfather, and you almost expect to see a group of grandchildren clamoring to sit in his lap to be regaled by stories of days that used to be, but are no more, and will never be again.

But there are no grandchildren waiting for a place at his knee to hear his stories. So it is for us to serve as surrogates to be enthralled as he tells about a segment of our country's lore that needs to be remembered because it should not be forgotten. No one else walked in his shoes, and no one else saw the world through his eyes. Only he can tell this story. This is Buck Leonard's story in *his own words*.

James A. Riley
August 10, 1993

# Part I

# The Early Years (1907–33)

# Chapter 1

## Roots (1907–32)

*Train up a child in the way he should go and when
he is old, he will not depart from it.*
—*Proverbs 22:6*

I was born September 8, 1907, in Rocky Mount, North Carolina,
and I've lived here all of my life. This is where Jim Thorpe played
his first professional baseball game, which later caused him to have
to give back all the medals that he had won in the Olympics. Of
course, I don't remember that because I was only two years old when
it happened, but I *do* remember people talking about it when I was
growing up. The ballpark where he played was right behind my
house on Raleigh Road, and years later I played on the same field.

My family roots are here in the Rocky Mount area. My
grandmomma, Lena Sesson, lived right here in Rocky Mount, and
my granddaddy, Spence Leonard, lived up in Castalia, North Carolina. That's about thirty miles from here. My father's name was
John Leonard, and he was a railroad fireman. He had to travel
from Rocky Mount to Washington and back, but he didn't have
to stay away from home overnight. My mother's maiden name
was Emma Sesson. She didn't work outside the home because
raising a family was a full-time job.

I had three sisters and two brothers. I was the oldest boy, but I had two sisters older than I was. Their names were Fannie and Willie. I was next in line, and then came my brothers Herman and Charlie. My youngest sister's name was Lena, and she was the baby of the family. My youngest brother, Charlie, was the one who gave me my nickname. My real name was Walter, but my parents called me "Buddy." My little brother couldn't say "Buddy" so he called me "Bucky," and that was shortened to "Buck" when I got older.

My parents were both active in the church, and we were raised in a Christian home. We had a family Bible, and my mother used to get us around and read to us in the evening. She also went to church about every Sunday and took us with her. At that time people went to the church closest to their home, and I started out in a Methodist church. But my parents were Baptists, and when we children got large enough, we went to the Baptist church on the other side of town.

I was about ten years old when I went there, and Reverend John Martin was the main preacher. They had a mourner's bench at the front of the church for people who wanted to be prayed for. I used to go up there about every Sunday morning and sit on the "button." Some people called it the "action seat." I went up there two or three years before I joined the church and was baptized. We had to be baptized down to the falls at Tar River. We used to throw some clothes on that we didn't mind getting wet in, and ride to the river in an automobile and ride back afterward. It was quite a celebration. All of us children joined down there.

We grew up in a part of town called Little Raleigh. It was a black neighborhood on the west side of town. Most of the people who lived in that section worked at the Atlantic Coastline Railroad Shop. That's where I worked later on. Almost everybody had a garden and raised collards, sweet potatoes, turnip salad, and things like that. At that time you could have chickens in the yards in town, so we had chickens and ducks and geese and all those kind of animals. You could also have hogs near the city limits, and we had two or three hogs in our pen out in the rural section, about three blocks from our house.

I started at Lincoln Elementary School in 1913. The first day they wouldn't let me write left-handed and changed me over. That's why I signed autographs right-handed until I had a stroke in 1986. Then I had to learn to write left-handed. I've always swung a bat left-handed because it just came natural that way, and I do everything else left-handed, too.

Back then I had a billy goat and when I would come home from school in the afternoon, I would hitch up my billy goat to a cart and go over into the white section of town and get slops for the hogs. When I wasn't busy doing that, I used to go down to the railroad tracks and hit rocks with a broom handle. Sometimes I did that in my backyard, too, pretending I was playing baseball.

I was about seven years old when I first got interested in base-ball. They had a white team in Rocky Mount that was in the Class B Virginia League. Their ballpark was not too far from my home, and ever since I was big enough, I would go over there and peep through the cracks or stand on boxes and look over the fence to watch them play. That's how we found out how to play baseball, by looking at them play.

The policemen used to get after us for what we were doing and that's when I got in trouble with the law. They came out there one evening and arrested everybody. We had to go to court and the judge told us we were trespassing on private property. Then about a year later, they built a black baseball park near my home and I could go to that one. Rocky Mount had a black semipro team that played all the local teams around the area I was out there every time they played. I was "keeping bats" at the black ballpark, but I had to look through the fence at the white ballpark.

Along about that time, the Lincoln Giants used to come through town playing exhibitions at the colored park against our local col-ored team. I was impressed with what they called "shadow base-ball." They'd play without a baseball. The fellow who was hitting around the infield practice would throw the ball up like he was hitting it and the third baseman came in like he was going to field it and throw it to first base. And the first baseman would take the ball and throw it back to home plate and the catcher would throw it to second base. But they didn't have a ball. They were just going through the motions.

That was about 1914, and the Lincoln Giants had the best team in the country. Dick Redding and Smokey Joe Williams were the big pitchers for them at that time. There were some other good black teams around, too. The Homestead Grays were in bloom, and the Chicago American Giants, the Philadelphia Giants, and the Baltimore Black Sox also had a team sometime around then.

Back then, too, A. G. Allen and Silas Green and all the other minstrel shows were going around the country, and most of them had a baseball team. They would come in and play baseball against the local semipro team in the afternoon and have their show at night.

They would start off with black comedians telling jokes and singing. Then the girls would come out on the stage and start dancing. Next they had a medicine show, and that was when the medicine doctor started selling his medicine that was good for everything. That old-time snake oil stuff. Whatever was wrong with you, his medicine was good for it.

The thing would always wind up with him selling medicine, and the comedians would go around through the crowd delivering the medicine. That was all one package, with the baseball team, the entertainment, and the medicine show. They wanted to take all of our money. Not that we had very much to begin with. I reckon we were poor, but I didn't know anything different. Everybody I knew was just like me.

My daddy died when I was eleven years old. That was when the influenza was bad in 1919, and when he died our main source of income was cut off. After the funeral, I remember my momma telling us that we were going to have to help out. She told me that as soon as I got out of school I was going to have to get a job to help support the family. And I understood that, since I was the oldest boy.

They had a colored hosiery mill and a white hosiery mill, and my oldest sister, Fannie, stopped school and went to work at the colored hosiery mill. The next year I started working at the same mill. When I went to work in the mill, my sister Willie went to Kittrell College in Raleigh.

We didn't know anything about making stockings, but they taught us. They taught me how to run what they called a ''ribber'' to make the leg of the stocking, and taught my sister how to make the foot of the stocking. They had some little ones to make the toe of the stocking, so it took three people to make one stocking.

The kind of stockings we made were the rib stockings that girls and boys were wearing back then. I worked there until May of 1921, when they closed the mill and never reopened it. That's when I went to the railroad station and started shining shoes. I was still going to school then, and working in the afternoon because we had to have some kind of income.

At that time, they didn't have high school in black schools in Rocky Mount, and we had to go off to some college to finish high school. That's the way most of us did it. We didn't expect anything else. You always had to remember that you were black, and it stayed on your mind all the time. There were certain places you couldn't go and things you couldn't do.

I went to the eighth grade and was supposed to go off to complete high school, but I didn't leave Rocky Mount when I came out of school. I was still shining shoes at the railroad station to help support my family. At that time they had a lot of trains running and we had bootblacks at the railroad station. We had one stand for whites and one stand for colored, and about four boys were working there shining shoes. Of course, we shined on both the white side and the black side. I worked there for about two years and then went to work at the Atlantic Coastline Railroad Shop when I was sixteen.

While I was working at the railroad shop, I saw my first major-league baseball game. The Yankees were going to play in Washington on the Fourth of July. Lou Gehrig was with them, and he was my favorite player. I later patterned myself after Gehrig in batting, fielding, and everything else. I was seventeen years old and went by myself. Since I was working at the railroad shop, I could get a pass to ride from Rocky Mount to Richmond, Virginia, but I had to pay my way from Richmond on to Washington. It was the thrill of my life up to that time.

I worked in the railroad shop nine years and four months. When I first started working there, I worked out in the yard picking up trash for about a year, at twenty-one and a quarter cents an hour. That came to a grand total of one dollar and eighty cents a day.

Then they wanted someone to work in the office, but they

wanted somebody who could read. They found out that I could read, so they sent me to the office to carry papers from one office to the other. I would go to work at seven o'clock in the morning before anyone else got there, and I had to go by the ice house to get about twenty pounds of ice and carry it over to the offices. Then I would chip off some ice and put it in each of the water coolers, and keep them filled with fresh water every day. I also had to sweep up and carry out the trash before the office group came to work at eight-thirty.

Then they would tell me what to do, where to go, who to see, and what to tell him. The telephone system in the shop wasn't so good, and when you picked up the receiver to call from one office to another, you had to wind up the phone. So sometimes I'd have to go to an office and tell a man something because they couldn't get him over the telephone system.

I worked there for a little over a year, and one evening I asked the foreman, E.R. Holliman, if he would give me a helper's job paying fifty-four cents an hour. After about a week he gave me a job down there to the air room working on air cylinders. I worked there seven years, putting brake cylinders on boxcars and cleaning them.

Blacks couldn't belong to the shop union, so we didn't have any job protection. They would have me working a mechanic's job and just pay me as a helper and I didn't have any way to make them pay me more because I couldn't get the union to speak for me. So they had me working on these brake cylinders and I had a laborer helping me where it should have been me helping a mechanic. That went on for seven years. Then the Depression hit and things got bad at the railroad shop.

They took me off from my job and put a white man on there and put me on the helper's job and cut him off. Both of us were colored. I worked there for about a year doing that and then they cut me all the way off. If you had more seniority than someone else, you could ''pull'' him, and it just kept backing up until they backed me out of there the last time.

When I got cut off at the railroad shop on the first of June 1932, I started to hang around the funeral home, working part-time. My future wife was there and, before we were married, we were friends. Whenever they had a funeral, I would drive one of the cars or go out and pick up a body or something like that. But I didn't have a regular job there.

There were two other fellows working there, and every night when we got off, they went by a bootlegger's house to buy a drink. I started going by there with them, drinking bootleg liquor. That's the kind they liked. They'd be carrying me home, but we'd go by there first, and every time when they were buying a drink, they'd ask me if I wanted a drink. So I started letting them pay for a drink for me, and I started tasting it. After a while I started buying a drink when they went by there. Back then, it cost fifty cents. And so I said to myself, "Now I know doggone well I don't like this whiskey and it don't taste good. I'm just going to stop going by there with them. That way I won't have to be refusing anything." So I just quit going with them. My brother Herman really drank, and that might be the reason why I understood his problem.

Anyway, I worked at the funeral home for a few months, and then that's when I started playing professional baseball in the spring of 1933. Up until then, I had only played semipro baseball.

# Chapter 2

## Semipro Star (1921–32)

*I played semipro baseball against Buck Leonard in North Carolina, way back before we ever played in the Negro Leagues. You could put a fastball in a shotgun and you couldn't shoot it by him.*
*—Dave Barnhill, New York Cubans*

I had started playing on the school baseball team when I was about ten years old and still in school. I never played any other sports, only baseball. I would have played football, but my mother wouldn't let me. She didn't say anything about baseball, but I could tell she didn't like it, either. She never did see me play.

I was in the grade school, but I was playing on the team with older boys who were in the upper grades. I started out as a right fielder and went from there to center field. I was too small to make the trips with the school team when I first started playing, but when I was about twelve, they let me go with the team to Smithfield, North Carolina, to play the Johnson County Training School. I was playing in the outfield and a ball was hit over my head and it went under the schoolhouse. When I crawled under there to get the ball, my belt got hung on a nail and I couldn't get loose. They were wondering why I didn't come out, but I was hung up under the schoolhouse. That was the same time when I struck out and cried because I struck out. That was one day I won't forget.

When I came out of school in 1921, I started playing on a city team called the Rocky Mount Elks. It was run by the Elks lodge for young local boys, and I was playing center field. After I got the job at the railroad shop, I played on the Elks team in my spare time. When the Elks stopped running the team, a fellow named J.K. Bullock took over, and we changed the name to the Rocky Mount Black Swans.

After working eight hours at the shop, I would get off from work at three-thirty in the afternoon, and the game would start at four o'clock. I had a bicycle and would ride from the railroad shop to the ballpark and then change clothes right across the street and play a baseball game.

My brother Charlie joined the team after I did. I was about four or five years older than him, and he was still in school. Charlie and I were pretty close. We were closer than my other brother, although Herman was between us in age. All three of us boys played a little bit of baseball together when we were growing up, but Herman didn't play much except around in the neighborhood. He never played on a semipro team like me and Charlie did.

I pitched a little with the team, too, but not enough to amount to anything. I reckon everybody gets the idea sometime that they're a pitcher. I was about fourteen then, and Raymond Stith was the manager. He saw me messing around trying to pitch and he just put me out there on the mound one day. It was odd for a left-hander to pitch at that time, and I didn't do so good. I was wild and I just had a fastball and that's all. I didn't learn to throw a curveball until later. I didn't win that first game, but I pitched two or three other games. I liked the pitching, but I didn't pitch any when I got older.

At that time they still called me Bucky. I learned to hit pretty good and played outfield because I could hit. Later on, when I was about seventeen, I started managing the team. We had a first baseman, a man named McIntyre, who worked in a tobacco factory, and on one of our trips he couldn't go because he couldn't get off from work. So I played first base and sent a pitcher to center field in my place. Then there was another trip and he couldn't go, and I played first base again. When he came back to the team I sent him to center field and I stayed at first base.

That was in 1931, when I started playing regular at first base. One reason why I did that was that when I played first base, I would be close to the umpire for some arguing and I wouldn't have to come all the way in from center field. That's a heck of a reason, but that's how I got started playing first base.

Since I was managing, I did all the booking for the games around here at Rocky Mount. In 1931 we had twenty-three men turn out for the three weeks of spring practice, and they put an advertisement in the *Norfolk Journal and Guide* to have anybody desiring games to write to me. If they wanted a game, I could tell them the name of the agent to contact.

We played High Point, Greensboro, Raleigh, Wilson, Salisbury, Statesville, Durham, Winston-Salem, Tarboro, and Smithfield. All those towns are in North Carolina. And we played Florence, South Carolina, and Richmond, Petersburg, Norfolk, and Newport News in Virginia. And all the other local teams around within a radius of a hundred to a hundred and fifty miles of Rocky Mount. The way we played around here was that if we had any money left after expenses, we would give everybody two or three dollars.

If we were going out of town and going on the road to play I had to get off from the railroad shop and lose a day's work. But my bossman understood how things were and he didn't mind me getting off and going. At that time we didn't play night ball and most of the games were played in the evening.

Sometime later on, Charlie went over to Wilson to play. That's about fifteen miles from Rocky Mount. He was the manager there and tried to talk me into coming over there to play. But I was playing ball here *and* working at the railroad shop, too, so I couldn't go.

But I *did* play some games with Wilson. Bill Bryan was the owner of their team and he used to come over here and get me to play for them against different teams. If they had a game and we didn't have a game, they would come over here and pick me up in a car. They would get to the railroad shop about three o'clock, wait until I got off at three-thirty, and then we'd go to

Wilson and play. Whatever time I got there, that's when the game would start. Usually it started around four o'clock or four-fifteen. I was paid about a dollar a day, but sometimes I got nothing.

Bill Bryan also used to get Dave Barnhill to play for him against some teams. Dave later played with the New York Cubans of the Negro National League, and with the Minneapolis Millers when organized baseball opened up to black players. The ballplayers called Barnhill "Skinny" because he was so little. And he *was* little! Not only short but slender, too. That's how he got his nickname. Later, when he played with the Ethiopian Clowns, they called him "Impo" because he looked like a little imp out there on the pitching mound.

Bryan finally got Barnhill to live in Wilson all the time and pitch on the baseball team. And whenever he could get a team to come in to play, "Skinny" was right there. Charlie was a pitcher, too, and he was staying over there at the same time that Barnhill was staying there. He was closer to Dave than I was because they were on the same team, while I just played *with* them occasionally. I played *against* them most of the time.

Barnhill's home is about forty-four miles from here, in Greenville, North Carolina. We were both playing out around here in the sandlots. The first time that I knew Dave I was playing on the Rocky Mount Black Swans and he was playing on a team in Greenville. We went down there to play them and he was pitching and he blinded us. I don't know how many he struck out, but he threw one of the fastest balls that we had faced. We went down there to play them again and he blinded us again. He was such a good pitcher on that team that Bill Bryan decided they would get him for the team in Wilson, and that's how Dave went from Greenville to Wilson.

Bryan was a black barber in a white barbershop. Back then blacks were the leading barbers for whites. Blacks couldn't get haircuts there and white barbers couldn't work there. All of the barbers were black.

I don't know how Bill got his money, but he operated the team. Whenever the game was over, whatever was cleared, the players got 75 percent of it and Bill got 25 percent. His profit came out of the 25 percent. He took what it cost to rent the baseball park and other expenses off the top. Then he gave what was left to the ballplayers and we divided it among ourselves. The team that won got sixty cents out of every dollar, and the team that lost got forty cents out of every dollar. The home team had to provide the umpires and, if a team came from pretty far away, we had to pay their board and lodging. If we went there they had to do the same thing. And that wasn't taken off the top. We had to pay that out of our part. The balls, umpires, and things like that were taken off the top.

Later, Bill Bryan left Wilson and went to New York, and a fellow named Herbert Woodard took over the team. He was a nightclub operator, and he was running a service station and had some cottages to rent out in the back. After he took the team, he built his own stadium behind his house. Before that we were playing in the city's baseball park, Band Street Stadium.

Another player I played against around Rocky Mount who later played in the Negro Leagues was Ray Dandridge. Around 1928, he was playing at Richmond, Virginia, and we used to play each other. We would go up there to play Richmond and they would come down here to play us. He was playing third base, and the thing I remember most about him from then was that he was the bowleggedest ballplayer I had ever seen. I didn't think at that time that he would become the ballplayer he *did* become. I also played against him later, when I was with Portsmouth, but none of us knew anything about black professional baseball. I was aware of the Negro National League's existence because I used to read about it in the Negro papers, but none of us had been up there and looked at it at that time.

My favorite player from the Negro Leagues was "Boojum" Wilson. He was a home run hitter, and he played first base with the Baltimore Black Sox. I never saw him play when I was a youngster, I just read about him. But in the latter years of his career he played with us on the Grays.

# Chapter 3

## Leaving Home (1933)

*Buck was the best first baseman that we had in the Negro Leagues. But I played against him a long time before that, when we were both playing in the sandlots.*

*—Ray Dandridge, Newark Eagles*

If it hadn't been for the Depression, I might have stayed in Rocky Mount playing sandlot ball all my life. I played and managed for Rocky Mount until I was twenty-five years old. I didn't go up to play professional baseball before that time, and I wouldn't have gone then had I not been cut off at the railroad shop in 1932, when the railroad business was going down. I was only playing baseball for a pastime and never thought about playing baseball for a living.

Then one Sunday afternoon, the manager of the Portsmouth team, Doc Daughtry, came up to my house and asked me if I would play with his team. I asked how much would he pay. He said, "Fifteen dollars a week." That was pretty good money back then, and I wasn't doing anything around here. So I left that Sunday and went back to Portsmouth with him in his car.

The team there had been called the Portsmouth Firefighters, but

17

they had an argument about what name to use. The year before, a man named I. D. Woodard was the manager of the Firefighters, and Daughtry was the owner. They said that Daughtry didn't have no business using the Firefighters name, so he used the name Daughtry's Black Revels.

When I was in Rocky Mount, I was still living at home but I was getting fifteen dollars a week and my board and lodging to play in Portsmouth. The owner got me a room with a big fat lady named Maggie Gates, and that's where I stayed and ate when we played home games. When the team went off somewhere to play, I went with them and roomed with a pitcher named King. He was a left-hander and we had to sleep together in the same bed.

We played every Saturday, and the first game that I played was in April, and we beat the Berkeley Black Sox, 6–4. They had me listed in the paper as "Bucky Lenox," and I played first base and batted third. Leon Ruffin, who later played with the Newark Eagles, was the catcher. When he left the team, Buster Haywood took his place, and he later played with the Indianapolis Clowns. None of the other players ever played with a professional team.

I remember when Rocky Mount came up to Portsmouth and played us. The game was played on Wednesday, May 17, 1933. Harry Sledge pitched a no-hitter for us, and my brother Charlie was pitching for Rocky Mount against us. I know he wanted to get me out, but I had a pretty good day. The headlines in the newspaper said, "Buck Leonard shines at bat in 9–0 victory." In that game, I went four for four, hit a triple, had four RBIs, and stole four bases. I don't know how I did that last part because I wasn't a speedster and didn't consider myself a base stealer.

We played at Washington Street Park and, after I hit a couple of home runs, I was well liked in Portsmouth. That was my first experience being away from home, and I was a little bit homesick. I had left a steady girlfriend in Rocky Mount, and when I left, we discussed it and I told her that I would be right back after the ball season closed. One thing they did in Portsmouth that helped me get over my homesickness was, they got me another girlfriend down there, and that kind of lightened the burden some. But I didn't stay there for the whole season. I only stayed about three months before the Baltimore Stars came down there to play us.

The Baltimore Stars were an independent team, and Charlie was with them when they came to Portsmouth. He had been with them about a week. They had come to Rocky Mount to play, and he got with them there. Then they came right on to Portsmouth, and I got with them. They had heard about me and they felt like if they picked him up, it would encourage me to go, too—which it did.

So I played with Portsmouth against Baltimore, and Ben Taylor, the Stars' manager, asked me how much I was making with Portsmouth and I told him. He said that I could make more than that going around with them. I asked him how much he would pay and he said, "Well, I don't pay no salary like you get here, but you can make more money playing on a percentage." Of course, I believed it. You know how those guys are. They're traveling around like they're big time and they know how to convince you.

When I decided to leave, I didn't tell Doc Daughtry anything but I told Buster Haywood. He said, "Don't you know if you go off with a team like that, you're gonna starve to death?" I said, "I'm leaving Portsmouth tonight." Other people had warned me against going with Ben Taylor's team. Traveling black teams had a hard time back then. They didn't have any money, they couldn't get many games, and things were just tough for black traveling teams.

There used to be a team that came down here from New Jersey named Pop Watkins' Stars, and we used to see how his players would be around and didn't have any games and all of them broke and their cars needed fixing and things like that. Thre was another fellow named Grady Johnson, who used to come around here with a traveling team. All of us who were playing ball around town here were warned not to get with these teams because you'd starve to death if you did.

But when Ben Taylor asked me if I would go with the Baltimore Stars, I told him, "All right," and left with him and went to Baltimore. Charlie was with the team already. We joined up in the same week, so both of us went to Baltimore together.

With the Stars we had a seven-passenger Buick and a 1929 Ford with a rumble seat. That's how we carried the ballplayers around. When I first started with them, we had some lean times for a while. We went to Winston-Salem, Charlotte, Statesville, Greensboro, and all around in North Carolina. It was a rough trip and I nearly starved to death. About three or four days after I got with them, we went to some town out there and had to ask the home team to feed us. We had fifteen men and we weren't getting our part of the gate, so there wasn't enough money to feed all of us.

When we got to Richmond, Virginia, we got into town a day or two before the game was to be played. We had to go out to Virginia Union University and ask the people out there if we could stay there because we didn't have any place to stay in Richmond. So they let us stay there until it was time to play the baseball game about two days later.

With Ben Taylor's team we would play some local teams and they'd pass around the hat after the game. Back then we weren't getting anything but board and lodging. When we finally got to Baltimore, all the games that we played in town were played at Druid Hill Park. It was just a big open park and didn't have a fence around it. We played five-o'clock twilight games and there would be between three and five thousand people sitting on the grass. They would pass the hat and we would get about twenty or thirty dollars for the team.

On weekends we played around Maryland, Pennsylvania, and West Virginia and made about fifty to seventy-five dollars a game. But Ben Taylor took most of that for the board and lodging. Sometimes he'd pay us about three dollars or maybe as much as six dollars, but mostly we were still just getting room and board, nothing else.

Ben Taylor wasn't too good with money—some of the players accused him of not sharing all the money that they were supposed to get. But he was a good manager. He handled players well, used good strategy, and most of the players respected him. Most of us were young and he felt like we needed strict discipline. And he was right, we did.

I didn't make much money with the Stars but that was the real beginning of my playing first base. I had played first base at Portsmouth and some at Rocky Mount but I got most of my learning from Ben Taylor. He helped me when I first broke in with his team. He had been the best first baseman in Negro baseball up until that time and he was the one who really taught me to play first base.

When I joined his team, he was the owner and manager of the team, and used to pinch hit a little, too. He was Candy Jim Taylor's brother and they used to play with the Indianapolis ABC's a long time ago. Candy Jim managed me ten years later when I was with the Homestead Grays, but at that time I only knew Ben. He was playing first base and the main reason that he got me was so he wouldn't have to play anymore. But in a few games, when he would pinch-hit somebody out of the ball game, he would come to first base and I would go out in the outfield and play. He was a line drive hitter, but he was old then. He must have been in his forties, but he still could hit the ball. I never did see him when he was in his prime.

In Baltimore, myself, Charlie and three more ballplayers were staying at Ben's house at 1315 Madison Avenue. He kept us right in the same house with him. We were staying upstairs and we ate right there, too. His wife wanted him to pay for us staying there and eating, and they got into an argument about it. We could hear them arguing but we never did say anything about it because that was their business.

One time I was going to leave the Baltimore Stars and go to the Baltimore Black Sox, but Ben had his wife got my clothes so I couldn't go. Back in those days, anything went. They would take a player's clothes and everything else to keep him from leaving.

We stayed and played around Baltimore for three or four weeks and we weren't making any money. Ben Taylor decided that if we moved to New York City we could get better booking. So we moved the team to New York City and played there for a while but things got bad and we still weren't making any money. We got rained out two or three ball games and we had some booking problems.

A white fellow named Nat Strong was the booking agent around New York City then, and he booked white and colored teams. Ben Taylor was supposed to pay Strong 10 percent of our take in exchange for booking us, but he failed to pay the percentage. So Nat Strong stopped booking us, and without him we couldn't get any games around New York and we had to break up.

At first, we players didn't know why he stopped booking us because we were playing fair ball for a semipro team. We thought that everything was all right and that everybody was being paid who was supposed to be paid. Then we found out later what had happened. That was my first experience with booking agents.

When we went to New York, at first we stayed at the Dumas Hotel on 135th Street. Old man Fein owned the place. About ten of us were staying in one room sleeping on cots, and five or six fellows were in the other room sleeping on cots. We paid six dollars a week to stay there, but without any booking we couldn't pay our hotel bill, and the hotel man told us that we were going to have to get out. He told us that unless we caught up the rent, he was going to get the manager and he was going to sell our cars to help pay for the lodging. We didn't think he could do that and we weren't paying him much mind. But we weren't getting any games and we were still staying in the hotel.

Then we woke up one morning and heard a lot of noise down there in front of the hotel. It sounded like somebody auctioning off things. I heard, "Three hundred fifty dollars . . . three hundred fifty dollars once . . . three hundred fifty dollars twice . . ." And I said, "Somebody look out the window and see what he's talking about." We looked out the window and the auctioneer was down there selling our cars out there in the street. And he sold them out there in front of the hotel that morning for three hundred fifty dollars.

Ben Taylor's niece was a hairdresser in New York and he was staying at her house while we were staying at the hotel. When he came to the hotel that morning, we told him that they had sold the cars downstairs and had put us out of the hotel. Apparently he already knew. I think the hotel owner had already told him what he was going to do.

The Baltimore Stars broke up after they sold our cars. We didn't play any more games because we didn't have no way to travel. And then we just had to do the best we could to get home from there. Some of the fellows from Baltimore went out on the highway and thumbed rides back to Baltimore. And some fellows who lived in New Jersey and in other parts of Maryland did, too. Everybody was getting back home the best way they could.

Charlie had to come home to Rocky Mount, because he was still going to school. But we didn't want to write home and ask for money, so when we broke up in New York, I had to get him back to Rocky Mount.

I was standing around down on the street one day, and Randolph Armstrong, who used to be coach at Booker T. Washington School, came by there. I said, "Mr. Armstrong, my brother Charlie needs a ride to Rocky Mount. Would you let Charlie ride with you to North Carolina in your car?" He said, "Yeah, you tell Charlie when I'll be leaving," and told me what day it would be. So I told Charlie to be down there, and he got the ride back to Rocky Mount from New York.

Now, my brother left from there and came back to Briggs Junior College. But he still wanted to play ball and wanted to play every game. Charlie was a pitcher and, when he didn't pitch, he played shortstop, and that meant he would be playing every day. When he was playing up there with us, I didn't think he was physically strong enough to play that caliber of ball. And I didn't want him to play because I wanted him to finish his education. I used to talk to Momma about that, and tell her to not let him play.

But somehow he stayed for about a year or two, playing in the summers while he was going to college. Sometimes he was called "Specs" or "Popeye" and, in 1935, he was voted the best short-stop in North Carolina. When he finished up at Junior College, he went down to Talladega, Alabama, for the next two years of college. After he finished, he taught in an elementary school up in Hollister, North Carolina, for three or four years. Then he married and started to work in the employment office, and that's where he was working when he died in 1952.

My brother Herman died about six years later, in 1958. He never left Rocky Mount, and lived here until he died. He worked in a grocery store, delivering groceries from the store to people's houses. He didn't go to college like Charlie did. I'm glad Charlie went back and got his education when he did, instead of staying around up there in New York City like I did.

That was about the first of September, when we got put out of the hotel, and I went and got a room at a rooming house and was staying there when I caught on with the Royal Giants.

# Chapter 4

## Brooklyn Royal Giants (1933)

*Buck and I went to the Brooklyn Royals at the same time. I tell him that if I had stayed, maybe I'd be in the Hall of Fame instead of him.*
*—Gene Benson, Philadelphia Stars*

After we broke up I found out that Dick Redding was the manager of the Brooklyn Royal Giants, and I went down there where the New York Black Yankees and Brooklyn Royal Giants hung out in the colored section in New York on the corner of 135th Street and Lenox Avenue. That was the baseball hangout for semi-pro teams around New York. I went around there and I asked some of the fellows about Dick Redding.

They showed me Dick Redding and I asked him about playing with his team and he said "All right." He had never seen me before but I was good-sized and I reckon I looked like I could play. He told me to be ready tomorrow and I could go with the team up to Nyack, New York. So I played right field that night, and from then on, I didn't have any more trouble about playing. That was in the latter part of 1933.

I got to know Dick Redding while I was with the Brooklyn Royal Giants. His pitching career had been excellent when he was in his prime and I understand that he was a humdinger. He still pitched on occasions while I was there, but he was more than forty years old and was over the hill then.

He wasn't too good as a manager. He didn't know the ins and outs of baseball like some of the fellows that I have known, but he was pretty good at maintaining discipline. He didn't drink himself and he didn't want the ballplayers drinking.

The Royal Giants played semipro baseball just like I used to play around Rocky Mount except they were a little better. They had some pretty good baseball players on the team that had played professional baseball, but they didn't play the same caliber of baseball that the league did. They were somewhere in between the Baltimore Stars and the Homestead Grays.

When I got to the Brooklyn Royal Giants they had a first baseman by the name of Highpockets Hudspeth. He only played about three more games after I got there and then he didn't play anymore. He was sick with the TB and died not too long after that.

Gene Benson joined the ballclub about the same time as I did. We used to hang around New York together, eating at the greasy spoon and like that. He was a first baseman then, too. But they had a fellow on the team named Huck Rile, who was a first baseman and a pitcher. He was a big fellow and an old-timer who used to play out West with Kansas City. When he would pitch, then I would play first base. And when he didn't pitch and was playing first base, then I would play right field. Benson didn't stay with the Royals. He went with another team, and a few years later got with the Philadelphia Stars.

There was another player named Leonard on the team, Bobo Leonard. He came from out West, too. They had a second baseman named Goldie Cephus, who came from western New York. Willie Williams was a shortstop, and he came from Scenectedy in upstate New York. Country Brown was the third baseman for us. He was a comedian. A boy named Jones was a catcher for us. Bergen was the left fielder. We had this Brooks fellow playing center field. He was an old-timer. Pitching they had Buck Buchanan and a big ol' boy named Cotton from down in North Carolina. Lefty Starks also pitched. He was an old-timer and he had been around New York for a few years.

We had one fellow there named Austin, who was a pitcher. He was a kind of goofy guy. We always felt like his parts were not all there. We never did know for sure, but we thought that he was using drugs. Sometimes when he would come to the team he would act funny and that's why we thought that he was on something. When they told me they thought this Austin was using drugs I didn't know what kind of drugs they were talking about. Because being from a small town down South, I didn't know anything about cocaine and marijuana and all those kinds of drugs.

Some of the older players would play jokes on young players, and I was no exception. They wanted to see how much baseball I knew, which wasn't much at that time. They would ask which side of the bat was best to hit the ball on and things like that. One time they told a pitcher to go down to the bullpen and warm up and they gave him a match to build a fire down there. They wanted me to think that he was supposed to build a fire under the pitcher for him to warm up and not to throw baseballs. When you first got with a team like that and you had old-timers on the team, they'd do everything they could to try you out.

But there was a fellow named Brooks, who was a center fielder, and he used to try to help me a little. He would tell me how to watch the pitchers and watch the balls and things like that. We used to call him "Beady," but I don't know what his real name might have been. He was a heck of an outfielder. When I got to the Royal Giants, he was still playing, but he was about through. He was a good player but he played on lesser teams throughout his career and never got the full recognition that he deserved.

Neither the Brooklyn Royal Giants nor the New York Black Yankees were in the league at that time. We played semipro teams around New York City and we would go upstate, up around Niagara Falls and in that area, and play around county fairs because we could pick up pretty good money around there. We traveled in two automobiles, a seven-passenger Pierce-Arrow and a five-passenger Cadillac. Sometimes we would go up there and stay three weeks playing around those county fairs.

We were booked in an area by the booking agent, who would tell us where to go, when to go, who to see, who we were going to play, and where we were going to play. Most of the teams played in the city baseball park, or maybe sometimes in the fair-grounds. We would dress at the hotel and then go to the ballpark.

Sometimes we'd be staying at the colored hotel in Buffalo, and we would dress there and ride up to Niagara Falls in our uniforms. After the game was over, we would get our money and go back to Buffalo and change clothes again. We never stayed around the fairgrounds *after* a game, but sometimes, if we got there early, we would park the cars out at the baseball field and walk down and look at some of the rides they had at the park. Of course we had our uniforms on, so they knew who we were.

I played with the Brooklyn Royal Giants that year until the weather got too cold. After we quite playing, a fellow named Ramirez wanted me to go to Puerto Rico with an all-star team to play during the winter, so I hung around New York hoping to go with them.

At that time I was staying with a fellow they called "King Kong." I had been staying with him even before the season ended. At first, after the Stars broke up, I went around to Dick Redding's house and stayed there a few nights. But he and his wife got in an argument and she put me out. She said that he wasn't paying for me to stay there no way. So then I went and got another room at King Kong's. I didn't know how he got his nickname. Maybe it was because of his size. He stood around six-foot-five and weighed about 250 pounds. He was big, and had bad feet and couldn't hardly walk. And he was a bootlegger.

At that time, in 1933, they used to make illegal whiskey—what we called "shakeup"—in the bathtub. And every Saturday night he would have a party and he would mix that stuff in the bathtub and shake it up and have sandwiches and other things to eat. And I had to wait on the guests that came up. He was a big gambler, too. They had poker games and he'd sell that stuff and sandwiches and all. And he had a "trick" girl working there and quite a few things went on at the party every Saturday night. And I would serve that stuff he had made up there and serve sandwiches and anything else he would tell me to do around the house that Satur-day night.

And in return, King Kong told me if I would help him sell liquor and help him keep his gambling game straight, I could stay there for nothing. But I had to buy my own food with what little money he paid me, and that's what I did.

Sometimes the law gave us some trouble. One night we were having a heck of a party there, and someone knocked on the door. We had a fellow named Jeff who answered the door and he had a peephole that he could peep out, but the folks on the outside couldn't see him on the inside. When he looked out, he saw it was the officers and warned everybody.

While the police banged on the door two or three times the fellows were taking the money off the table and splitting it up and hiding everything. When everything was cleared away, Jeff opened the door and let the policemen come in. They carried all of us down to the 135th Street precinct. King Kong told them that I didn't have anything to do with the gambling or anything else and that I was a baseball player and was just rooming there. So they let me go.

When I got back to the house, they had left a policeman there and he got me and carried me back down to the station again. But of course they let me out again and I came back to the house at 205 West 142nd Street in Harlem. The neighborhood was cleaner then than it is now, but the same illegal activities that are going on now were going on then.

I stayed there until Ramirez told me I couldn't go to Puerto Rico. At first he told me that he was going to carry fifteen players, but then he decided that he was only going to carry twelve players. One of the players who was going was Rap Dixon. Rap was a good hitter, a good outfielder, had a good arm, and was a better ballplayer than I was at that time. But he drank a lot and Ramirez thought that he might not show up and told me that if Rap didn't show up, then he was going to take me. I was going to play right field and Showboat Thomas was going to play first base down there.

This was in October and they didn't leave until the fifteenth of November. So I stayed there until the morning they were going to take the boat out of Brooklyn to go to San Juan, Puerto Rico. Rap Dixon showed up the day before they were supposed to leave and Ramirez told me that he couldn't take me, and so I had to come home. Ramirez gave me five dollars and told me that would help buy my ticket to Rocky Mount. I stayed there about a week after the fellows left for Puerto Rico and then I went back home.

I had an old girlfriend from Rocky Mount there in New York. She was living in Yonkers, and she used to come down to New York City every Thursday evening on her day off. And I used to see her and she would hand me enough change to eat and pay for my room there. Around November it really got cold in New York and had snowed a couple of times. But I didn't have enough money to come home. The bus fare to Rocky Mount was ten dollars and seventy-five cents. I told her about it and she said that she would give me money to stay in New York, but not to come home. So I told her, "Well, all right, then." She gave me twenty dollars and told me to buy an overcoat and a pair of shoes for the winter months.

Back then, I could get an overcoat for fifteen dollars and a pair of Thom McAnn shoes for about four dollars and change. Twenty dollars would have got me in good shape for the winter. But I took the twenty dollars and bought a bus ticket that same night to Rocky Mount. I had been working on a percentage, and when the team broke up, the five dollars from Ramirez and that twenty dollars was all I had.

After leaving a small town like Rocky Mount and going to the "Big Apple," it was quite a change. I was not too happy with New York City at first and I never really got used to it. Although I stayed there the rest of 1933, I still didn't like New York and I was glad to get back home.

# Part II

# The Prime Years (1934–50)

# Chapter 5

## The Big Time (1934)

*The baseball team rocked to the sensational play-*
*ing of a youngster by the name of Leonard, whom*
*experts agreed had everything. He was a first base-*
*man and showed class and finish.*

—Pittsburgh Courier

In the spring of 1934, I went back to New York to play another season with the Brooklyn Royal Giants. They played their home games up at the Catholic Protectory Oval, and so did the New York Black Yankees. After I first got there I practiced with them a little bit, but didn't stay long because I got a better offer.

Smokey Joe Williams, who used to pitch with the Lincoln Giants and had been with the Homestead Grays, too, came up there one Sunday and saw me play. He talked to me after the game and said that he thought I could make the Grays' team. He seemed to be a nice fellow. He had retired from the Homestead Grays and was working as a bartender on Lenox Avenue near 135th Street. I wasn't drinking but I used to go there pretty often and we would talk about baseball.

Not too many ballplayers hung out there. They used to hang out on 135th Street at Mom's and Pop's Place. The owner there wasn't a baseball man, but we could get hot dogs and soft drinks on credit. After we played a ball game we could come in there that night and then pay whatever we owed the next day or some-time later.

Smokey Joe had told some of the fellows to tell me to come around to the bar where he worked. So one night I went down to where he was tending bar and talked to him. He asked me, "Do you want to play with a good team?" I told him "Yes," and he said that he could get me a job with the Homestead Grays. But I told him that I didn't think I wanted to go to Pittsburgh because I didn't know anybody out there and all my friends were around New York.

He said, "Well, you come back here about midnight, and I'll get you together with the Homestead Grays." He thought that Cum Posey, who owned the Grays at that time, would be more likely to be at home by then. And he said, "I'm going to call Cum Posey and then you can talk to him and see what kind of arrangements you can make."

So I went back down there around midnight and he called Cum Posey. Now, Smokey Joe had seen me play with the Royals, and he told Cum that I was a good ballplayer and could hit, and told him how old I was. I had got a late start in professional baseball and was already twenty-six then.

Then I talked to Cum and he asked me how much money I wanted to play. I told him I didn't know, because I was playing on a percentage when I was with the Brooklyn Royal Giants and sometimes we would make two dollars a game and sometimes only one dollar a game. So we talked and got together on the price. Cum said he would pay me a hundred twenty-five dollars a month for four and a half months if I would come out there to play. But he said, "I'm going to get another first baseman from Fort Wayne, Indiana, named Joe Scott. You can play first base until he comes and then I don't know what I'm going to do with you."

He made that offer based on Smokey Joe Williams' word be-cause Smokey Joe had seen me play. So I said, "All right." Then Cum said, "I'll send you the money and you come on out here on the bus." He didn't know me, so he sent the money to Smokey

Joe for my transportation to Pittsburgh. Smokey Joe got me a ticket and gave me five dollars to go out there. I don't know whether he got a commission or not, but when I got my first check they held out fifty dollars and I know it didn't cost forty-five dollars for a ticket.

The Homestead Grays were spring training in Bridgeport, Ohio, just across the Ohio River from Wheeling, West Virginia. A fellow named Tex Burnett also went to play with the Grays at the same time I did. He was a catcher and an old-timer who had played all around New York and all out West. He was over the hill and only stayed with the team about a year. But we went to the Homestead Grays together on the bus that night. We left New York about twelve o'clock that night and got to Wheeling the next afternoon. When we got there, snow was on the ground "half a leg" deep, even though it was in the spring of the year, and we couldn't practice for two or three days. But then the weather broke and we got a chance to practice.

When I first got there, Cum Posey said, "I was looking for a bigger man than you. Can you play first base?" I was five-foot-ten and weighed 185 pounds. Joe Scott, who was playing for the Berghoff Beer Company's team in Fort Wayne, was about six-foot-two. The Homestead Grays liked big men, just like the Yankees did. That summer he was supposed to quit his job and come down and play first base for the Grays. I said, "Well, I'll stay until you get the other man."

So I stayed there and after a few days of practice they said, "Well, you look like you can play," and they never sent for him. The Grays saw that I could play first base *and* I could hit. I wouldn't have ever played except that I could hit. That was my main point, hitting the ball. So they wanted to keep me. And I stayed with the Homestead Grays for seventeen years, until they broke up at the end of the 1950 season.

The team had been started back in 1910. This was what Cum Posey, who owned the team, said. He had been with the team since 1912, so he had seen a lot of players come and go. Homestead was a steel mill town with a population of about twenty-eight thousand. U. S. Steel had the biggest steel mill in the country there and that was the only thing worth anything in Homestead. The black work-

ers formed a baseball team for weekend recreation. They had a
field out there in Homestead called West Field. It was an open
field and the fellows who worked in the steel mills used to go up
there and play and that's how the team was first organized.

The fellows were working until around four o'clock in the afternoon, and they played a lot of twilight games. The team was all
black and they would get together with a white semipro ballclub
and they would have a game. They would play from about six
o'clock until it got dark. That's how they started out.

Cum Posey was a railway mail worker then. He had played
football and basketball at Penn State, and joined the steelworkers
to play baseball with the team. They kept getting new players and
playing better baseball until their reputation had grown to where
they were the leading attraction in the tristate area. They played
hard and added a little comedy to the game to make them enough
different so that they were a good gate attraction. Cum started
handling the team's affairs and it became a full-time job. There
was a lot of gambling going on and quite a bit of money around
town, and he felt like the folks would support a baseball team.

Everybody wanted to play them, but Cum still played all the
leading teams around the Pittsburgh area where the team was already established. Every year from 1912 to 1929 they made a
good profit, but when the Depression hit in the thirties there were
some lean years for the Grays.

In 1932 Cum Posey organized the East-West League, but it
didn't even last out the year and folded in June. The Depression
got the league about the same time that it got my job at the
railroad shop. By then the Negro National League had reorganized,
and the Grays joined up and stayed in the league until it broke
up after the 1948 season.

When I came up in 1934 Cum Posey was still running the team
by himself. He was the owner and also the manager of the Homestead Grays. Cum was tops as a teacher of baseball, too. He could
tell you how to play. He taught me how to hit left-handed pitchers.

The first thing that he told me was about the best way to grip
a bat. I was holding the bat with my hands a little apart and he
made me put both hands together on the bat. Next he showed me
how to adjust my stance. Against right-handers, I had a closed

stance, and he told me to open up my stance a little against left-handers. Then I could face the left-handed pitcher and I wouldn't duck from his curveball.

So many guys helped me with my hitting through the years that I can't pick just one who helped me most. When you play twenty-four years, you get a lot of "do this" and "do that" during your career. Cum was very helpful at a time when I needed to learn some things, not only about hitting but about other things, too.

Cum knew the game and he wanted you to play to win. He would tell us to play hard but clean. Ballplayers can play hard and want to win and still play clean and not try to hurt anybody. All of us are trying to make a living and nobody would want to have to play hurt or be out of the game with an injury. There's no need in trying to put five or six stitches in somebody's leg or something like that. He didn't want us to go down to first base and deliberately run into the first baseman and try to knock the ball out of his hand. He just wanted us to go down there and try to get safe or make a close play of it.

That year we got sixty cents a day to eat and we could eat good for that. We couldn't eat steak, but we could eat good. Later they raised it to seventy-five cents and then to a dollar. When they raised it to a dollar, I saved some money. Back then I could get a haircut for fifteen cents and a shave for ten cents. Cum Posey treated me good. I got along all right with him until I asked for more money. Eventually I was one of the highest-paid players, but it wasn't until around the early forties that we started making some money.

That first year I was with the Grays I hurt my shoulder in the first part of the season when I fell on it one night in Akron, Ohio. Since I wasn't playing because of it, when we got to Chicago, they sent me to a doctor to have it treated. He told me that I had pulled some muscles and not to play for the next couple of weeks. So I didn't play for a couple of weeks, but I still started back too early. I thought they were going to send me home then, but they didn't, and my shoulder got all right.

I could still hit, and that's what kept me there. I knew I could hit when I went out there, but I wasn't such a fancy fielder. I didn't really learn how to field until I went to Puerto Rico with the Brooklyn Eagles during the winter of 1935. That's when I could emphasize and work on my fielding.

I had some doubts about going out West to begin with. After I got out to Homestead, though, I found the people were kinda good out there. They had plenty of money around the steel mills. Homestead was just across the river from Pittsburgh. I was still a bachelor at that time, so at first I stayed on Wiley Avenue in Pittsburgh with Tex Burnette, Jim Williams, and couple of other ballplayers. We three were staying in Pittsburgh and most of the players were staying in Homestead.

That was when we were playing up and down the river. Whenever we were going off to stay a couple of weeks they always came through there from Homestead and picked us up and we would go on to play. But we weren't going to bed like we should when we were in Pittsburgh and were running around at night. So a few years later, Cum Posey made all of us stay in Homestead, where they could keep an eye on us.

The first year I joined the Grays, I was the captain of the team, and Cum wanted me to have the team on the field, too. So I managed the team briefly. But I didn't really want to because I was one of the youngest members of the team, and the older players like Harry Salmon, Joe Strong, and Jim Binder and those fellows wouldn't do what I told them. Whenever I would say bunt or do something like that, they didn't want to do it because I was a whole lot younger than they were.

One night Strong was pitching and I was going to take him out of the box, but he said that I was taking him out too early and didn't want to leave. I didn't know the game like those fellows did because they had been there ten to fifteen years, and they knew strategy. And whenever they got a few hits off of a pitcher I would be ready to take him out and it would be the early part of the game. They said that as soon as he settled down he would be all right. But I didn't know anything about that. Of course, I told Cum about what happened when I saw him again. He was still the official manager until the next year, when Vic Harris rejoined the team.

That first year with the Grays was a learning experience for me in a lot of ways. Before I left Rocky Mount, I went to church almost every Sunday, but when I joined the Grays, we played games on Sunday and we were traveling so much, we didn't have time to go to church. I took a Bible with me when I left home, and I used to read two or three verses in the Bible about every night before I went to bed. I used to read about Job a lot. There's a man who lost everything he had, but he came back and had a little more. One time I had a roommate who asked what I was reading, and I told him I was reading the Bible. He thought that was all right as long as *he* didn't have to read it.

And during that time is when I started working crossword puzzles. I never had worked one before. But I had a lot of time and I didn't gamble. I didn't play pinochle, poker, or any kind of cards, and I didn't shoot dice or nothing like that. So I just started doing crossword puzzles. It was just a pastime, when I was sitting around in the hotel lobby when we got rained out and couldn't play. I bought a crossword puzzle book and a dictionary for crossword puzzles, and I specialized in it for some years. When I quit playing ball with the Grays in 1950, I quit working crossword puzzles, too. I gave it up when I went to Mexico, and I haven't worked a crossword puzzle since.

And in my first year with the Grays, we were still an independent team and only associate members of the Negro National League. The games we played against league teams didn't count in the standings, because we didn't have a good team and couldn't stand up with the teams in the Negro National League at that time.

The best teams in the league then were the Pittsburgh Crawfords, the Philadelphia Stars, and the Chicago American Giants. They were on the same level as the Grays when we had our good teams. In 1933 the Crawfords' owner, Gus Greenlee, was the league president, and he had awarded the championship to his team, but that was disputed by the American Giants, who said they had finished in first place.

Chicago had good ballplayers when I first went out there. They had Mule Suttles and Willie Wells, but they came East a few years later. And they had some more boys out there who were good ballplayers. They had Steel Arm Davis and Nat Rogers, but they both must have been forty-some when I saw them and they were about through. Steel Arm had bad feet and couldn't move

much and had moved in to first base. Double Duty Radcliffe's
brother, Alec, was at third base. And Turkey Stearnes had come
over there when the Detroit Stars folded. He was a good hitter
and could hit the ball a long way.

Their best pitcher was Willie Foster. He was one of the best
left-handers ever in black baseball. He played most of his career
out West, but he came East in 1936 to play with Gus Greenlee's
Crawfords. After his playing career ended, he was a baseball instructor at Alcorn College, and had just retired from that position
shortly before he passed away in 1978. The last time I saw him,
he came up here and stopped and stayed all night with me. The
next day he went on up to Oxonhill, Maryland, to visit his son,
who had a newborn baby. Not too long afterward, I heard that
he died.

One time he struck me out with the bases loaded when we
played out there after the end of the 1937 season. He was playing
on a team of Chicago and Kansas City players and we beat them
almost all of the games we played. But that was a few years later.
In 1934, they won the first-half championship, and we went out
to Chicago to play and lost three straight games. Then we came
back the next week to Philadelphia and lost two and tied one
against the Stars, and they won the second-half championship.

The Philadelphia Stars had "Boojum" playing first base. That's
what we called Jud Wilson. He was the one I had read about years
before, when he played with the Baltimore Black Sox, and years
later he played with us. Dick Seay was at second base, Dewey
Creacy was at third base, and Jake Stevens was shortstop. A few
years earlier, he had played for the Homestead Grays. He was a
good fielder and could run bases, too, but he was a light hitter.

He and Boojum were friends and roommates, but one time Boojum held him out of a hotel room window by the ankle and threatened to drop him. Jake Stevens was drunk, and he was kicking
Boojum's arm, trying to get loose. But if he had got loose, he
would have been killed when Boojum dropped him. Now, that
happened before I had ever played with Boojum, and I only heard
about it later.

Chaney White was a good ballplayer. He could hit the ball and
was a good outfielder but didn't have such a good arm. He was

a good runner earlier in his career, when he was younger, but he had slowed down. Biz Mackey was catching for the Stars. He was rifling the ball to second, but his arm got sore that same year and a boy named Casey had to fill in until Mackey's arm got better.

Slim Jones was one of their pitchers, and he could throw just as hard as Satchel. He was a humdinger. They used to feature him against Satchel Paige in Yankee Stadium and the Polo Grounds when they had the four-team doubleheaders. The opening game would be Slim Jones against Satchel Paige and the score would always be 2–1, 3–2, or something like that when they matched up. I've not seen a left-hander, except Koufax, who could throw harder than Slim Jones. We used to barnstorm against Lefty Grove and the major leaguers in Baltimore every summer, and between Slim Jones and Lefty Grove, I'd say Slim was a little faster.

Slim Jones was one pitcher I couldn't hit. But he didn't really last too long, only about three years. I played with him on an All-Star team that we took to Puerto Rico after the 1935 season, but he didn't last long after that. He drank and, the way that I understand it, during one winter he caught the pneumonia somehow and died. He was still young, but his arm had gotten bad.

Another good pitcher for the Philadelphia Stars was Webster McDonald. He was the manager of the Stars in 1934 and was an underhand pitcher. Now, he was in the evening of his career, but he was still pitching good ball even back then. He wasn't like Slim Jones. He was a slowball pitcher and had good control. He had a pretty good curveball, and he kept the ball down.

Soon after I first joined the Grays, I hit a home run in the eleventh inning and won a game against the Stars. They went on and beat Chicago in the playoff, but they had a big argument about one of the games, when Boojum hit an umpire and was put out of the game but wouldn't leave. After it was all over, the Philadelphia Stars were declared champions.

Both of these teams were good, but the most dominant team in the league when I first broke in with the Grays was Gus Greenlee's Pittsburgh Crawfords. I didn't know Gus Greenlee too well. I just knew him when I saw him and that's all. He was a numbers banker and had an assistant named Woogie, who handled a lot of that kind of business.

In addition to being in the numbers racket, Gus had a stable of about five or six good fighters. The best known were John Henry Lewis and Red Bruce. John Henry Lewis won the light-heavyweight championship in 1935 and held it for three years. Gus also had several lesser fighters of different weights. He said the only reasons why he was making money off those fighters was because when they were fighting he'd keep most of the money and just give them board and lodging.

He also owned a restaurant called the Crawford Grill, and it was just a front for the numbers racket and everything else that he was doing. We ballplayers hung out at the grill. That was our favorite spot. When the Crawfords were playing in Pittsburgh, we were on the road, and when we were in Pittsburgh, they were on the road. The two teams weren't in town at the same time except when we were going to play each other. On those occasions the Grays players and the Crawford players sometimes got together off the field. I already knew Josh Gibson and Satchel Paige from the year before, when I was with the Royal Giants.

In my first year with the Grays, we played the Crawfords a doubleheader on the Fourth of July at Greenlee Field, and that became an annual event. I remember that first doubleheader. Satchel Paige started the first game. He was a big name and I was only a rookie. I didn't get a hit against him, but neither did anybody else. Satchel pitched a no-hitter and struck out seventeen batters and beat us 4–0. But in the second game he came back in to relieve with the score tied, and we beat him 4–3.

As a pitcher Satchel was a humdinger. But I didn't know much about him as a person. I played on an All-Star team with Satchel in 1936, but I never did play with him on a regular team. I just know how he was in baseball. I remember one time when we were playing the Crawfords an exhibition game up in a coal mining town, somewhere near New Kensington. They had Satchel playing right field, just because of his name. And somebody for us hit a fly ball to right field and all of us were looking out in right field for Satchel to catch the ball—or try to catch it—and he was over there on the sideline lighting a cigarette from one of the fans.

That was typical of Satchel. When we were barnstorming, he

had to pitch the first three innings everywhere we went, and then we could put in another pitcher to finish the game. Satchel didn't ride on the bus with the other players. He kept a Cadillac about all the time, and would drive to the games in his car.

One time we were playing an exhibition game in Franklin, Kentucky, and he was supposed to pitch the first three innings against the local team. But on the way to the game, he stopped at some pond somewhere and was fishing. And when we got to where we were going to play that night and got dressed, he wasn't there. So we told the man in Franklin, "Look here, Satchel's not here yet. Do you want to wait a little while?" He said, "Yeah." So we waited for about half an hour and Satchel didn't show up. So we had to start the game with another pitcher and Satchel got there about the fifth inning and we let him pitch the last two innings. And he said that he stopped somewhere along the road and caught some fish. We knew that he was doing things like that.

That was during the time the Grays were rebuilding. They had been one of the best black teams of all time in 1930 and 1931, but Gus Greenlee signed most of them when he organized his team. That's why our team was weaker in 1934 than it had been a few years earlier. We hadn't built back up yet.

They say Greenlee took advantage of Cum Posey because Cum didn't really have any money. When he was running the team by himself, he wouldn't half pay you. He would pay you part of the time, and part of the time he wasn't paying. Cum was poor and couldn't pay the ballplayers and, since Greenlee did have some money, he was able to persuade the fellows to leave Posey and come to him. Cum did manage to keep Smokey Joe Williams, but most of the other players went to the Crawfords because that's where the money was. They stayed with him until 1936 and then they started coming back to us.

After Greenlee's raids Cum realized that he needed more money behind the team and that's why he needed Rufus "Sonnyman" Jackson. Sonnyman was a different kind of person from Cum Posey. Cum was a college man with a few educational accomplishments, was a columnist for the *Pittsburgh Courier,* worked for the city of Homestead, and was on the city council and involved in things like that.

And Sonnyman Jackson was a gambler. He played cards all around Hot Springs, Arkansas, and everywhere there was a big poker game. And he had all these illegitimate businesses going. He was in the numbers business and he had thousands of piccolos— nickelodeons—all up and down the Monongahela, Allegheny, and Ohio rivers. You'd put ten cents in there and get some music. And he had some fellows going around who did nothing but take money out of these machines and repair them. And he did not depend on baseball for his money. We weren't getting paid from what we were making playing ball. Those piccolos and numbers were bringing in the money and we were getting paid from those businesses.

But Sonnyman Jackson had some money, so Cum got him in to help finance the team. Cum became the team's traveling secretary and he made Jackson president and treasurer. When Sonnyman took over, the Homestead Grays got some fresh money, and that's when we started getting *our* money. And Sonnyman got the ballplayers back to the Homestead Grays because we could pay them. At that time a lot of teams needed money, and any player that a team would sell to us, Sonnyman bought him. That's when we started getting good ballplayers. When I got there in 1934 we didn't have twelve ballplayers and we were just picking up players wherever we could get them because Cum Posey didn't have any money then.

I talked to Leon Day about coming to the Homestead Grays that year. He was with the Baltimore Black Sox, and I had seen him play. I asked him if he wanted to play with the Grays. If he had said "Yes," then I was going to tell Posey, but Posey didn't tell me to talk to him. I did that on my own. I think his manager, Rap Dixon, did something to keep him like Ben Taylor had done with me when he hid my clothes. Day had a good fastball and a good curve, and he turned out to be one of the best pitchers in our league.

We didn't get Day, but we got Vic Harris back from the Pittsburgh Crawfords right after that. He had been with the Homestead Grays earlier in his career, but when the Grays got shaky financially, he left and went to play with the Crawfords when Greenlee was raiding the Grays. After we got him back, he stayed with the

Grays for the next fourteen years. Vic was a good outfielder, but he wasn't among the top ones.

Sonnyman Jackson also bought a new bus for the team. The business manager was the bus driver back then. Sonnyman also made arrangements around town for our lodging and fixed it so that the people would trust us to stay at their houses in Pittsburgh. That was at the beginning of the first season that I went out there, and a couple of years after the team had been raided by Greenlee.

By then the Grays had become too much for one man to handle by himself and, within the next year, Cum made some other changes. Near the end of 1935 he named his brother, See Posey, as business manager. See rode around with us and took care of details. He was all right, but he didn't have too much to say about playing the game.

Cum also stopped managing on the field and Vic Harris became the manager when he came back in 1935. But Vic couldn't tell you how to play. He never did tell any ballplayer how to play. A seasoned manager would tell a youngster coming up, "Throw the ball this way. Get on the pitcher's mound this way. Hold the bat this way. Step this way," and all like that. And here's something else important. If you are at bat and you swing and miss the ball, you had to know how you missed it. Whether you're over it or under it, and correct it the next time. But Vic Harris didn't do that.

Now, Vic was one of those ballplayers who would do anything to win. One time I saw him do something and I've never been so disgusted with my own ballplayer in my life. We were playing in Buffalo against the Newark Eagles one night and we made a double play, and the umpire called the man out at second but reversed his decision and called him safe. He was a white umpire. And Vic went out there and was arguing with him about the play. Vic said that he ought to have been in position to have seen the play at second and then he spit in that man's face—right on the jaw. The umpire was so scared and so surprised that he just put him out of the game. I walked down there and I said, "Anybody who would do a common trick as that ought to be run out of the ballpark." Not only be put out of the ball game but out of the ballpark. But Vic would do anything to win.

If you go into a base and jump into a fellow and spike him, we call that "undressing" him. Vic Harris was one of the guys that really tried to undress a fellow. The others were Rap Dixon, Ted Page, Oscar Charleston, and Willie Wells. Those five fellows were the worst I've ever seen. And Vic was one of them.

We were playing the Eagles in Newark one Sunday. Willie Wells was playing shortstop and Vic went into second base and jumped right into him with his baseball spikes and tore his uniform all the way down his leg. That kind of play is uncalled for. Wells had to go in the clubhouse and change uniforms. When he came back out he was going to get even, but Vic was in the outfield, and he spiked me instead. I said, "Hey, Wells, I thought we were friends. Why did that happen?" And he said, "Because you're playing with Vic and against me." He didn't cut me very bad, and I didn't leave the game. But that's the way Wells played, and that's the way Vic played.

Vic never had any trouble with his own players. He didn't fight with his own players that I know of, and I played for him for about twelve years. Everybody knew how he was and knew he wouldn't take no stuff, so we wouldn't try to do anything that we thought he'd be dissatisfied with. I knew what kind of egg he was. I knew he was just as rotten as anybody you ever saw in your life. But I just never did say anything to him about it. I didn't let him know what I thought. The way I got along with him was, I'd ask him things. With some guys, you have to let them think that you're interested in what strategies they used. And I got along with him fine.

After the Grays reorganized, we fielded a good team almost every year. But in my first year with them, we were still struggling. That year the traveling secretary for the Pittsburgh Crawfords was Harry Deal, and he picked a "dream team" and put me on there. For a first-year man that was an honor. I reckon, just like now, a guy who can hit will get more recognition than anybody who can't hit.

We were just an average ballclub then. Some of the players who were with us at that time were Jim Binder, a third baseman, and Buddy Burbage, an outfielder we got from the Bacharach Giants in Philadelphia. And we had Tommy Dukes and Rab Roy

Gaston catching. Dukes was a better player than Gaston, but Dukes was a "boxer." What a boxer is, in baseball terms, is sometimes he would catch the ball and sometimes he would knock it down and pick it up and throw to wherever he had to throw. He was a pretty fair hitter, though. He was little but he could hit with some power.

Neil Robinson played with us when he first came up. We got him from an independent team, the Cincinnati Tigers. He was a good hitter and had good power, but he didn't stay with us long. I hate to say this, but when we had him in 1934 and '35, he drank quite a lot. He and a fellow named Johnny Lyles were on the team with us, and then we got rid of them. But later Robinson got with the Memphis Red Sox and stopped drinking, and had his best years.

Tom Parker stayed with us for maybe ten years because of his size. They stay with any big ballplayer longer than an average-size ballplayer. He was big and had a fastball and that's why we kept him. He wasn't one of our better pitchers because he couldn't throw the ball over the plate. He was a good hitter, too, and played some in the outfield. The Grays were noted for good-hitting pitchers.

Willie Gisentaner was a left-handed pitcher and he had some fingers missing, the index and middle fingers, on his throwing hand. It made the ball curve every time he threw a pitch. But he got so he could throw it over the plate, and he stayed with the team about three years after I got there.

Joe Strong was a good tough-nut pitcher for us during that time, but he'd cut the ball, though. He got a good job at American Rolling Mills in Middletown, Ohio. We weren't paying too much. We had some ballplayers who were just getting eighty-five dollars a month, and if a ballplayer got a good job at the mill, he left the team.

Harry Salmon was an old-timer and was with the Grays when I got there. He and Strong were both old-timers. They knew how to pitch and could throw the ball across the plate. Salmon was one of those mean guys, too. He'd throw at your head and everything. He had been the ace down at Birmingham when Satchel was on the same staff.

Louis Dula was a young fellow and a fastball pitcher. He pitched for about two years and his arm got sore. We sent him back to Cincinnati, and we brought him back later, but he still couldn't pitch because his arm was still sore. We carried him with us hoping his arm would do better but it didn't, so we just let him go. A young player will give over to an ailment. If he gets a sore arm he quits, but an old ballplayer will try to pitch it out. He'll keep right on throwing. Like Satchel, his arm got sore in 1935 and he didn't sit down or anything. But Dula just quit pitching any after his arm got sore.

Harry Williams was an underrated ballplayer. He was a good hitter and could do everything. He was born and raised in Pittsburgh and he had been playing around with the Pittsburgh Crawfords and with the Homestead Grays before I got there. He decided to go to New York to play with the New York Black Yankees because he was going to get more money. So he went to the Black Yankees and stayed with them until about 1935. At that time Cum Posey would "steal" ballplayers. That's what we used to call it then. We went up there to play them in New York, and Cum talked to Harry on the side there at the game. Cum told him to come on and sit on the bus and talk about it. And while he was sitting there on the bus talking to Cum, we drove off with him. We went on to Pittsburgh and carried him with us.

He didn't say anything about it because he got more money again. The Black Yankees weren't in the league at that time so they couldn't say anything about it either. Harry stayed with us about two years, then he left because the Black Yankees offered him more money again, and he went back out there. There was more money out East than there was out West.

Another player who jumped back and forth from the Grays to the Black Yankees was George Scales. He did know baseball and I think he had the ability to manage wherever he went. He was a good manager in Puerto Rico. The old ballplayers, from back there in the twenties, could tell you how to play.

Now here's something else. In spring training they would give the pitchers a ball and he kept that ball in his hand day and night until spring training was over. He had to carry it with him to the picture show, and he carried it with him to eat. He kept the ball with him all the time. You had to get the feel of it.

We had several players who didn't stay with us long, but we kept looking for players and collecting more players until we got a pretty good team together.

# Chapter 6

## Young All-Star

*This year his work has been superb, a flashy, consistent, fielding genius, a superman at the plate and a player of the old school, who eats and dreams baseball.*

—Pittsburgh Courier

We trained in Wilson, North Carolina, in 1935. Beginning then, we were full members of the Negro National League, and the league play gave the team more prestige. And our team was stronger than the year before. We got Jerry Benjamin, Matthew Carlisle, and Bozo Jackson from the Birmingham Black Barons at the same time. They came to us because we were going to pay them more money, and they all became regulars.

The regular season began with a bang. The opening game was in New York, at Dyckman Oval against the New York Cubans. Bozo Jackson was playing shortstop for us and he slid into second base and spiked the Cubans' shortstop, Horacio Martinez. They got to fighting at second base and when they started swinging at each other the fans ran out of the grandstand, especially those Spanish-speaking folks. They had mostly Cuban players, and a lot of Cuban people were in the stands at that time. You know how

51

it is when something like that happens, the players all come out
of the dugouts. When the Cuban fans saw us players running out
there, they thought we were going to help Bozo Jackson, and they
ran out there. And the American fans ran out on the field, too. It
took a while to get the field cleared so we could finish the game.

The next time we came to New York, on July 21, they issued
a program advertising the second game between the two teams.
The program's cover said, "Caramba! We will keel the Homestead
Grays if they try these riot again. See the fiery Latins from Man-
hattan get their just revenge." And it had a picture of the "riot
scene" from the May 26 game. Inside it said, "See the renewal
of baseball's blood feud." They tried to stir it up by making them
think we were going to fight, just to publicize the game and to
get more fans there. But there was not really any "bad blood"
between us, and nothing happened in that game.

That was in July, and when they came to Pittsburgh to play us
we tried to stir it up again over there. They would do anything
that they could to get more folks in the ballpark. Alex Pompez
was the owner of their team. He was a Cuban, but he was born
in Tampa. He had a business on Lenox Avenue, where he had
about six or seven fellows in a building and they made handmade
cigars like they did in Cuba. They had some stationery equipment
that they used for rolling tobacco and everything like that to
make cigars.

He was in the numbers racket, too. That was his main concern.
One time an Italian who was running the numbers racket, too, got
at him in New York. Pompez got on a bus with two suitcases of
money and was going somewhere out West. The bus stopped at
some town and these Italians got on and took him off the bus and
took the money away from him, and took him back to New York.
That's the way it was.

If somebody would hit the numbers for a big sum of money
the owner would have to leave town and stay a week or so, until
he could pick up enough money to pay off that hit. Our owner,
Rufus Jackson, used to do that if he didn't have enough money
to pay off on a big hit. He would go to New York and stay until
he took in enough money to pay it.

Another thing the numbers bankers used to do, when a number

was heavily played on a given day, was to give part of that play to an Italian banker so that if somebody hit, then the Italian would have to pay off some of it, too. Now, it hadn't hit, but it was played heavy. That was common among the bankers.

Later Pompez got mixed up with Dutch Schultz's mob, and testified against him. And lived to tell about it. But I didn't know anything about that except what I heard and what the papers said.

Martin Dihigo was the New York Cubans' manager, and he would pitch, too. He wanted to pitch all the important games. Like when they had a doubleheader on a Sunday, he would pitch the first game. Dihigo was the best all-around ballplayer I ever saw. He could play any position, and I mean play it good. I've seen him play all of them, except I never saw him catch. But he could catch, I reckon, if he wanted to. If I had to put him at one position, I'd pitch him. He excelled as a pitcher.

He played mostly down in Mexico, because he could make more money on all those Mexican teams. I played on his team in Mexico in later years. He wasn't over here too much, but he was over here playing with the Cubans when they were in the Negro National League around 1935.

He pitched for the Homestead Grays in the late twenties, before I came there. I didn't see the Grays back there then, and all I can say is how they used to talk about him when he was with the Grays. But I saw him when he was pitching with the Cubans.

Other New York Cuban pitchers were Johnny Taylor, a boy named Blake, and Luis Tiant, the father of the Tiant that played in the major leagues. Taylor and Blake were good pitchers and so was Tiant, when he felt like it. In July we played them a doubleheader, and Tiant shut *us* out in the first game and Ray Brown shut *them* out in the second game. And they had some more Cuban boys. "Yo Yo" Diaz was a pretty good pitcher, for one.

Other players they had were Rap Dixon, Alejandro Oms, Lazaro Salazar, and Clyde Spearman. But they didn't have them, except for Oms, when we first played them. They got the others later in the year. Oms was a Cuban and was just about through when I saw him, but he could still hit the ball. Salazar was a Cuban, too. He pitched and played the outfield.

Spearman was an American boy. His brother, Henry, played

third base with us on the Grays a few years later. We used to call them ''Big Splo'' and ''Little Splo.'' Henry was older than Clyde, so he was ''Big Splo'' and Clyde was ''Little Splo.'' Henry was just an ordinary third baseman, but he could hit pretty good and had pretty good power. Clyde was a good ballplayer and went to Cuba with us a few years later when we took an all-star team down there to play one winter. He was a good fly chaser, could run the bases, and could hit.

The New York Cubans had a good team in 1935, but the Pittsburgh Crawfords were a better team. After the Crawfords had won the first half of the split season, the Cubans won the second half, but the Crawfords beat them in a playoff.

Satchel and Josh Gibson were the big stars on the Crawfords. Gus Greenlee advertised them as the greatest battery in baseball, and they *were* the biggest attraction in black baseball. When we were playing against Gibson when he was with the Crawfords, we'd play the right fielder over toward right-center, and the left fielder toward left-center, and we'd pull the third baseman out close to shortstop, and I'd play out close to the second baseman and let the second baseman and shortstop play deep. And we'd put the center fielder as far out as he could and still be in the ballpark. Then we'd throw the ball straight down the middle of the plate. That's how we pitched to him.

The Crawford teams of that time were great. The Pittsburgh Crawfords of 1935 was the best black team I've ever seen. They had five Hall of Famers on the team. In addition to Satchel and Josh, they had Oscar Charleston, Cool Papa Bell, and Judy Johnson. Satchel spent almost all that season in North Dakota, and they still won.

Oscar Charleston was the manager, and he was also one of the best hitters in the whole Negro Leagues. Even though he had gotten fat and was just about through, I'd say that as far as batting was concerned, Charleston was just as good at that time as Josh. But Josh could hit the ball farther than Charleston.

Charleston was one of the tough ballplayers. I remember one game on July 4, 1934, when we were playing the Crawfords in Pittsburgh at Greenlee Field. Satchel was pitching for the Crawfords and Dula was pitching for us. Charleston was on third base and somebody hit a ball to the infield. Tex Burnette was catching for us and Charleston cut him all the way from his thigh right down to his knee. They had to put stitches in his legs. Charleston was a tough slider, and when he was young, he was fast. That combination of speed and aggressiveness made him a good base runner.

Talking about baserunning, the Crawfords had the best in Cool Papa Bell. He was the best base runner I ever saw. People tell all kinds of stories on him. Some of them are true. He *could run*. They used to talk about how Cool Papa would run out from under his hat and how he used to go from first to third on an out. But the way he used to go, he would catch the umpire looking at first base and he would cut right across the diamond and go to third base. He would never touch second base. We would joke him about that.

When he got on first base, we'd just throw over there three or four times and try to outwait him. But even if we kept him from getting a good break on the pitch, it was still hard as the devil to get him at second base, as fast as he could run. He could even steal on a pitchout. And if a throw was off, even a little bit, he would be safe. He knew how to slide, too, and had what we called a "swan slide." It was really just a hook slide, but the way he did it looked special.

We tried to keep him off the bases. They say you can't steal first base, but with Cool Papa, you couldn't be sure of that. We knew he could bunt and we knew that if he got on first, it was as good as a double because he was going to steal second anyway. So we used to play the infield in close to keep him from bunting. We'd bring in the third baseman and I would come in, and the shortstop and second baseman would come in, and we'd just let him try to hit the ball by us if he wanted to. Cool Papa was a good hitter at that time and sometimes he would hit it by us and get two or three bases on it. But if we played back, he could beat out a ground ball for a base hit. They used to say if the ball bounced twice, just put it in your pocket, Cool Papa had already got safe.

Satchel said that Cool Papa could turn off the light and get in bed before the room got dark. I roomed with him when he came to the Grays about ten years later, but I never did see anything like that. By that time, we were having to help him in and out of bed. He was older then, but he was still fast when he got on the field.

Judy Johnson was the other Hall of Famer on that team. His best years were behind him, but he was still one of the best ballplayers up there at that time. He is one of the best third basemen of all time in black baseball. He could hit and he could field. But he didn't hit with power and he wasn't as quick as Dandridge at third base. Dandridge could field more balls than he could. Judy knew the game and he was a gentleman all the time. He used to wear a shin guard on one leg, but I don't remember which one it was. And with players like Vic Harris, Oscar Charleston, and Chaney White, infielders needed shinguards.

They had an outfield that Satchel said could catch the raindrops before they hit the ground. Of course they had Cool Papa in center field, and they had Jimmy Crutchfield and Sam Bankhead in the other two outfield positions. Crutch was a nice little fellow and a good all-around ballplayer. He could run bases good, but he didn't hit the long ball because he was little. Sam Bankhead came to us a few years later when we had our good teams.

Ted Page and Rap Dixon had played outfield with the Crawfords a couple of years earlier. Rap Dixon was a good outfielder. I saw him before he finished, when he played with us. And he was a good hitter and a good thrower, too. And in his day they say he was a humdinger. But I didn't see him in his prime.

Ted Page was pretty good. He was killed a few years ago when somebody broke into his house and beat him to death with a baseball bat. Before he was killed he was one of the players who was really clamoring for the Hall of Fame. There's a lot of them who were better outfielders, and a lot of fellows who I think were better ballplayers than he was. He was playing when I went up there in 1933, and he played about ten years before he retired.

Chester Williams was their shortstop, and he played with us during the early forties. He was another player who was killed after he got out of baseball. He was shot to death down in Louisiana around the time that I was in Mexico. The Crawfords had different players at second base. Pat Patterson, Dick Seay, John

Henry Russell, and Leroy Morney all played there at one time or another, and they were all good fielders.

Bill Perkins was Satchel's catcher. They had been together down in Birmingham before they came to the Crawfords. I've heard that Perkins had the words "Thou shalt not steal" written across the front of his chest protector, but I never saw it. But Perkins was that kind of fellow and he might have done it. With Josh on the team and doing most of the catching, Perkins played in the outfield some, too.

Pitching they had Leroy Matlock, Bert Hunter, Harry Kincannon, and Spoon Carter. Kincannon and Carter both later played with us. Matlock was another pitcher who gave me trouble. He was a left-hander and he was extremely tough for me to hit. He gave me a fit. I had more trouble with him than with any other left-hander. I don't know how he was so effective against me, he seemed to throw what I wasn't looking for. I guess he just had my number. Other left-handers I did fair against, except Slim Jones. But Matlock wasn't a fast ball pitcher. He could just get me out. With other fellows, I could tell when they were going to throw the curveball, but with Matlock, I couldn't tell when he was going to throw a curveball. He was their top pitcher in 1935, after Satchel jumped the team, and didn't lose a game.

Hunter was one of the good pitchers on the team, and they also had Bill Harvey and Sam Streeter. Streeter was a spitball pitcher. I remember one time when I batted against him, and there was so much spit coming off the ball, I didn't know whether to hit the spit or the ball. He had it loaded up so much, the spit was flying everywhere.

Satchel's arm got sore and he left and went up into North Dakota and pitched for a white team and his arm got better. When he came back to our league, his arm was better and he could throw a curveball. Now, who taught him, I don't know. But when he came back in 1936, he was throwing a curveball and before that he wasn't throwing no curveball. Satchel threw fire. He didn't have to throw anything else. Not against us. We knew Satchel was going to throw a fastball and we still couldn't hit it.

But he pitched up there in Bismarck for about a year or so. He stayed up there the rest of 1935, but even without him, they had

a great team. We all go along with Satchel being the best pitcher
in black baseball history. He gave me more trouble than anyone
else. Satchel had an exceptional fastball. It had a little hop. It
would get up to the plate and rise up just a little bit, enough for
you to miss it. And if you did get a piece of it, it wasn't much.
One time I asked to see the ball and the umpire threw two or
three balls out of play. Satchel said, "They're all going to hop
today, so you might as well throw them all out." And he was
right, too.

I didn't do much good against him, but I did fair. Some batters
said that his fastball got smaller as it got close to the plate and it
was like trying to hit a pea. As long as I played against him, I
can't remember getting a clean hit off him. I haven't seen anybody, black or white, as good as Satchel.

Our best pitcher was Ray Brown, and in 1935, he got married
at home plate on the Fourth of July. The ceremonies took place
right there on the field. We were going to play a ten-thirty game
at Greenlee Field in Pittsburgh, and Brown married Cum Posey's
daughter about nine-thirty that morning. I think that Cum was the
instigator of them getting married like that. It was the Fourth of
July and we were playing the Pittsburgh Crawfords, so the two
local teams were playing. It was a pretty good show to draw the
people and it did raise a big crowd.

Cum wanted her to get married in the ballpark *during* the game,
and Brown would have gone along with it. He was going to Wil-
berforce College and he didn't have any money, and he's going
to marry into a family that he thinks has got some money. You
know how that is. But Cum's daughter didn't want to, so they got
married before the ball game started.

At first, before they ever got engaged or anything, Cum Posey
didn't want his daughter to go with Ray Brown, but she was
determined. And you know how it is when a young girl gets
something in her head. And you know how it is with some fellows,
they like to see their daughters marry a college fellow rather than
just the run-of-the-mill fellow like we were. So Cum was kind of
proud of it.

I don't think Raymond Brown was favored because he was
Cum's son-in-law. If anything, I think it was against him. Brown

was going to college in Ohio, and when the season would open and college classes were not over yet, he wanted to quit college and join the team. But Cum didn't want him to quit college. He wanted him to stay until school closed. And it looked to Cum like Brown was leaning on being his son-in-law. And Brown had an attitude about baseball that Cum just didn't like.

Now, he was the best pitcher we had on the team, and we think he was one of the best in the league. When it was Brown's turn to pitch, he pitched and he pitched hard and wanted to win. Vic Harris, our manager, didn't favor him because he married the boss's daughter. When he got to the ballpark after having married Cum's daughter that morning, Vic made him pitch. We thought it was a good thing since he hadn't had a chance to go on a honeymoon or anything. Because Vic knew he wouldn't be worth ten cents the next day. I figure he was right. I think that's the reason that he made Brown pitch.

Later we had another fellow, Roy Welmaker, who married a schoolteacher. And he just got married the year he joined us. Now, a young boy who has just married has got to go home every now and then. You can't get him on the road and stay three weeks or more and think that he doesn't want to go home. In the later years, if we got a young ballplayer and he got married, every chance that we could get, we'd let him go home for a few days.

Now usually, if a fellow pitched a game and asked to go home to his wife after the game was over, we'd let him go home the next day and stay two or three days. And we would tell him when and where to meet us. A manager should let him go on home and do what he's going to do. And when he would come back from home, we would not pitch him the same night that he got back, because you know he's wore out. We would wait and let him get a chance to recuperate for a couple of days. Then he's ready to go. And that's what we used to do.

We had a third baseman, and his wife lived in Baltimore. We'd be playing in Washington and he'd ask Vic Harris on a Sunday evening, "Look here, my wife's in Baltimore and I want to go on back there." Then he would met us back in Washington the next day. But with a young ballplayer that way, you can keep him in good spirits as long as you let him go home every now and then. When I first got married I felt the same way.

You know how it is when you first get married, you miss your wife. So about the first of June, I wanted to go home and be with my wife. So I got "sick." At least I said I was sick. We were playing in Cleveland and the team was going to leave that Sunday morning. It was about a hundred-mile trip and they were going to come by and pick me up about eight o'clock. I told the manager that I was sick and felt bad and that I couldn't make the trip. He said, "All right, you stay here and we'll be back Thursday and you can join us then."

I had my things packed and setting there in my room. When I heard that bus pull off from downstairs going on to Cleveland, I called a taxi and went on to the railroad station. They left that Sunday morning about eight o'clock going to Cleveland to play and I left about eight-thirty on the train going to Rocky Mount. I went on home and stayed two or three days with my wife until that Wednesday and got back in Pittsburgh before the team got back. They never even knew that I had been home.

Now, when a player gets older, it doesn't make any difference, but with a young ballplayer you've got to let him go home ever now and then. Anyway, that's the way it was with Welmaker.

He was a pitcher, and he could think like the devil. He went to Clark University down in Atlanta, and when we first got him from down there, he had a screwball. We were playing a game in Toledo, Ohio, and he was pitching. Josh was catching for us and he got down and gave a sign. He put down two fingers and Welmaker shook his head. Josh gave him three fingers and he shook his head. Josh gave him one finger and he shook his head. Josh said, "Come on, Homey." Josh called him that because both of them were from Georgia. Josh started over again and Welmaker still shook his head. Josh called time and went out to the mound.

When Josh came out to the pitcher's mound I went over there from first base. I said, "What's going on here?" Josh said, "Homey don't want to throw what I say." He said, "Welmaker just came up here and I've been here eight or ten years. I know these fellows, and I know what they can hit and what they can't hit. But he wants to use his own judgment."

By that time Vic Harris came out there and he's the manager. He said, "Now listen, throw what Josh signs for." Welmaker said, "I want to throw my screwball." Vic said, "You ain't got no screwball. Throw what Josh signals for." Some college boys have to be straightened out, you know. They come up there and they think they know more than we do, and we've been there for ten or twenty years. They have their own ideas about what should be, and we just have to straighten them out. A player has to do what he is told by the manager. All of us had to do that.

Along about that time was the first time I played in a major-league park. It was in Griffith Stadium in Washington, D.C. We used to play in Griffith Stadium and in Municipal Stadium in Cleveland under the football lights because they didn't have baseball lights at that time. They would turn on the football lights and that's what we played baseball by, but they weren't as bright as baseball lights.

The first time I played in Yankee Stadium was also around 1935. It wasn't like Griffith Stadium. It was short down the right-field line, and I liked the right-field fence but I didn't like center. In the first four or five games I played there I hit a home run. I would have liked Yankee Stadium for a home park, but I don't know how many home runs I would have hit if we had played all of our games there. At that time we were playing 154 ball games, so we would be playing 77 in Yankee Stadium and 77 on the road. It would depend on the pitching. If the pitching was tough it wouldn't have been as many as if the pitching was weak, but I would have hit my share.

We played in Yankee Stadium on special occasions and when we played the New York Black Yankees, who used it as their home park. At first the Black Yankees were an independent team for a long time, and then they got in the Negro National League, but they never did win anything. In addition to playing league games, they played all the leading white semipro teams around the area. They played the Bushwicks, Parkway, Farmers, Springfield Grays, and teams around New York City. And they'd play in towns like Ossining, Pleasantville, and all around East New York and in New Jersey. And then they'd go up into New York State and play. It was very seldom that they went very far from

New York. The Black Yankees used to specialize in that kind of playing, but all of us used to do it, too. We'd go up to upstate New York and take up around Dunkirk, Olean, Saranek Lake, Poughkeepsie, Peekskill, Hudson, and all those places like that up and down the Hudson River.

We would play one team today, then play another team tomorrow. We would even go up into Lewiston, Maine, Manchester, New Hampshire, and Lynn, Massachusetts. Some of them had county fairs in summertime, and we'd play on Saturday night. We would stay up there about two weeks just playing different white teams around in county fairs and get about a hundred dollars a day. And that was all right. As long as I was with the Grays, we played up around those county fairs. Later we got a bus, and we would take that up there when we went but, when I first joined the team, we were traveling in two cars. We had a seven-passenger car and then we'd have another car that would have six in it. That was thirteen men on the entire squad.

Around that time we used to take a Hawaiian All-Star team on a tour. We would go out around Pittsburgh and take them all around the area and play eight or ten games. In one doubleheader, I went four for six with a double and a triple, but the Hawaiian team wasn't as good as our team. They had a fellow managing the team named Buck Lei, and his son played on the team, too. Buck Lei had also played third base for the Bushwicks in New York and that's where we first saw him. After he got his name established, he organized a team and called them the Hawaiian All-Stars. He was from Hawaii but his son was born in California and had never been to Hawaii and didn't even know anything about Hawaii.

In league play, the season was divided into two halves, and the first half ended on the Fourth of July, when we lost a doubleheader to the Pittsburgh Crawfords. That Independence Day doubleheader between us got to be an annual affair. I was batting .337 at the break, and I made my first All-Star game appearance that year. I had led in the fans' voting right up until the last week, but Oscar Charleston beat me out for a starting position by 109 votes. I don't know anything about the voting or how it was handled or nothing like that. But I was picked for the All-Star squad as a non-starter and got to play in the game anyway.

Our East-West All-Star game had started in 1933, the same year as the white major leagues' All-Star game. Usually the Grays played on the East squad, but in 1935 we were playing with the West. The West team consisted of players from the Pittsburgh Crawfords, Homestead Grays, Chicago American Giants, and Columbus Elite Giants. The Elite Giants had not gone to Baltimore yet. The East team came from the Newark Dodgers, Philadelphia Stars, New York Cubans, and Brooklyn Eagles. Only two of us from our team were selected to play in the All-Star game, myself and Raymond Brown. Around the time of the All-Star break the Philadelphia Stars' manager, Webster McDonald, offered to trade four players for the two of us.

We played most of our games out of Pittsburgh and on the road, and we did a lot of traveling. And Webster McDonald said that if Brown and I had been in Philadelphia, where we could play in the same location instead of traveling around, then we would draw a better crowd for the league and for all the teams that came to Philadelphia. But Cum Posey just laughed him down.

So when we left for the All-Star game we were still with the Grays. We left Newark, New Jersey, on a plane, and that was the first time that I had ever been on a plane. The fare from Newark to Chicago at that time was forty-four dollars, and it took the plane three hours and fifty-nine minutes to make the trip. They used to have a big sign on there that advertised how long it took to fly back.

That was my first trip to the All-Star game. In the bottom of the sixth inning Josh Gibson hit a four-hundred-foot line drive to the left-center-field fence for a double. Martin Dihigo ran into the fence trying to catch the ball and was injured. They stopped the game and everybody went out there and gathered around him. But he was all right and stayed in the game. I pinch hit for Leroy Matlock in the sixth inning against Leon Day. Slim Jones had started the game, and Day relieved him. They had Tiant warming up in the bullpen. I liked hitting against right-handers better and I was a fastball hitter, but I grounded out back to Day. And then I stayed in the game to play first base in place of Charleston.

When I came up to bat in the tenth inning, Dihigo was pitching and we were one run behind. On the first pitch, I hit a sacrifice fly to tie the ball game. Then the next inning, we had the winning run on base and two outs and Josh Gibson at bat. They decided to walk Josh to pitch to Mule Suttles, and we won the game when Mule hit a home run with two outs and two on in the bottom of the eleventh inning.

The Grays had finished a half game above .500 for the first half, and then we finished a half game under .500 for the second half, which made us dead even at the end of the season. That was our first year back in the league, and only my second year with the Grays. At the end of the season, Cum Posey picked me on his All-America team for the year. Vic Harris and I were the only two from the Grays that he picked. We were on his team and he had to pick somebody else from other teams for the other positions. Cum wrote an article every week for the *Pittsburgh Courier,* but the other newspapers had guys picking All-Star teams, too.

One time I asked Cum whey he didn't pick Lick Carlisle for his All-Star team, and he said that anybody that he publicized by picking them on the All-Star team would want more money. I don't think that Carlisle really deserved to be on the All-Star team, though. He could run the bases but he wasn't that good a hitter or fielder and couldn't make the double play like some of them that we had after that.

That winter was the first year I went to Puerto Rico. Abe Manley owned the Brooklyn Eagles in 1935, and he signed me to go with them. We took a good team down there. Vic Harris managed the team and played left field. In center field we had Ray Brown from the Grays, who also pitched. In right field we had Ed Stone. At third base we had Ray Dandridge. At shortstop we had a fellow named Bill Sadler. He didn't play in Negro baseball long. At second base we had Dick Seay. He played for the Philadelphia Stars at that time, over here in the States. I was playing first base. Catching we had Frank Duncan from the Kansas City Monarchs and Johnny Hayes from the Brooklyn Royal Giants. Pitching we had Slim Jones, Raymond Brown, Leon Day, Terris McDuffie, and a fellow named Slim Lewis.

That was the year we played the Cincinnati Reds in exhibitions.

We had been down there since October and had played all winter and were in good condition. They were spring training there and were just getting started. They got down there about the first of February in 1936, and we were supposed to leave there the fifteenth of February, but we stayed there another month in order to play them.

We played three games and beat them two out of three. That's all they wanted to play, and that one year was the only time we played them. I was impressed with the major leaguers. They were a whole lot better than the Negro League teams. Paul Derringer was the pitcher I was most impressed with. He gave me a hard time. They also had Calvin Chapman, Lew Riggs, and Kiki Cuyler with them. They had a good team. Some of them were the same players they had in 1939–40 when they won back-to-back pennants. They didn't make any comments or talk to us either during the game or after the game.

The game that they won, I lost for us. A ground ball went right between my legs at first base and they beat us, 3–2. Johnny Peacock, their catcher, was the batter. It was late in the game, about the seventh or eighth inning, and a man was on third base when it happened. Nobody said anything about it because they knew it was just an error, that's all. I didn't make many errors, but it seemed like sometimes when I *did* make them, it cost a lot.

Slim Jones mowed them down when he pitched. He was in good shape because he'd been down there all the winter. Slim was still in his prime and was the best pitcher in our league at that time. After we played the Reds, a team from Cuba came down to Puerto Rico and beat them two straight. And then we mixed together with the Cubans and beat them bad then. The score was about 12–4 or something like that.

Hi Bithorn pitched for us in one game against the Reds. He was a white Puerto Rican. He was just a youngster when he played for us and we told him a few things that might have helped him. Then the Cubs got him and put him in the minor leagues for two or three years. He developed on the farm and Chicago finally took him up there to pitch for the Cubs. He stayed with them four or five years, and won eighteen games for the Chicago Cubs the last

year before he went into the service during World War II. He was
about as good as Johnny Wright, who pitched for us.

In Puerto Rico, fans would throw oranges and lemons at the
players on the field. That was something we were not used to.
But we were the champions down there. I hit .346 and, as I said,
that winter was when I really learned to play first base. That's
another thing about winter baseball, you can practice whatever
you're weak on. They'll send somebody out to the ballpark with
you in the morning and you can hit for two hours if you want to.
You can field for hours if you want to, and the local boys will
help you out. They'll send two or three of them out there and
they'll pitch to you just as long as you want to hit, or they'll hit
ground balls to you just as long as you want to field. That is really
how you improve your baseball skills, by playing winter baseball.
Because at that time, they only played games on Saturday evening,
Sunday morning, and Sunday evening. All the rest of the time you
could practice if you wanted to.

Baseball wasn't the only thing we learned down there that winter. I remember one thing that happened off the field. A whole lot
of players got ''burnt'' down there by going up in the red-light
district. Five or six players went down there to pick up some girls
and picked up something else, too. They caught a social disease
down there. That's when salvo-salve first came out, and that's
what the team doctor used. Penicillin hadn't been developed yet,
and sulfa drugs came out later, too. When we got down there they
told us not to go in that district. They said, ''Don't go up on
Lomas Street, that's the red-light district and it's 85 percent
syphilitic.''

But you know how it is when somebody gets full of beer. They
can't remember one street from another. And some guys went up
there one night. And all of them got burnt down there and had to
go to the doctor. And when it was time to leave they still wasn't
in good shape. But nobody missed any games down there because
of the condition they were in. The doctor had told them what to
do when they got back here to the States. Ballplayers back in
those days were bad about that kind of thing. They'd tell us where
to go and where not to go. But with ballplayers, when you tell
them not to go somewhere, that's where they're going to go.

That wasn't the only time something like that happened. It was pretty commonplace. The girls were waiting outside the clubhouse. I was still single then, but most of us were married. And when we went to another town, we told them we weren't married. We used to say, "Let every town furnish its own women." One time a young player joined the Grays out of Wiley College and he found himself in the same situation as the guys did down in Puerto Rico, and asked what to do about it. Another player told him to take some concoction, and he took it and got real sick. *Then* he went to the doctor.

Before we left Puerto Rico, they gave us a farewell lunch on March 11, 1936, at the Escambron Baseball Park. We got back to the States about the fifteenth of April and I was here in Rocky Mount for a few days, and then it was time to go to spring training.

# Chapter 7

## Prelude to a Dynasty (1936)

*Buck is one of the best players in the league, steady as a clock, stays in condition and makes all hard plays look easy.*

*—Cum Posey, Homestead Grays*

We trained in Atlanta in 1936. Vic Harris, Ray Brown, and I had just got back from Puerto Rico and we were in good playing shape when we reported to spring training camp. The reason we trained there was because we could play the college teams. The four colleges there were Morris Brown, Spelman, Clark, and Morehead. And we could also play the Fort Benning Army Barracks' team.

We only trained in Atlanta for a year. It wasn't far enough south, and it got too chilly. So then we had spring training in Florida for eight or ten years, until the wartime restrictions made us have to train near home. Then we went back to Florida again after the war. Regardless of where we trained, each spring we played our way into shape. That's what we called playing "strong-arm baseball." We learned by playing. We traveled around the South playing exhibition games before the regular season began.

With the other teams that I had been on, we traveled in cars, but on the Grays we traveled on the bus that Sonnyman Jackson bought for the team. Cum Posey didn't allow gambling, but a whole lot of gambling was going on anyway, both in the back of the bus and in the rooms at night. There was a lot of fast living among baseball players. At that time most players were gamblers, and they liked to play cards and dice. And they were rough. And sometimes they got loud. They would talk about girls in a certain kind of way, and things like that. I didn't go for that. I just wouldn't pay no attention to what they said.

We'd be riding along the highway and I would try to keep everybody quiet. But you know how that is. When I tried to talk about the Bible or something like that, well, that was foreign to them. I'm not a preacher, I'm just a Christian man. And it was difficult sometimes. I'm not perfect by any means, but I tried to do what was right. And if I couldn't do anything to help somebody, I wouldn't do anything to hurt him. But on the ball teams, we didn't talk about things like that much. The other ballplayers would rather play cards, and they used to pass the time by teasing the bus driver. I would tell him not to pay any attention to what they said, that they were just joking him.

And we used to sing on the Grays' bus. We were doing a lot of traveling, and to pass the time on the bus trips we had a quartet. George Scales was the leader of the quartet, and when he left the team, Jelly Jackson took his place. Jerry Benjamin was singing tenor. I was singing baritone. And Matthew Carlisle was singing something, I don't know what. And that was our quartet. We were the four that did the most singing. But sometimes Vic Harris took Carlisle's place and, after Jelly left the team, Vic took his place. Sometimes others would take part in the singing. What we specialized in was barbershop singing, four-part harmony, and we sang just about every night when we was traveling. It sounded good late at night, and it seemed like it made the trips a little shorter. Sometimes we would all be singing, and we would keep singing until we fell off to sleep.

We tried to sound like the Mills Brothers. We tried to sing their songs. You know, they went around with us on the bus for a while. We were staying at the Woodside Hotel in New York and they had singing engagements downtown and were staying there, too. When we would go out somewhere to play on their off-days, they would go with us wherever we were going that evening. But they had to be back to perform that night at one of the big theaters.

They were from Ohio originally, and they were baseball fans. Two of them, Harry and John, were the ones who used to go out there and mess around with baseball. The youngest brother used to work out at shortstop for us when we played white semipro teams. He was out of shape, of course, but he'd go out there and work out at shortstop with us, taking infield practice before the game. He even played a game once. He played outfield in one game against a semipro team, but they didn't hit the ball to him. He wanted to hit and we let him bat for somebody one time. Part of the time the old man, their daddy, went, too, but he never played.

That's the only singing group that went around with us, and they were my favorites. Donald sang lead. Herbert sang tenor. He was the quiet one. Harry sang baritone, and he went blind later in life, about 1967. John sang bass but he died in 1936, and his daddy, who was also named John, took his place. They had a big hit with a song called "Paper Doll" in 1941.

Of course, we all liked the Mills Brothers and we liked the Inkspots and one or two other groups. But I was a quartet singer, period. I was in the choir down at the St. James Baptist Church for a long time. We sang religious hymns and I sang baritone, but I don't sing in the church choir anymore because I lost my singing voice. I don't know how long ago that was, but it's been a good while. I've mellowed a whole lot, but I still like the quartet singing better than any other kind of singing. Four-part harmony. Even now, I'd rather hear quartet singing.

We also had a radio on the bus and sometimes when we weren't singing, we listened to all kinds of music on the radio. I didn't like jazz too much, but I like some hillbilly singing and we would turn on country music sometimes. Gene Autry was our favorite western singer at that time.

I talked with him at Cooperstown about eight or ten years ago for a long time. We talked about baseball and about country singing and about several other things. I told him I used to sit on the front seat and look at his western movies. He laughed and said that he was glad I was patronizing him.

And I talked about how high-priced his team was, but still didn't do anything, and he said that he was going to have a shakeup. Gene Mauch was his coach and was sitting right there at the table. We asked Gene Autry why he didn't make Mauch the manager. He just said that he had somebody in mind, but then he *did* make Mauch his manager the next year, and they finished in second place, only one game behind Kansas City in their division. Then they won their division the next year, but lost to Boston in the League Championship Series. That was in 1986. The Angels still haven't won a pennant for Gene Autry. But back there in 1936, he was still a cowboy singer in the movies.

That was the same year that Cum Posey wanted to take a ten-day leave of absence from league play so he could take the team on a barnstorming exhibition tour in the Northwest around Montana, but that never did happen. At the end of July the league did let fifteen of us from different teams form an all-star team and go to Denver, Colorado, to play in the *Denver Post* Tournament.

We had Felton Snow from Baltimore at third base, but he was nursing a spike injury, and Jack Marshall played most of the time at third base. And we had Chester Williams from the Pittsburgh Crawfords playing shortstop, Sammy T. Hughes from the Baltimore Elite Giants playing second base, and I was playing first base. That was our infield. We had Vic Harris playing left field, Cool Papa Bell playing center field, and Bill Wright playing right field. That was our outfield. We had Josh Gibson catching. A boy named Paul Hardy from Birmingham was the second-string catcher. Of course we knew Josh was going to do all the catching. Pitching was Satchel Paige, Raymond Brown, Robert Griffith, and Sam Streeter. Streeter was a relief pitcher. He wasn't one of the starters. Candy Jim Taylor was the manager and See Posey was the business manager for the team. We were called the Negro National League All-Star team, and that was the best team I ever played on.

Going out there we stopped in Des Moines, Iowa. That was when we first met Bob Feller. He hadn't gone to the major leagues yet. We beat the Des Moines team, 17–0, but Feller didn't play in the game. From Des Moines we went to Omaha, Nebraska, and played a team there. Then we went on to Denver and played in the tournament.

It was an amateur double-elimination tournament. They called it the Little World Series. They were semipro ballplayers and we didn't have any trouble with them. We won the tournament and didn't lose a game. We won all seven games that we played and none of them was close. The closest score was 7–2. The last night we played Enid, Oklahoma, and we had to beat them twice. They hadn't lost a game to anybody else and we beat them, 15–3 and 7–0. Satchel shut them out and struck out eighteen in the final game.

Everybody hit good in the tournament, but Cool Papa hit .481, and that was the highest on the team. I hit .360, and there was one game where I hit a triple to break up the game. They gave prizes for the tournament, and most of them were won by players on our team. Satchel was the best pitcher. Chester Williams was the best infielder and Vic Harris was the best outfielder. Josh Gibson had the most RBIs and Cool Papa stole the most bases. I didn't win anything. They gave a box of cigars for the first three home runs, but I didn't get any of them either. But I wasn't smoking at that time, anyway. I started smoking them later.

We dominated the tournament, but they had semipro teams out there. We weren't supposed to be there. We were playing in organized baseball, but we weren't recognized as organized ballplayers. That's how we were able to play in the tournament.

Some players on the other teams had been to the major leagues and had gotten out of the major leagues, but they didn't bring anybody that was still in the major leagues. They might have played under assumed names, but I don't know about that. If they did, they didn't get caught.

They barred us after we won. After we won they paid us and told us not to come back no more. And we never did go back again. We were going to leave there and go to Wichita for that tournament. But they called out there and said for us not to come to Wichita because we couldn't play. And we didn't play.

Now, in the Denver tournament first prize was $5,092 and some cents. We were supposed to get a certain amount apiece. After we played our last game in Denver that night, we left the next morning and had not divided the money. At first they said they were going to divide the money there. Then they decided to wait until we got to Chicago. We went to a town called Oxford, Nebraska, and played that next night and then we came on to Chicago and when we got to Chicago they decided to wait until we got back out East. Gus Greenlee was not there and he was the head man of us going out there. He got a quarter of it and we didn't get much. When we got the money about a week later, it had dwindled down to just about nothing. We got some recognition but not much money.

Fortunately, our salaries were still going with our teams, and we came back to our regular teams and finished the season. The Elites were in Washington that year and they won the first half, but the Philadelphia Stars disputed their title, and the commissioner made them play two protested games after the end of the second half to decide who won the first half. The Pittsburgh Crawfords won the second half. That was the year they had Willie Foster and Satchel Paige both pitching for them. In our traditional Fourth of July doubleheader with them, Ray Brown won the first game for us, 2–1, but Satchel shut us out in the second game, 8–0, in seven innings.

Later in the year, Dan Parker, a sportswriter for the *New York Daily Mirror,* accused the Crawfords of "throwing" a ball game against the Bushwicks. But he later admitted that he was wrong, and had received a "bad tip" from somebody.

The Grays finished in the second division with a losing record but, according to the newspapers, I hit .436 and 33 home runs for the year. After the season, we were scheduled to play a series of games in Kansas City, but we were rained out. We came back East and played some exhibition games against some black teams in Durham and Winston-Salem. That was in October, and the weather was beginning to get too cold to keep playing.

That's when I went to Cuba and played with Marianao in the winter league. Martin Dihigo managed me down there. He was also the top pitcher and the top home-run hitter on our team. I ate down at his house almost every Sunday, and I knew his wife and I knew his daddy. We also had Silvio Garcia pitching for us.

That was before he hurt his arm and started playing shortstop full time. I hit .304 for the winter and we won the pennant by one game over Santa Clara. Ray Brown, from the Grays, was Santa Clara's top pitcher and led the league with twenty-one wins.

That might have been the year I got thrown out of a game in Cuba. The umpire called a runner safe at first base on a double play and I thought he was out. And I got to arguing with the Cuban umpire. He couldn't understand what I was saying and I couldn't understand what he was saying. He put me out of the ball game and said that I called him a name and I had to pay ten dollars before I could play the next day. I *did* call him a couple of names. I learned to speak Spanish a little bit, but I was talking in English and I knew he couldn't understand English. That's why I was telling him that. I thought he couldn't understand what I was saying, but maybe he did understand *some* English! At least he made a good guess about what I was saying. He looked at that expression on my face and could tell that I wasn't saying nothing good.

That was the first time I got thrown out of a game. Another time in Cuba, a fellow was throwing at me and I started out there toward the mound, but the catcher got between us and I never got to him. We just argued.

There was only one more time in my career that I got thrown out of a game. We went down to Norfolk to play Birmingham one night. It was an exhibition game and we were using local umpires. I didn't think he would put me out of the ball game because he was a local umpire. Now, had it been a league umpire, I wouldn't have said what I did. But he put me out of the game. And those were the only two times that I ever got put out of a ball game.

# Chapter 8

## First Pennant (1937)

*Buck Leonard is the greatest player to enter big-time Negro baseball in the past five years.*
— Philadelphia Tribune

In 1937 they organized the Negro American League. They had teams in the Midwest and South and, at that same time, the Negro National League became an eastern league. The Chicago American Giants and the Kansas City Monarchs had been in the Negro National League a long time but had dropped out, and were in the new league. A lot of teams were in and out of the league, but by the forties, they were pretty much set after the Cleveland Buckeyes and Indianapolis Clowns joined. They had the Birmingham Black Barons and Memphis Red Sox from the South. Some other southern teams, the Jacksonville Red Caps and the Atlanta Black Crackers, were also in the league for a year or two.

Kansas City won the league's first pennant in 1937. They were owned by J. L. Wilkinson. He was a white man, and I understand that he owned property around town there. In earlier years, Kansas City had some of those old-timers like Bullet Rogan and all of them guys, but they were there a long time ago. In later years the Monarchs got some younger ballplayers. Hilton Smith was a good

77

pitcher, and when Satchel joined the Monarchs, Hilton Smith got
well known as Satchel's relief. Satchel was the top pitcher in the
Negro Leagues at that time. But Leon Day, Bill Byrd, and Raymond Brown in our league were just as good as Hilton Smith, or
a little better.

Birmingham had their best teams in the forties, when Piper
Davis and all of those players were there. They had Tommy Sampson, Artie Wilson, Lester Lockett, and Lyman Bostock. After a
while Birmingham got some younger ballplayers, including Willie
Mays. So did the Memphis Red Sox. They got some younger
ballplayers, too. They used to have Jelly Taylor, Red Longley,
and Larry Brown. Longley and Brown were catchers. Jelly Taylor
was a first baseman. Johnny Lyles played third base for a while,
and Neil Robinson was playing left field. They had a boy named
T. J. Brown playing shortstop and one of the Bankheads, Fred,
playing second base. He was Sam Bankhead's brother. And another Bankhead, Dan, the one that went to the Dodgers, pitched
with them later. And they had Verdell Mathis pitching. They were
in there with the younger group in the forties.

The Jacksonville team got their name because they started as
Red Caps working at the train station there, and playing ball, too.
They had Preacher Henry, and old Preacher had a dropball like
Dwight Gooden of the Mets. They also had Skindown Robinson,
Dad Turner, and Fluke Mitchell, their manager. In 1940 they
moved up North and played as the Cleveland Bears. After a couple
of years in Cleveland, they moved back to Jacksonville, and a
new team started in Cleveland.

That was the Buckeyes. They started in Cincinnati before mov-
ing to Cleveland and, in 1942, some of their players were killed
in an automobile accident. They were riding in a car and had a
flat tire one night. When they got out to fix it, someone was
standing in front of the taillight and a car came along and didn't
see them and ran right into the back of their car and killed three
of them.

Some of the owners in the West were in the numbers business
like the owners out East. The man in Birmingham was in the
rackets and ran a restaurant. The man at Cleveland ran a chicken
farm and did a little gambling, too. Now, in Memphis, there were

two Martin brothers and they were medical doctors. One was a dentist. And there were two more Martin brothers, too. One was the owner of the Chicago American Giants. Syd Pollock was the owner of the Indianapolis Clowns, and Abe Saperstein, who owned the Harlem Globetrotters basketball team, also worked with the Clowns baseball team. He was a booking agent and had done some booking for the Black Barons, too.

In the East Gus Greenlee with the Crawfords, Abe Manley with the Newark Eagles, and Rufus Jackson with the Grays were all in the numbers racket. In Baltimore Tom Wilson was the owner of the Elite Giants, and he was in the rackets. Alex Pompez, owner of the New York Cubans, was in the numbers business, too. And so were Ed Bolden in Philadelphia and a fellow named James Semler, who owned the Black Yankees in New York City when they were operating. Most blacks who had money to finance a baseball team were in the numbers racket.

Had it not been for that, we might not have got Josh Gibson with us. Josh joined the Grays in January of 1937. One of our owners, Sonnyman Jackson, bought him from Gus Greenlee to pay off a hit in the numbers lottery. Greenlee had a big hit on his number, and our man paid Greenlee for Josh. That's how we got him, because Greenlee needed the money to pay off a hit.

Jackson was a nice fellow, but he didn't care anything about baseball at first. But he got interested when he started riding around with us in the bus and heard how we talked and the lies we told. And he got used to that. You know, sometimes when a man doesn't have an interest in a thing and goes out with the guys and hears how they joke and talk, it makes a difference. We were playing pretty good ball, and he just got interested and got Josh from the Crawfords.

Josh had been a holdout, and he wanted more money from Greenlee. He had hit .444 the year before and hit 18 home runs in 45 league games, which would have been over 60 in a full 154-game season like the major leagues were playing at that time. When Josh was sold to us, the papers called it "The biggest player deal in the history of Negro baseball." They said that Josh and Judy Johnson were traded for Pepper Bassett and Henry Spearman and twenty-five hundred dollars. I don't know about Judy, he didn't play with us that year. I reckon he retired at that time, but we *did* get Josh.

That's when we started winning. Josh made the whole team better. He put life into everybody. Before that we were just an ordinary ballclub. Josh made the difference. I know I started getting a lot of good pitches because they were pitching around Josh. They weren't watching me so much. They were watching him those first years he was with us. That was the reason I ended up the first half of the season leading the league in batting with an average of .500 that year. Their main interest was to get Josh out.

I was also tied with Josh for the league lead in home runs with 7 at the end of the first half of 1937. That only included league games, and Josh had missed five weeks during June and part of July when he went to Santo Domingo to play with Satchel for Trujillo's All-Stars. When he left to go down there, he told me, "Buck, you hold them close until I get back." I tried to do just that. One day we beat the Pittsburgh Crawfords a doubleheader and, in the second game, I had three hits, including a grand-slam homerun, and we won, 20–0.

Tommy Dukes did most of the catching for us while Josh was gone, and he did all right. But when Josh came back from Santo Domingo, we were glad to get him back and get his bat in the lineup. There was no resentment at all about him leaving the team. He got along with the rest of the players, and he was welcomed back with open arms. The Elites protested us using him when we played them. They were in first place at the time, but we swept them in a five-game series soon after that. In one of the games, Josh hit three home runs over the center-field fence in four times up.

Josh Gibson was a big, strong, right-handed hitter like Jimmie Foxx but had more power than Foxx. Josh was a good curveball hitter. You could get him out with a fastball, but if you threw him a curveball, he'd hit it a mile. Even missing that much time, he was still credited with 62 home runs for the season. But that total included games against all levels of competition, not just league games. Had we been in the same league and played against Foxx every day, I don't know how Josh would have stacked up.

When Josh came back to us, Cum Posey was glad to have him

back, but some of the other owners whose players jumped down there were mad about it and they were going to bar them out of the league. But Satchel just formed a team from the players and they called themselves the Trujillo All-Stars. With Satchel pitching, they attracted bigger crowds than most league teams, so they couldn't really make the suspension stick. I think Greenlee and Satchel had a falling out, but I don't know what really happened except that Satchel jumped the team and didn't go back.

When Josh left to come to us, Greenlee got Pepper Bassett to take Josh's place with the Crawfords and promoted him as being better than Josh. He had Bassett catch an inning while sitting in a rocking chair and promoted that act real big. They would advertise him as catching in a rocking chair, and they used to go around in the streets with that rocking chair on a truck, saying Pepper Bassett would catch the game tonight in this rocking chair.

When the game would start he would sit down in that rocking chair catching, but if somebody tried to steal second base he would get out of the chair and throw the man out at second and then sit back down. He did that for a couple of innings each game as a gate attraction for a year or two. But that was all just show business.

Greenlee touted Bassett because he was with his team then, but Bassett wasn't anywhere near the baseball player that Josh Gibson was. Bassett had been with us the year before, but compared to Josh, he wasn't no good at all.

After Josh left the Crawfords, they had gone down and they weren't the team they were the previous two or three years. The Crawfords were spring training in Monroe, Louisiana, that year, and we played them a four-game series down there in April, and we beat them three games and tied one. I hit three home runs in that series, and in one of the games I hit two home runs and Josh hit one.

Satchel had left them the year before and gone out to North Dakota to play for a white team there. When he came back, he didn't stay long before Trujillo's men cornered him outside a hotel in New Orleans and he was gone again. Cool Papa was still with the Crawfords at the beginning of the season, but he left soon after that to join Satchel in Santo Domingo. Leroy Matlock, Sam

Bankhead, and Harry Williams went down there, too. Most of their other good ballplayers also went somewhere else.

Along about that time is when Oscar Charleston caught two Santo Domincans at the Crawford Grill inquiring about players. And they were asking about the Grays, too. Bill Perkins and Thad Christopher signed with Martin Dihigo and Lazaro Salazar, who were recruiting players to play in Cuba, too.

Gus Greenlee's Crawfords suffered more than any other team from the raids. And they lost other players for other reasons. Jimmy Crutchfield went to Newark, and Ted Page had already retired a year earlier. The Crawfords fielded a team for a couple of more years before they folded, but they were never the same again. They finally went to Toledo to play out their last year.

Greenlee had built a park in Pittsburgh for the Crawfords, and it was one of the few Negro ballparks in the country. We didn't have a ballpark in Homestead and we played most of our home games at Greenlee Field. Our other home games in Pittsburgh were played at Forbes Field, the Pirates' home park, when they were out of town. And that season was the first time we started playing some home games at Griffith Stadium in Washington, D.C. We wore a "W" on the sleeve of our uniform in recognition of this, and that was when we first started being referred to as the Washington-Homestead Grays.

Playing at the major-league parks was a lot different from playing at Greenlee Field. I hate to even mention Greenlee Field because it was so dilapidated. It didn't have no top on it. Not on any part of it. The fence was close to 400 feet in left field, and center field was about 500 feet. Left field and center field were open, but there were bleachers in right field. It was about 350 to 375 feet in right field. The capacity of the ballfield was roughly eight or ten thousand.

We dressed at home because there were no clubhouses there. Between games of a doubleheader, we would just sit around out there on the field. But we only played a doubleheader there two or three times. None of the stands was covered, so there was no protection from the weather. The stands had a chicken wire screen in front. I didn't know of no gamblers that hung out at the park, but there might have been some. Greenlee built the ballpark when he bought the Crawfords in 1932, and they tore it down after the 1938 season. That's when we started using the Pirates' park when we played in Pittsburgh.

I preferred to play in Forbes Field. It was a pretty good ballfield, and we used all the facilities there. They had a trolleycar that went around by the ballpark. We were staying in Pittsburgh when I first started playing, and we caught the trolleycar to the ballpark. When we moved to Homestead and I was staying with Sonnyman Jackson, we took the bus to the ballpark. If we were playing a doubleheader at Forbes Field, I got up about eight or nine o'clock. We ate at the Sky Rocket Grill before going to the game. Usually we ate a standard breakfast, something like ham and eggs, and then we went on the bus to the ballpark.

When we played at Griffith Stadium, we would would leave Pittsburgh at four o'clock Sunday morning and get in Washington at a quarter to twelve that same day. It was 290 miles from Pittsburgh to Washington on the turnpike. We stopped on the way to eat, about halfway there. We'd play a doubleheader and go back to Pittsburgh that same day. We would leave at about nine o'clock that night to come back home, and we would get back about five o'clock in the morning. We would sleep in the bus and play a Monday evening game against somebody around Pittsburgh. Sometimes we played around Pittsburgh against semipro teams and didn't take no batting practice. We'd get off the bus and play. We were professionals and it didn't take much to play those teams.

In the spring that year, some sportswriter wrote an article that said, "Grays boast a new superstar in Buck Leonard." But I never paid no attention to what they wrote in the papers. I was just happy to be playing baseball.

We went South to Jacksonville, Florida, for spring training and played a series against the Ethiopian Clowns in Miami. That was when Dave Barnhill was still with them, before he joined the New York Cubans. We played on a high school grounds and the fences weren't too far. One game against them I hit a home run and a triple but Josh hit two home runs and a double and he got the headlines. That's the way it was. When you played with Josh, he got the headlines. He was the drawing card. Everybody came out to see him play because he was advertised above everybody else.

He was the only real star we had. So we just had to give him the most publicity.

I guess that the two of us were the team leaders. I mostly lead by example. I always played hard and played to win. Maybe the other fellows saw that and it helped them to play harder, too. That spring we played a game against the Indianapolis team of the American Association in Bowling Green, Kentucky. That was the first time that a white team and a black team had played against each other in the South.

In 1937 we won our first pennant, and that started our string of nine straight league championships. I was the first baseman all those years. Jerry Benjamin was in the outfield, and Ray Brown was our top pitcher. We were the only three players who played as regulars in all nine seasons, but I would say we had good continuity during this time. Vic Harris was there each season, but he spent two years working in a defense job and didn't manage or play full time those years. Josh Gibson was the catcher except for the two years that he was in Mexico. And Edsall Walker only missed one year, 1942, when he was in a defense job and playing with the Philly Stars.

Lick Carlisle was the second baseman from '37 through '42, and he was a fair player but he never made the All-Star team. He finally quit because he would get tired in the season and want to rest. He got a defense job during the war and just decided that he would quit playing and started working. Our bossman had a tavern and he started tending bar there around 1947.

When Carlisle began working in the defense plant, Joe Spencer came in. He was a wartime ballplayer, somebody we picked up because we didn't have anybody else to play. He didn't have any speed or power to speak of and was below average in fielding.

Jelly Jackson was the shortstop from '37 through '40. Jelly was not a good hitter, but he was good defensively and was a good base runner. He didn't go into the Army, but he got a defense job. He was out about three years, and when we got him back, he'd slowed down. We finally had to let him go because he couldn't move. Being out of sports like that has a tendency to slow you down. Your reflexes slow and your coordination is off. In those three years that Jelly worked in a defense job, Chester

Williams and Sam Bankhead were the shortstops. Chester played
in 1941 and part of '42, but Bankhead played most of the time
from '42 on.

We had a lot of third basemen, but Howard Easterling played
more than anybody else there. Blue Perez was the third baseman
in 1937, and we got Henry Spearman during the next season.
Boojum Wilson played third base with us during the war years.
Easterling went into the Army at about that time or a little after
that. And then we had Dock Battle, who played some at third base
for us a couple of years during the war. He wasn't such a good
hitter and had no power and didn't have such a good arm. He
was just a replacement. Just somebody to stand over there because
we couldn't get anybody else. I carried him from my hometown
up there to Homestead.

Rev Cannady came with us and stayed until he and Cum Posey
got in an argument about some money and Rev left. He was over
the hill and his speed had gone, but he was still able to field, and
he was a fair hitter. And one other thing about him, he didn't
want to play with us. The way we were playing, traveling so
much. That wasn't his type of baseball.

Vic was our left fielder most of the time, but he stopped playing
in '43. He was managing but he wasn't playing regular. That was
the year that we got Cool Papa, and Cool played for the next three
years until he retired. Vic didn't manage two of the last three
years of our nine straight pennants. That's when he got a defense
job and Candy Jim Taylor managed the team.

One outfield position seemed like it was always changing. Ray
Brown played in the outfield some of the time, especially when
he first joined the team. He was pitching for us and he was also
a good hitter, and hit from both sides of the plate. Big Jim Williams was there about 1934, way back when I first went to the
team, and he played about four more years after I got there. He
was a big fellow, about as big as Josh, and was a pretty good
hitter. He could hit the ball a long ways. But he wasn't such a
good outfielder, though. He was our right fielder the first two years
we won the pennant.

Then Dave Whatley joined the team in 1939 and was our regular
right fielder for the next four years. He was real fast and a fair

hitter. His outfielding wasn't so good and his throwing wasn't so good, but he could fly. He was nicknamed "Speed" and was the fastest man we had except for Cool Papa. We had five fellows who could run the bases. They were Whatley, Bell, Benjamin, Carlisle, and Jelly Jackson. They were our base stealers.

Whatley played until the war. He didn't go into the service, he just quit and decided to go back to Griffin, Georgia. We don't know what happened to him. He didn't stay with us but a few years. He didn't like the traveling we were doing, that was one thing. And we thought that was the reason he didn't come back. We had another boy named Dave Hoskins, who played about '44 or '45. He later played with the Cleveland Indians as a pitcher.

Pitching was Ray Brown and Edsall Walker. And we had Johnny Wright, Roy Partlow, and Roy Welmaker. Wright wasn't there in 1937, he came along later, around 1942. He was one of our top pitchers, too. Partlow, Walker, and Welmaker were left-handers. Terris McDuffie pitched with us one year, too. Those were the ones who did most of the pitching during those nine years when we were winning pennants. Brown was our best pitcher, and Wright was about next to him.

Some of our other pitchers during that time were Tom Parker and J. C. Hamilton. Hamilton was a fair left-handed pitcher from Sarasota, Florida, and he used to be Dizzy Dean's caddie. Dizzy Dean used to come down for spring training with St. Louis and they had some time off for golf, and Hamilton was his caddie. J. C. Hamilton could hit the golf ball just as far as anybody you could think of. We used to go to the range and buy a bucket of balls and the man wouldn't let him use the regular driver, he had to use a smaller iron, something like a number three or number four iron so that he would stay within the range. Now, he could drive, but he couldn't play golf, because he couldn't putt or chip or do nothing like that. But he could hit the ball four miles.

And we had Spoon Carter. He had a good screwball and he *was* a screwball. I don't remember his real name. We just called him Spoon. We had two Walkers. We had Edsall Walker and we had another boy, R. T. Walker. We called them "Big" Walker and "Little" Walker. Edsall was the "big" half of it. R. T. Walker pitched for us for three or four years, but he wasn't one of our main pitchers. He just pitched against white teams most of the time.

Red Ferrell was from Birmingham and he stayed with us for maybe a couple of years. But he never was a top-notch pitcher. We used to pitch him against white teams in exhibitions. We had a pitcher named Jess Houston. We got him from the Cincinnati Tigers. He was a good pitcher, too, but he was brief. He didn't last long. Arnold Waite was with us but he was brief, too, and didn't stay but about a year or so.

Tommy Dukes was the catcher part of the time before we got Josh, and Rab Roy Gaston and Eddie Napier were backups. Gaston was just an average player. He wasn't such a good hitter and didn't have such a good arm and he never did become our regular catcher. He was always a substitute. He and Napier caught when Josh was in Mexico. Napier was a better hitter and a better fielder than Gaston. Napier was a pretty good receiver and a fair hitter, but he wasn't one of the top ones either way. He was not with the team as long as Gaston.

Josh Johnson was a catcher with us for a while when we were looking for a replacement for Josh Gibson. We had Johnson when we couldn't get anybody better. He wasn't what you would call a real top-notch player. And we also had a catcher named Joe Greene. He went to Kansas City later, but we had him first. We picked him up from Stone Mountain, Georgia, and he played with us for not quite a year. We didn't keep him because he couldn't hit. He learned to hit like the devil later, when he got to be with Kansas City.

Those were the main players we had with us during those nine seasons, 1937–45. That's what they call the "dynasty years." Those seasons paralleled the great Yankee teams of the same era. But I don't think the Grays would have fared so well against the Yankees in head-to-head competition, because we just didn't stack up as a team. If we had played the other major-league teams it would have been about the same thing.

It depended on who pitched. If we had our best pitchers pitching we had a pretty good ball team. But if we had to use some of the other pitchers, I don't believe we would have done so good. We put a pitcher out there who could throw the ball over the plate and who could pitch nine innings. If he couldn't pitch nine innings, he didn't stay on the team. And we didn't have a lot of walks. We had about three or four good pitchers and about three or four just ordinary pitchers. Back there then, the major-league teams had four good pitchers and a couple of good relief pitchers.

And they had good players at each position, two good catchers and bench strength. We didn't have depth like that. From 1934 to 1950 I was the only first baseman for the Grays. We had a utility infielder or outfielder and one good catcher and one fair catcher. We just didn't have the bench that major-league teams had. We had three or four ballplayers on the team who could hit the ball, and some others who could hit pretty good. In our league, we didn't have a lot of players who couldn't hit, but there are a lot of players now a days who just can't hit.

Ordinarily we had eighteen players on the roster but during the war we had less, and we didn't have good players at each position. Man for man and position for position we were not as good as the major leaguers. We didn't fool ourselves. None of the Negro League teams were major-league teams, and we knew it. We didn't claim to have major-league teams. But there were some of us on some of the teams that felt like we could have made it in the major leagues. Just about all of our regular players could have gone into the major leagues, but I don't know about being starters. Somebody else may have played the same positions that they did. Some of the fellows from our league had to change positions when they went into the major leagues, like Larry Doby and Monte Irvin.

And when we were barnstorming in the fall of the year, we had an All-Star team and the major leaguers had an All-Star team. Both squads had fellows from different teams, and those fellows were not going to play together all year. So you don't know what would have happened had we played 154 games like they played in the major leagues. Now, one time they were talking about getting a black team and putting it intact into the major leagues, but we didn't think that was going to work because we would have had to get some players from other teams for us to make a representative showing in the major leagues.

We didn't have a star player at every position like the majors did. They've got star players at every position. From our team, Josh and I were picked on the All-Star team almost every year. Benjamin made the All-Star team several years. So did Bankhead after he joined the team. And Easterling was an All-Star, but he didn't join us until after Bankhead. Vic Harris and Ray Brown both played in the All-Star games and were with us during our best years.

I started at first base for the East squad in the All-Star game in 1937, and I got the highest vote total of any East player that year. That started a streak of a sort. Except for two years, I was the starting first baseman for the East for the next twelve years until the Negro National League broke up. I always considered it an honor to be selected for the All-Star game.

Josh was banned from the East-West game that year because of having jumped the league to go to play for Trujillo's team. So Jerry Benjamin, our center fielder, was the only other player from our team to be selected that year. Jerry was the leadoff hitter for the All-Stars, and I batted cleanup. I had two hits, including a home run, and we won the game, 7–2. That was my first All-Star home run, but I don't remember now who was pitching then.

But most important of all, the team was in first place at the All-Star break, and we went on to win our first pennant that year to start a streak of nine consecutive Negro National League championships for the Grays. I don't think any other team in major professional sports has ever matched that.

When we beat the Newark Eagles three straight games late in the season, that about wrapped up the pennant. But there wasn't a playoff or a World Series in 1937. That was the first year that the Negro American League had been in existence. But we did have a postseason series between players from the top two teams in each league. The papers called that a World Series. We picked up Willie Wells, Ray Dandridge, Leon Day, and Terris McDuffie from the Newark Eagles, who had finished second, and played a combination of Kansas City and Chicago players from the other league. Candy Jim Taylor, who later managed us, was their manager. See Posey decided who could play from the Eagles for us. He talked to the manager about it, though, and we got the best players.

Willie Wells was the best shortstop in the Negro Leagues, and the best shortstop I ever saw. He could hit, run, and field. He wasn't big, but he had pretty good power, and he didn't have a strong arm, but he'd throw you out. And he wanted to *win*.

Leon Day was a good pitcher. He had good control, a good curveball, a good fastball, and he knew how to pitch. And he was an excellent fielder. All the bunts around the pitching mound, he was on them like a chicken on a june bug. And he was very good at that. The third baseman and first baseman could play back when he was pitching because he was going to field any slow-hit ball around the mound. He was just an excellent baseball player. But one thing, Day said he struck me out three times in a game, but he didn't. Nobody never struck me out three times in one ball game. Not even once.

Everybody knows how Ray Dandridge could field. When it come to fielding grounders around third base, he was a shark. There's not any question about his ability. He could run, had a good arm, and he could hit. He was a first-ball hitter. If you threw that first pitch across the plate, he'd knock the devil out of the ball.

Now, he should have realized that the fellows know it, too, and that he's got to stop hitting that first pitch and hit the second pitch or the third pitch sometimes. I'd say, I know they know I'm going to hit the first pitch, and sooner or later they'll curveball me and I'm going to have to stop hitting that first pitch. But he didn't think like that, and he wasn't a heads-up ballplayer. Now, he could play like the devil, but you've got to be able to think, too. That was his shortcoming. But there were some who could think and couldn't play.

When we picked up those four players, we were strong at every position and had good pitching depth. And we won the Series against the Negro American League team without too much trouble. We won the first two games, 4–2 and 5–3. Josh hit a home run over the left-field fence in the first game, and I hit a home run over the right-field fence in the second game. We were going to play them eleven straight games in different towns, but we had already won six games and only lost one after seven games.

That was the series when I got in a shouting match with a writer in the stands. In the barnstorming days we just didn't keep box scores. We couldn't get anybody to keep score in those games, and he was going around and keeping scores. His name was Hall, and he was a sports writer for the *Chicago Defender,* a black newspaper, but he didn't know anything.

The umpire called some kind of decision out there on the field one night in Indianapolis, and Hall kept raising sand with the umpire and calling him names and all like that. He was sitting behind our dugout and I stood up and looked up over the dugout and told him he ought to keep his damn mouth shut. And we had two or three words.

That series was billed as a World Series, but while we were playing those games, Satchel's All-Stars and a team of All-Stars from our league were playing in New York City and they drew bigger crowds than what we were drawing. That's when Johnny Taylor beat Satchel with a no-hitter, but Satchel won the next game in a rematch.

We won most of the games in our series and were the Negro League champions. According to the newspapers, I finished the season with a .383 batting average and 36 home runs. But Josh was credited with 74 home runs for the season. Maybe that's why I didn't get noticed by some people as much. But I still got some recognition at the end of the season. Cum Posey picked me both on his All-American dream team *and* on his all-time Grays team.

Those honors were all real nice, but the most important thing to happen to me that year just barely got in under the wire before the year ended. It was on New Year's Eve—December 31, 1937— when I got married.

My wife's maiden name was Sarah Wroten. She was from Jalisbury, North Carolina. That's about 150 miles from here over on the coast. We met right here in Rocky Mount. Her first husband was running the funeral home, but he died in 1935, and then she was running the funeral home by herself and teaching school. She had a fellow there named Joe Crudup, and he helped her with the business end. He stayed there for a while, but I don't remember how long. I was off playing ball and was away when he left. When we talked about getting married, I had her sell the funeral home. I told her I was not going to stay here and run the funeral home, and she sold the funeral home that summer. And we got married in December.

I was thirty years old before I got married, and I was staying with my momma at home. I traveled a lot when I was with Homestead, but before I started with them, I hadn't traveled much. I stayed around the Rocky Mount area. I had sisters and brothers here but they weren't making any money. And I was the main support for the family. We had already paid for our home, but there were a lot of expenses. I had a brother that wasn't no good and another brother who was in college down in Alabama. One of my sisters, Willie, had died from TB in 1922. I had another sister, Fannie, who worked making dresses, and the family spent all of her money. Then she got married and, from that time on, I took care of everything around the house. Then, when I got married, I still had to help out up there.

When we got married, there wasn't a big to-do. Me and my wife went to the preacher's *house* and got married. The preacher's name was Reverend Dudley. We didn't go anywhere on a honeymoon, we just stayed in Rocky Mount.

We both had strong ties to the church. I'm an active Christian and my wife was active in church, too. Both of us went to Sunday school, but we didn't belong to the same church. I belonged to St. James Baptist Church and she belonged to Mount Zion Baptist Church. On Sunday morning we'd get up and get breakfast, and I would carry her to her church and I'd go to my church. When service was over some Sundays she'd beat me back home and, if she didn't, I would go to pick her up. I believe that faith in the Lord serves as a solid foundation for a marriage, and we had a long and happy marriage together.

When we first got married, my wife was working, teaching the first grade at our school. She wanted to know how I could play ball and help her pay for this house, when I wasn't working but four and a half months a year and making $125 a month. I told her, "Well, I'm going to play some winter baseball, too." But what kept me going was my wife teaching school. That's the main thing. At first she was making $48 a month. Then she got some raises and got up to about $78 a month, and we were able to make it.

Most of the fellows who were playing ball back then in the thirties weren't married or, if they were married, they either weren't staying with their wives or their wives were working and helping take care of them. You couldn't depend on black baseball. If she hadn't been teaching school, I would have had to quit playing baseball.

# Chapter 9

# The Best Team (1938)

*There is no better fielder in the majors in smart-
ness, speed, thinking, and throwing than Buck Leonard. He is equal to the best in the game.*
                        *—Overton Tremper, Springfield Grays*

In spring training, when I got back to the team, I told the
fellows that I had got married. I said to Vic Harris, "Vic, I got
married." And he said, "Man, you mean you cut that kind of a
hog? You got married?" He was joking me. That means to do
something extraordinary.

Married life must have agreed with me. I had a good season
and we had our best team ever that year. We won the first half
pretty easy, with an .813 winning percentage. The papers said we
"completely outstripped all competition." We beat the Crawfords
six straight games at the end of the first half, winning a doubleheader on the Fourth of July. I hit a home run in the second game.

With Josh still batting behind me, I was leading the league in
hitting again at the halfway mark, this time with a .480 average.
Josh was hitting .375 and led the league in home runs. Vic Harris
was hitting .374 and Big Jim Williams .355 at that time. That's
not bad hitting for a team. They were calling us "Murderer's

Row.'' They also called us the ''Gashouse Gang'' because Cum Posey said that hustle was the key to our success.

Ray Brown was our top pitcher. We also had Jerry Benjamin, Lick Carlisle, Jelly Jackson, Roy Welmaker, Edsall Walker, Tommy Dukes, and Louis Dula playing. There was not much turnover in players from 1937 to 1938. The only change in the starting lineup was at third base. They said we needed some more local fellows, so we picked up a boy named Jack Johnson. He was from Pittsburgh and he'd been working in a steel mill. He was a third baseman but he just didn't make it. He was awkward and couldn't hit, field, or run. He quit and went back to the steel mill. A lot of times we would pick up a ballplayer and he would stay for a month and we'd let him go.

A pitcher named Hannibal was another one who didn't make it. But we had to pick up some local boys. And Vic Harris's brother Bill, who was an outfielder, didn't make it. He became an umpire, and we were accused of having some home cooking.

There were two umpires in our league named Harris. The other one, Mo Harris, wasn't any relation to Vic. Other teams complained sometimes about Vic's brother umpiring, but it was Mo Harris who was our home umpire. He used to play for the Grays and, when he started umpiring, we expected a favor from him. Sometimes he came through and sometimes he didn't. Other teams got mad and said that they called things in our favor. But it didn't always work that way.

If you were going to play a tough series with a team that was tied for the top or second place, you would want certain umpires to work during that series, and you could ask the league to send you a certain umpire. Sometimes they would and sometimes they wouldn't. And there was some teams who didn't want Vic Harris's brother to umpire when we were playing them, because they seemed to think that he would favor our team. I don't know whether he favored us or not. Sometimes a fellow would be more rough on a team to avoid criticism.

I remember one night when we were playing the Pittsburgh Crawfords in Griffith Stadium by the football lights. We were ahead and it was raining, so we told Mo Harris, ''Mo, call the game now. Its gone five innings and that takes care of the money and we're ahead." But he said, "Let's play one more inning." Then Oscar Charleston hit a home run and they beat us. Well, we cussed him out. I'm telling you, we cursed him!

Let me tell you something else about Mo Harris. During the winter months he would pawn his umpiring stuff—his mask, chest protector, shin guards, his indicator, and everything. He pawned them so much that we learned the pawnshop man's name. His name was Hymie. Every spring when we were getting ready to play the first game in Pittsburgh, Mo Harris's umpire stuff was in Hymie's because he had pawned it during the winter. He would come to Forbes Field in Pittsburgh and tell us his umpiring stuff was in the pawnshop so he could get the money right then. Then he'd get a taxi and go down there and get his stuff from Hymie, and come back and umpire the ball game. Now, that's why we were looking for a favor from him.

Sometimes we looked for a favor from a sportswriter or an official scorer, too. There was a sportswriter for the *Norfolk* (Va.) *Journal and Guide* named Mr. Rea, who was keeping score. And I found out he smoked Tampa Nuggets and I gave him a box of Tampa Nuggets so he would write something about what I did. And he gave me a good write-up in the paper. That was about 1933, and I was at Portsmouth. He might have helped me out on the scoring, too, and given me a hit on anything that was close. In fact, the cigars were for him to do that very thing, but I don't know if it helped or not. Another time, in Mexico, I bought the scorer a box of cigars for changing errors to hits if it was close.

I never kept up with batting averages much, mine or anybody else's, because it wasn't official. Some white newspapers told us they would run the scores in their paper if we mailed the scores to them every night. But sometimes we weren't near a mailbox where we could mail them in every night, so that idea never really worked out.

When the Elias Bureau and the Howe Bureau began keeping league statistics, we'd give a player the job of keeping the scorebook. Sometimes a pitcher who pitched the night before kept the scorebook, and maybe he didn't know how to keep it or he didn't know what was a hit or what was an error. Or maybe in the middle of the game he'd have to go in and pitch and some other player would have to finish the scorebook.

One Negro newspaper sent a reporter to be our official scorer and travel with the team. The paper paid his salary, but he said he couldn't live on what they paid, so the team had to add a little something to it. But he wouldn't get to the game on time, and he'd show up in the third inning and ask one of the players on the bench what happened in the first inning. He'd ask, "What did this man do?" And maybe the player couldn't remember, or just made it up. And he would write down what we said. Sometimes one of the fellows would make up something and he didn't know the difference. And if the guy keeping score didn't see what happened on the field, he put down "singled to center" or "flied out to center" and the next day the newspaper story was filled with things like "he singled to center." We used to joke about that, and we gave him the nickname "Single to Center."

So you can see, the scorekeeping in the Negro Leagues was not good. It was not consistent. They didn't keep accurate statistics like they do now. Sometimes the league would keep the statistics but they just counted what was reported to them. Some teams didn't always call in the results. And some teams would keep their own totals and it might include all games, not just league games. Some newspapers would keep their own statistics, and sometimes they published them all and sometimes only part of them, or maybe not at all. During four or five years in the forties, the owners hired some sports bureaus to keep them, and some of the newspaper people didn't like that. We didn't think much about it at that time. We were just playing ball and didn't worry about it.

Anytime I talk about statistics, it's from whatever was printed at the time or has been found since then. I don't think we can ever have complete statistics like they have in baseball now, so we can't prove some things.

One of the big attractions in black baseball around this time was to play four-team doubleheaders in Yankee Stadium. During the season two southern teams from the Negro American League came up to play us and the Newark Eagles in one of these promotions. All of these games always attracted about twenty thousand people, so we had a good crowd as usual. In the first game, Mule

Suttles hit a home run into the right-center-field bleachers, and Newark beat Birmingham. In the second game, I hit a home run into the right-field stands, and we beat Memphis. Then Memphis went on to win their league's championship that year.

Suttles had good power. Later in the year Tom Parker was pitching for us in Newark, New Jersey, and Suttles hit a 460-foot home run over the scoreboard at Ruppert Stadium in the sixteenth inning to win the game for the Eagles. But I wasn't there for that game. I had gone to the All-Star game in Chicago. I only heard about it after I got back.

We lost the All-Star game that year, 5–4, even though we jumped on Sug Cornelius for three runs in the first inning. He pitched for the Chicago American Giants. Edsall Walker, who pitched for the Grays, was the starting pitcher for us on the East squad and took the loss. The Monarchs' Hilton Smith relieved Cornelius and was credited with the win. I batted cleanup and had one hit. Josh didn't play for the second straight year. Biz Mackey caught for us, and Walker was used to Josh catching him, and had some difficulty pitching to Mackey for some reason. Walker said that Josh had him keep everything down and Mackey wanted his fastball high.

That year Mule Suttles got more votes in the balloting, but they picked me to play instead. Josh Gibson and Ray Dandridge also won the balloting at their position but did not play in the All-Star game. I don't know how it happened, but they arranged it somehow or other. It must have been the owners. After the West won, there were some people who thought we should have won. So another All-Star game was played, at the Polo Grounds, and those three players played. We felt like the All-Star teams would draw more in another town. In those years when we played two games, the second games were usually played later in the year, around September. The East won, 5–4, in the second game that year.

Sometime during baseball's winter meetings before the season started, Chester Washington, a sportswriter for the *Pittsburgh Courier,* sent a telegram to Pittsburgh Pirate manager Pie Traynor about signing some black ballplayers. The telegram said that he had the answer to Traynor's prayers right there in Pittsburgh because Josh Gibson, Satchel Paige, Cool Papa Bell, Ray Brown, and myself were available at reasonable figures, and that if they signed us that the Pirates would be guaranteed the pennant. I don't know about that guarantee, but the Pirates only lost by a game that year, so maybe we would have made a difference.

Around that time I had told the newspapers that Satchel could stack up against any big-league pitchers I'd ever seen and that Josh was one of the hardest sluggers in the game and was as smart and cagey a catcher as Bill Dickey or any of the rest of them. We all know about Cool Papa. He could have played between the Waner brothers to give the Pirates a Hall of Fame outfield. Ray Brown was in his prime at that time and could have pitched better than any pitcher they had. We would have had to face major-league pitching every day, and we hadn't faced major-league-level pitching every day in the Negro Leagues. But to add four future Hall of Fame ballplayers and one of the best pitchers in the country to any team's roster certainly would not have hurt any.

I don't know what would have happened among the fans if they had signed us. There weren't any blacks in the league at that time, and we just don't know what the reaction would have been overall, or even with the local players.

Around about that time, Jimmy Powers, sports editor of the New York *Daily News*, tried to get Burleigh Grimes to hire Satchel Paige and several other black stars. Burleigh told him he would like to but said, "You know why I can't do that." But I don't think he would have liked to hire black players. He was from the old days. You know, if a guy is prejudiced, he's just prejudiced. Whether it's in the major leagues or in the grocery store. That was about 1936, back there then. And some of them guys were just like Dixie Walker was when Jackie Robinson first broke in. They boasted to others, "I'm not going to play with him. I don't want those guys in the league." Other players didn't say anything but they were thinking the same thing.

I never thought much about racial prejudice. Of course, it was always our ambition to get into the major leagues, because of the prestige and money. I felt regardless of what color you were, if you could play baseball, you ought to be allowed to play anywhere that you could play. But we just weren't considering it too much.

I thought integration would come, but I didn't think it would come as quickly as it did.

In 1938, Powers had picked a dream team for the New York Giants that included Josh at catcher and me at first base. And he picked some other black players that he thought could play for the Giants. At the end of the season the newspapers were nominating players to go to the major leagues. To be included in this group was quite a compliment, but we black players didn't even think about things like that. But there were some baseball people who did.

It was around about this time that Clark Griffith called me and Josh up to his office to discuss the possibilities of playing in the major leagues. It seems like we met with Clark Griffith the second year that we played there in Washington. That would be 1938, but it might have been later, after Josh came back from Mexico.

One Sunday evening we played a doubleheader in Griffith Stadium, and Clark Griffith saw both of the ball games. So he told the fellow down there at the gate to tell us when we changed clothes to come up to his office. So we went up there and he said, "I saw the ball games. You fellows had a pretty good day." We said, "Yeah, we did all right." He said, "Would you all like to play in the major leagues?" We said, "Yeah, we'd like to play in the major leagues." He said, "Do you all think you could make the major leagues?" We said, "Well, we're hoping so. We believe if we got a chance, we could play major-league baseball." He said, "Well first of all we have seen some of you fellows play and we'd like to have you in the major leagues with us. But nobody wants to be the first one to hire black ballplayers. That's where the problem is right now."

So we said, "Well, we would like to play in the major leagues and some of us believe we could make the team. And we'd like to have a tryout anyway." He said, "Well, that's the problem now. Don't nobody want to be the first one to hire you fellows." So that was that.

But we thought that it was just a matter of time until they signed black ballplayers. One reason we thought that was coming about was because during the war years, in 1942 or 1943, a lot of major-league ballplayers were going to the Army and they were getting short of players. We thought that since they were in need of players, they were going to use us. But it didn't never happen. Not back there then. We told him we were interested, but nothing ever came of our meeting.

Clark Griffith had told us up there when Josh and I went to talk to him, "Well, if we take you fellows into the major leagues, we're going to take the best ones and it's going to break up the Negro Leagues." And that's what it did. He had told us that back there then, and that really is what happened. When they started taking blacks into the white leagues, majors and minors, the black leagues started going down.

I wasn't in favor of too much agitating toward opening the doors of white organized baseball, but I let them know that I would be willing to join up if the chance was available. And I told them that if I did get the opportunity I would not desire to socialize with the white players after I was through playing the games and that I would be content to find a respectable hotel for coloreds to stay in. You know, if they don't want you in a place, I don't believe you ought to go there. If they didn't want us in Forbes Field, then I don't think we ought to have gone.

I thought at that time if the color bar were ever let down that the teams in the West would be the first to do so. My last year I was a member of an All-Star team that toured the West and played the Western League teams. We beat them every game we played by scores of 9–1 on up and we had no embarrassing moments whatever. And those were white teams we were playing. Prejudice was more out East than out West. We could play Fort Wayne, Indiana, and South Bend and Toledo and Tulsa and didn't have the same kind of behavior as we had out East.

One of the biggest drawbacks to breaking the color bar was the black owners. They knew that if the major leagues started taking in black ballplayers that it would hurt their own teams. They were more interested in their own welfare. I also told the writers that the gate receipts would play the largest part in the issue. If the colored fans would only demand that colored players would get their chance before they spent their money at the ballparks, then I felt it would make a difference.

Everywhere we would go there would be someone saying,

"Wouldn't you like to play in the major leagues? Wouldn't you like to play on a white team?" Especially the NAACP and a newspaper in New York called *The Daily Worker*. Anytime we went to New York to play in Yankee Stadium or the Polo Grounds, there was a group that used to come around asking, "Wouldn't you like to play in the major leagues?" I said, "Sure I'd like to play in the major leagues." They would say, "Don't you think you could make it in the major leagues?" And I would say, "Yeah, I would be trying." Then they would say, "Well, why don't you join us in demonstrating?" We would say, "You people go on and demonstrate—we're going to play the ball game."

And I told them that I was not in favor of too much agitation because, if owners were forced to take black players before the owners were ready, the players would have a hard job staying on the team for more reasons than one. The major leagues didn't see the need for black ballplayers at that time. I told the writers at the time that I was certain that they would take blacks into the major leagues someday, but that it would be after it was too late for me. I thought the time would come but I thought it would come after I was too old to take advantage of the opportunity. And I was right. That's exactly what happened. I could see that even then.

In 1938 we won both the first and second half of the split season, so there was no playoff for the pennant. And we hadn't started playing a World Series yet, so after the season was over that year, we took a tour of Cuba with an all-star team.

We picked up Willie Wells to go along with us and he took a hairdresser with him. We knew she wasn't his wife, and we kicked on that. She was from Jacksonville, Florida, and he used to go down there every winter when the baseball season was over and hang around, and she would take care of him. He used to like big Buick automobiles. He had one and she had one, too. One year he carried it to Havana, Cuba, with him. The team paid their way and nobody said anything about it. Ray Brown took his wife down there that year, too. Sometimes my wife traveled with me when school was out. She would come down there during the Christmas holidays.

See Posey was the business manager, and most of the Grays
went with us that year. We left New York in November and went
down to Miami. Then we went from Miami to Havana on a boat.
There weren't any planes running down there back then. If they
*were* running, we didn't ever ride one.

On that all-star team we took to Cuba that year was Gibson
catching, me at first base, Sammy T. Hughes at second base, Willie
Wells at shortstop, and Felton Snow at third base. That was the
infield. In the outfield we had Sam Bankhead in left field, Henry
Kimbro in center field, and Fats Jenkins in right field. Pitching
we had Roy Partlow, Edsall Walker, Bud Barbee, and Oscar
Owens. That was a pretty good ballclub.

# Chapter 10

# Tarnished Flag (1939)

*Buck was one of the best hitters I've ever seen. He
had a real quick bat. You couldn't get a fastball
by him and he hit the curve real well, too.*
— *Roy Campanella, Baltimore Elite Giants*

When we got back from Cuba I went home for a few days and
then it was time to go to spring training. We trained at the colored
high school grounds at Orlando, Florida, that year, and the facilities were not very good. Orlando was our main training base for
quite a few years. It must have been six or seven years altogether.
One reason why we stayed in Orlando so long was because the
Washington Senators were training in Orlando at the same time,
and they would let us play all the Negro League teams over there
at their park, Tinker Field. They were one of the teams in Florida
that would let us do that.

A few years later, around 1947, we were spring training in
Daytona Beach at the colored high school. And Rochester, a farm
team with St. Louis, was training in Daytona, too, over near the
waterfront. They complained about it being so breezy over there.
Fellows would work up a sweat and then the wind was blowing
and they would get chilly. And they wanted to come over and

103

train where we were. The high school grounds belonged to the
city, and they talked to the city officials, who decided to let them
come over there and train in the morning, and we had to move
our training to the evening.

And the facilities were bad. They didn't have good showers and
the infield wasn't up to par. They got some groundskeepers from
somewhere, fixed the grounds, remodeled the clubhouse, and put
training tables in there and everything. That's how they made the
facilities good in Daytona. Otherwise they would have stayed like
they had been.

Black baseball was tough in the thirties. It seems like I remember the bad days better than the good days because we were scuf-
flin' then. As I said before, we played what we called "strongarm
ball." We'd play our way into shape. We didn't have time for
somebody to teach us fundamentals and inside baseball like the
major leaguers did in the spring. As for things like backup plays,
relays, cutoffs, and things like that, we learned by playing. We'd
play every day. Anybody, anywhere, anytime. We were booked
every day. For a player to miss a game, something had to be
broken. You played with sprains, bruises, and anything else.

We'd come North from Florida and stopped in New Orleans at
the Patterson Hotel. We used to call it a "chinch parlor." A
chinch is what we called bedbugs. As soon as the lights would
go out there, the chinches would come out. We used to get newspapers out and spread them on the bed and sleep on top of them.
The bedbugs couldn't crawl up on the paper. Then we'd leave the
lights on all night.

In New Orleans we played the Kansas City Monarchs in a doubleheader on Easter Sunday and beat them both games. That Easter
series in New Orleans with the Monarchs became an annual event
each spring, just like the Crawfords series, which had became a
Fourth of July tradition until they broke up.

When we got back up North, Cum Posey made those of us who
were living in Pittsburgh move over to Homestead to stay. He
said that we were running around too much at night and he felt
like he could watch us better over there. Now, you can't control
*all* of the fellows because some of them were young and they
were erratic.

They didn't want us to hang out at the Crawford Grill. The Pittsburgh Crawford baseball team owner, Gus Greenlee, had a grill, and a lot of wayward girls used to hang out around there. And they didn't want us hanging out around there with prostitutes and all like that. They felt like if we hung around the Crawford Grill, then that's what we were doing.

Sonnyman Jackson had a grill, the Skyrocket Grill. It was out in Homestead, and he opened it October 19, 1936. Sonnyman didn't allow those prostitutes to hang out at the Skyrocket Grill. All of us ballplayers hung out there and ate there. He hired a good cook to cook for us. There was about ten of us out there in Pittsburgh, and when Cum made us move over to Homestead, I went to Jackson's house in 1940 and stayed there from then on until the Grays broke up in 1950.

When the Crawfords and the Birmingham Black Barons broke up, Cum Posey signed some of their players. That made some of the other owners mad and they wanted compensation for them. We got Sam Bankhead and David Whatley, a couple of pretty good players, that way. Cum gave away Lick Carlisle, Jim Williams, and Tommy Dukes to the Crawfords as compensation, but they didn't report. The Crawfords moved from Pittsburgh to Toledo, and those fellows didn't feel like Toledo was going to last, which it didn't, and they refused to go. They might have gone to the Crawfords for a few days, but not for long, because that team broke up before the year was over. Benjamin went to the Crawfords, too, for a short time and played under the name Christopher. But Cum got him back.

The players on the 1939 Grays were about the same as in 1938, and we had another one of our good teams. We had Josh Gibson catching and myself at first base. The rest of the infield was Sam Bankhead, second base, and Jelly Jackson, shortstop, and Henry Spearman, third base. We had Vic Harris, who was left field and manager, and the rest of the outfield was Jerry Benjamin in center field and Dave Whatley in right field. Rab Roy Gaston was our other catcher. Pitching we had Ray Brown, Edsall Walker, Roy Partlow, Big Tom Parker, Specs Roberts, Red Ferrell, and a boy named Waites.

We had a good ballclub and I had another pretty good year. In one game against the Philadelphia Stars I hit two home runs, and one of them was an inside-the-park home run. I might have hit some other home runs inside the park during my career, but I don't remember any. I wasn't really that fast going around the bases.

In June we lost a doubleheader by big scores to the Newark Eagles at Buffalo. They scored 34 runs and had 34 hits. Willie Wells hit for the cycle in both games that day and, according to one of the newspapers, Mule Suttles hit four home runs. Nobody could hit the ball farther than Mule. Not even Josh.

At that time, Suttles was leading the league in batting and I was second with a .458 average and Josh was third with a .435 average. Jerry Benjamin was leading the league with 27 stolen bases and Specs Roberts had won about 17 straight games, but we were still in second place. We finished strong and overtook Newark to win the first half. The *Pittsburgh Courier* said, "Led by Buck Leonard and Josh Gibson, the Grays came down the stretch with a burst of speed that left their rivals drowned in the wake of their triumphant march." And they said that if the major leagues ever *did* open their doors to black ballplayers that Josh and I would lead the parade. Now, that's what they said in the paper.

Up through July, Josh had hit 42 home runs and I had hit 31 home runs. That's what they put in the papers, and that's counting all games, against everybody. In league play he had 13 and I had 8 at that time. We were both voted by the fans to start in the All-Star game, and heavyweight champion Joe Louis threw out the first pitch for the game.

We lost that year, when Dan Wilson of the St. Louis Stars hit a two-run home run in the bottom of the eighth inning. Roy Partlow was the losing pitcher. That was the second year in a row that one of our Grays pitchers got the All-Star loss. Neither me nor Josh got a hit, but they had a second All-Star game again that year, and the outcome was different. It was played in Yankee Stadium in September and I had two hits and Josh hit a bases-loaded triple, and we won, 10–2, to make up some for the first loss.

They had a special day for Josh Gibson at Forbes Field in August to show their appreciation for the way he played. The year before, Walter Johnson had seen Josh play at Tinker Field in

Orlando during spring training and compared him to Bill Dickey. But most often, Josh and I were called the black Babe Ruth and Lou Gehrig. Sometimes people asked us what the difference was between them and us. Well, the only thing that we said was, they were white and we were black. That was the difference. They were white and could play in the major leagues, and we had to play in black baseball. That was the only difference.

But we were not the only home-run hitters in the Negro Leagues. There were quite a few long-ball hitters. With Newark there was Mule Suttles, Monte Irvin, Johnny Davis, and Lennie Pearson. And in later years, Larry Doby hit the long ball when he was with the Eagles. Philadelphia had Jake Dunn and Red Parnell. Jim West hit the ball a long way, and Boojum Wilson was playing with Philadelphia at that time. And on the Baltimore team was Bill Wright, Zollie Wright, Sammy T. Hughes, and a boy named Bill Hoskins. And Roy Campanella was there, too. The Blank Yankees were in the league, and they had Harry Williams for a while.

Turkey Stearnes was a power hitter, and he played out West most of the time. Chicago had Steel Arm Davis, and out West they also had Tom Young, who used to catch with Kansas City. He was a long-ball hitter. With the Cleveland Buckeyes they had Quincy Trouppe and Sam Jethroe. They were the long-ball hitters for them. And another boy named Joe Atkins, who played later for a while. There were quite a few. I just can't name all of them. Other than us, I reckon the Eagles had the most power in their lineup.

Dick Lundy, the Eagles' manager, had them playing good ball and they were in first place going into the stretch. There was some bad blood between the Grays and the Newark Eagles that had built up over the years. There were some fights and near riots at games and several times we had beanball battles.

At one game in Buffalo, Willie Wells wore a batting helmet for the first time. It was an old coal miner's hat that he had cut down, but it didn't have the light on it. Well, Wells came into the ballpark with that helmet on and our big pitcher, Tom Parker, was pitching. We told Wells that Parker was going to knock that hat off of him. And sure enough, the first pitch was right at his head and knocked him down. But Wells got back up and hit a triple. Parker was just carrying out what we had said, when he threw the first pitch at his head. We were trying to get him out of the ball game. Not that he had done anything to us. He was a mainstay in the ball game and we knew that if we could get him out then it would reduce their strength.

Another time, when we were playing the Newark Eagles in Newark, Wells had been ''picking'' shortstop, catching everything that came down there. And Vic Harris, our manager, was on first base and somebody hit a ball where Wells had to cover second base and Vic slid right into him and tore his pants and everything. But that wasn't the main fracas.

We had a fellow named Blue Perez playing third base for us at that time, and a little later in the game somebody went to third base and was going to get even with us and ran into Blue Perez and cut him. And we had a free-for-all. The fans and everybody came out on the field, and policemen on horseback came out on the field to break up the fight. They had to bring the horses out there because the fans got into it. When the fight broke out, I never jumped on anybody. I never got in a fight in a ball game. I stayed out of them.

Another incident happened a few years later, in 1942, when Wells cut Lick Carlisle, our second baseman, and later in the game Josh Gibson jumped at Ray Dandridge and injured him. That led to another free-for-all and a near riot.

During the years there were some other fights between our players and other teams. There was one between Vic Harris and Horacio Martinez of the New York Cubans, one between George Scales and Bill Wright of the Baltimore Elites, and another fight between Wright and Jelly Jackson. There were probably many others that I can't remember. Both Bill Wright and Vic Harris played hard, and they were the kind that *would* get in a fight with somebody.

Sometimes we used to have footrace exhibitions before a game between the fastest man on each team. We had Jelly Jackson and Jerry Benjamin, and we'd race them against the other team's fastest players. If we were going to play Baltimore, they had Bill Wright and Henry Kimbro, who were fast. And we'd have a race between them before a game and we would advertise it. Jerry

Benjamin was one of the fastest on our team. He was faster than Whatley and Jelly Jackson, but he wasn't faster than Cool Papa after he joined the Grays a few years later.

Sometimes Jesse Owens would put on an exhibition before a game against the fastest player on the team. And sometimes we would have wrestling matches between our mascots and the other team's mascots. We would do a lot of things to bring in a crowd.

The two teams that usually gave us the hardest time were the Eagles and the Elites. The Eagles were the second best team in the league that year, and the games were always hard fought. The Baltimore Elites also had a good team. I remember one double-header against them when I had a pretty good day. I was four for four in the first game and hit a home run in the second game.

The Elite Giants came up there from Nashville, Tennessee, and started playing out of Baltimore. They had played in Washington D.C., for a couple of years before going to Baltimore and had played in Columbus, Ohio, for a year before that. The Elites had Sammy T. Hughes at second base. He had a real nice personality. I got along with him fine, and he got along with his teammates, too. I saw him play a lot and he was tops. He was my all-time second baseman. He could hit, field, run, throw, and think. He could do all of it. He wasn't a home-run hitter but he would get extra-base hits, and he was a good hit-and-run man.

Red Moore was playing first base in 1939. Jim West was their regular first baseman when I first went with the Grays, but he got with the Philadelphia Stars, and Johnny Washington was the Elites' first baseman most of the time while I was playing. Later they had a boy named Doc Dennis playing first base while Washington was in the service.

Felton Snow played third base and Pee Wee Butts was the shortstop. They got him from Atlanta that year, and he stayed with them a long time. He was a good fielder and a fast base runner, but he was a light hitter. He couldn't hit the curveball.

In the outfield that year they had Bill Wright, Henry Kimbro, and Bill Hoskins. Hoskins wasn't related to Dave Hoskins, who played with us several years later, and Bill he was a better hitter than our Hoskins. He made the All-Star team a few years. Before Kimbro and Hoskins joined the team, they had two Wrights in the outfield, Bill Wright and Zollie Wright. Zollie had been there about as long as I had been with the Grays before then.

Bill Wright was big and fast, and he could run, hit, and throw. He could do all of it. And Bill Wright was a mean ballplayer. He didn't carry on a lot of fun and jokes like some of the rest of the ballplayers did. He didn't fraternize like most of us did. Now, it could have been just his ways. The year before, he was fined twenty-five dollars and suspended for three games for hitting an umpire, but he showed up to play against us anyway. When the umpire at that game told him to leave, he refused, and the game was forfeited to us.

He was one of the top players way back in the thirties, and he remained one of the top players until he went to Mexico around 1940, when Josh and all of them went down there. He was a good player down there, too. He came back to the Elites for a year or so during the war, but he went back again when Sal Maglie, Max Lanier, Danny Gardella, and the other major leaguers went to Mexico. When he went down there that time, he stayed and never came back after that. He's down there now, in Aquascalientes.

Henry Kimbro was a good center fielder. He was fast in the outfield and could run bases. He was a good all-around ballplayer. He could hit and had some power but was not considered a home-run hitter. Kimbro was not easy to get along with, for some reason. He was kind of moody.

I don't know why it is that some players don't get along with their teammates. Sometimes a fellow has different moods. Sometimes he's in a bad mood because of something that happened the night before. One thing that causes a ballplayer to get moody is when he's in a batting slump, because he's thinking about he's not hitting. And then sometimes a player makes an error that loses a ball game and that'll give him a bad attitude for a few days. Sometimes, if he doesn't get a hit that he knows would have won the ball game, he's still thinking about that.

Sometimes a pitcher will lose a ball game or make a pitch that a fellow hits for a home run and he feels like he should have made another pitch and that'll put him in a bad mood. There's several things that can happen in those kind of situations that put a fellow in a bad mood for the next two or three days. But it seemed like Kimbro was moody all the time.

Catching for the Elites around that time was Biz Mackey. He was the best receiver I ever saw. Even though he was old, he could still get a lot out of a pitcher. He had more advice for the pitcher than any catcher I ever saw. He'd go out and tell the pitcher, "Start your curve at the batter, so it will break over the plate." If a pitcher was wild high, he would stay down. If he was wild low, he would stand up.

He was a jovial fellow, full of fun, and he always had something funny to say. When you'd go up to bat, he was talking to you and trying to get your mind on something else besides hitting. He would use psychology, you know. He'd say, "You're standing too close to the plate." Or he'd say, "What kind of bat are you using?" And he'd tell the umpire, "Look at his bat there, I don't believe that bat's legal." He'd say just anything to upset you.

He'd say, "I hear you're hitting over .400. Well, let's see how much you can hit today." You know, he'd say anything to throw you off. "Where did you all play last night? How did you do last night? Where did you all sleep last night? Did you all sleep on the bus last night? Aren't you tired? Don't you need no rest? You mean you rode all night last night and you all think you're going to win this ball game?" He would keep talking like that, trying to distract you from what you're doing. That's the way he was.

Mackey had already been playing about twenty years at that time. He started away back about 1920, and played with Hilldale when they had their good teams. Then he got with the Philadelphia Stars for a while. He had been the catcher for the Elites for about three years, but he left to join Newark with about two months left in the 1939 season, and Roy Campanella took over catching for the rest of the year. He was just a youngster then, but he had learned a lot from Mackey.

Bill Byrd pitched for Baltimore. He was a spitball pitcher. That was his best pitch. I don't know whether that takes anything away from him or not. Sometimes he would act like he was spitting on his fingers but he wouldn't spit on his fingers, and then he'd throw you a fastball. Spitters were legal in the Negro Leagues. The way they did it in the Negro Leagues was all the spitball pitchers who already were in the league could continue, but no new ones could come in. We had Byrd, Phil Cockrell, Roosevelt Davis, and Sam Streeter in the league. There may have been one or two more that we didn't know of, but these were the real spitball pitchers. There were several players who scratched the ball. They say that there are still some spitballers around today, in the major leagues.

The Elites also had Jonas Gaines. He was a left-hander and another pitcher that I had some trouble with. A few years later they had another left-hander, Tom Glover, and he was a pretty good pitcher, but I didn't have any trouble with him, like I did Gaines. Glover would set up his fingers like he was going to throw a curveball. That was to fool me, and I would think he was going to throw a curveball and he would throw a fastball.

During the years that I played, they had some other pretty good pitchers. Two of them were Robert Griffith, who had pitched on our team in the *Denver Post* Tournament in 1936, and Andrew Porter. We called him Pullman Porter. Then they also had a pitcher named Ace Adams.

In 1939 we were in a four-way playoff with the Elite Giants after the end of the regular season. We won the pennant by about four games over Newark, with Baltimore finishing third and the Philadelphia Stars in fourth place. We didn't have a split season like we had in previous years, and there wasn't any World Series, so we decided to have a four-team tourney in our league. The top four teams played. We finished first, so we played the Philadelphia Stars, and the Eagles and the Elites played each other. That was the first round. We beat the Stars, and the Elites won over the Eagles, so we faced the Elites in the finals of the playoffs.

Partlow beat Bill Byrd, 2–1, in the opener, but we didn't win again. We tied one game that was called after five innings with the score 1–1, because of the curfew. Parker and Roberts both lost games, and then Partlow lost the final game, 2–0, in Yankee Stadium. So the Elites won the playoffs and the Ruppert Memorial Trophy, which was donated to the winner by the owner of the New York Yankees. Baltimore claimed that they were the league champions because they won the tournament, and we claimed that we were the champions because we won the regular-season pennant.

After the playoffs we picked up Leon Day and Ray Dandridge and toured through the South playing against the New York Black Yankees until the weather got too cold.

Cum Posey selected me on his All-American team at the end of the season, and I went back down to Cuba again with another All-Star team that was mostly our Grays players. We left in November, and in December we swept a six-game series in Havana against a major-league team that included Dolph Luque and Mike Gonzalez.

While I was playing in Cuba that winter, Josh Gibson was playing in Puerto Rico. Along about that time, somebody rated us and Satchel as the "Big Three" of black baseball. And over thirty years later, we were the first three players from the Negro Leagues inducted into the Hall of Fame at Cooperstown.

This is my whole family in 1918. That's my momma and daddy sitting in the rocking chairs. My brother Herman is standing between them and my brother Charlie is standing in front of my daddy. My youngest sister, Lena, was the baby of the family and she's sitting on the step in front of Herman. My two older sisters, Fannie and Willie, are the two on the right. And I'm sitting on the top step wearing a necktie. I was eleven years old then, and my daddy died from the influenza epidemic not too long after this picture was taken.

Here's a picture of my mother. Her maiden name was Emma Sesson.

This picture was taken in 1934 in Akron,
Ohio. That was my first year with the Grays.

Here I am with the bat that I donated to the Smithsonian Institute. Visitors can still see the bat.

This is the 1937 Homestead Grays. That year we started our string of nine straight pennants. Front row (front left to right): Tommy Dukes, Jelly Jackson, Matthew Carlisle, Roy Welmaker, Louis Dula, Vic Harris, Clifford Allen, Jerry Benjamin. Back row: me, Arnold Waite, Blue Perez, George Walker, Tom Parker, Jim Williams, Josh Gibson, Raymond Brown, Edsall Walker.

BANKHEAD
S.S.

GIBSON
C

LEONARD
1 ST

HOSKINS
R.F.

BENJAMIN
C.F.

1946 WASHINGTON, D.

This was taken at Griffith Stadium in Washington, D.C. in 1946. They called us the Grays' Murderers Row. That's Sam Bankhead, Josh Gibson, me, Dave Hoskins and Jerry Benjamin. Gibson had more power than Jimmy Foxx. There's no telling what he would have done in the major leagues.

This was in 1939 at the Yankee Stadium, with Josh Gibson and Sam Bankhead congratulating me as I cross homeplate. We were playing the Black Yankees and I had hit a homerun with Bankhead (#7) on base. Josh was the next hitter and that's why you see him with the bat. I think a boy named Forest was pitching that game.

TORNER

CANNADY

GIBSON

LEONARD

Somebody found this picture in a bar that was closing down and gave it to me. This is Satchel Paige, Josh Gibson and me—the first three players from the Negro Leagues voted into the Hall of Fame.

This is our last championship team, the 1948 Homestead Grays. We won the last pennant and the last World Series before the league broke up. This picture was taken in Homestead, Pennsylvania. Front row (front left to right): Sam Bankhead, Luke Easter, Matthew Carlisle, Charles Gary, Tom Parker, Wilmer Fields, R.T. Walker. Back row: me, Luis Marquez, Garnett Bankhead, Clarence Bruce, Unknown, J.C. Hamilton, Eudie Napier, Unknown, Groundhog Thompson, Vic Harris.

(Upper left) Here are some of the wives at the All-Star game in Cominskey Park. My wife, Sarah, is the one on the right in the front row and that's Vic Harris' wife next to her.

(Upper right) This is Sarah and I dancing at a nightclub in Cuba. At least I was trying to dance.

This is the 1945 All-Star team that we took to Venezuela. When we were getting ready to catch the plane to go to South America, Branch Rickey came down there to the airport to talk to Jackie Robinson and signed him with the Brooklyn Dodgers. Kneeling (front left to right): Jackie Robinson, Gene Benson, Felton Snow, Verdell Mathis, Sam Jethroe, Unknown (trainer). Standing: Blanco Chataing (Venezuela consulate official), Roy Campanella, Hank Barker, Bill Anderson, Quincy Trouppe, George Jefferson, Parnell Woods, Roy Welmaker, me.

(Upper left) This one was taken in Durango, Mexico. Durango is the last team that I played for. They were in the Mexican Central League and I played there two summers, 1954 and 1955.

(Upper right) I took a correspondence course and then, after I passed my real estate test, I opened up my own realty agency.

(Bottom left) This picture of me with my present wife, Lugenia, was taken at Cooperstown in 1972, before we were married.

(Bottom right) Here I am in 1972 with a plaque that was given to me when I was inducted into the Hall of Fame in Cooperstown.

This was taken at the White House on Friday, March 27, 1981. I'm the one on the right. I didn't get the other guy's name.

# Chapter 11

## Narrow Victory (1940)

*Buck Leonard was an outstanding hitter, and he had a lot of power. I would rather pitch to Josh Gibson than to Buck.*
*—Leon Day, Newark Eagles*

Josh Gibson decided to play in Mexico for the 1940 season. When Josh jumped to the Mexican League, Sam Bankhead went with him. That was our catcher and starting shortstop, and both of them were good hitters. We had traded for Terris McDuffie, and he and Roy Partlow also went to Mexico. They were two of the pitchers we were counting on for the whole year. We also lost Henry Spearman, our third baseman.

Losing those ballplayers weakened our team quite a bit, but we added Howard Easterling and Boojum Wilson to help make up for some of the hitting we lost. We didn't have one of our better teams that year, but we still were good enough to win the pennant over Baltimore and Newark in a race that went down to the wire.

The fact that we won without Josh shows how solid the Grays were as a team. I felt like I had to do more and carry a bigger piece of the load with him gone. The day that Josh left, we played that same night in Toledo, Ohio, against Newark. The players said then that I was going to have to pick up the slack since Josh was gone, and I pretty much did what they said had to be done.

Some people called me a ballplayer's ballplayer, and I guess I was. I was a natural ballplayer, and I thank God for giving me my talent. I was strictly business when I was on the ballfield. I wasn't out there to clown. I was out there to play ball, and I was out there to win. Sometimes they thought that I played hard unnecessarily because, even with the score 12–1, I still played just as hard. Some of the rest of the players might not have played that hard or wouldn't take extra bases and things like that.

When the baseball season first started, we didn't know that we were going to lose Josh for the whole year. About the middle of March, they came by Rocky Mount and picked me up and we went on to Orlando for spring training. We expected Josh to be there, too, but we soon found out that he was not going to play with us that year. So we had to do without him and, after a few weeks of training, we left Florida and started playing our way North. We won the traditional Easter doubleheader in New Orleans against the Kansas City Monarchs, and they went on to win the Negro American League pennant again.

On opening day of the regular season, Raymond Brown won for us, and we beat the New York Cubans all three games of the series to get off to a good start for the year. In a later series against the Cubans in Portsmouth, Virginia, I hit a long fly ball right next to the fence in my first time at bat. The next time up, I hit a home run over the right-center-field fence. Then the next time up, they walked me intentionally. In another game, I hit a home run into the center-field bleachers, and they talked about it being the longest ball ever hit in Portsmouth Park.

But the Baltimore Elites jumped out in front of us in June. One weekend against the Elites I was 4 for 10, including two home runs in a Saturday single game and a Sunday doubleheader, and by July we were back on top. But later in the month they beat us a doubleheader and moved back ahead of us again. Then Brown shut them out on three hits, giving him a perfect 12–0 record for the season and 27 straight wins carrying over from the year before.

He had been our ace pitcher for several years and was one player who helped us win without Josh. In 1940 we only had three pitchers

doing most of the pitching—Raymond Brown, Edsall Walker, and
J. C. Hamilton. Brown finished with about half of our team's victo-
ries and was the best pitcher in the league. I think he was a better
pitcher than Leon Day and Bill Byrd. But I may be partial because
he was on our team, and somebody else might not agree.

I believe Raymond Brown and Sam Bankhead were the best
players on the Grays other than Josh and myself. Brown pitched
in the All-Star game that year and we shut out the West, 11–0. I
had two hits and also stole a base, which was a rare occurrence
since I was not noted for my baserunning. That time I ran on my
own, the manager didn't give me the steal sign. I thought I had
a good lead, and I left. My wife was at that game and she got at
me about that. She told me to quit trying to steal bases because I
might get hurt.

When I first came up to the Grays, I was trying to run bases.
I went to steal and we lost a couple of games we should have
won. One night in Toledo they threw me out three times trying
to steal second base. They stopped me from stealing bases because
I was slow, and also because I hurt my knee. Cum Posey told me,
"You're not as fast as you think you are. Don't you ever run no
more trying to steal a base!" And I quit from then on. That was
the first year I was with the Homestead Grays, in 1934. And I
quit running bases from then on.

Another time in my early years with the Grays, we were playing
a game in Syracuse, New York, and I hit a ground ball to the second
baseman, and while I was running to first base, my hat fell off and I
stopped to pick it up and got thrown out. Vic Harris was managing
then, and he asked me why I didn't keep running. I didn't have an
answer, so he fined me ten dollars—just enough for me not to do it
again. And it never did happen again. I still have no idea why I did
it that one time. I never did anything like that before or after that
time. My hat came off a lot of other times but I didn't stop to pick it
up. That one time happened early in my career.

I'll tell you another thing that happened when I was running
the bases. In a game sometime around 1940, I hit a ball down the
right-field line and I slid into second base, and the throw came in
from right field and the ball hit me right in my armpit. I caught
it right there in my armpit. And I got up and ran on home holding

that ball right under there. They didn't know where the ball was. Nobody else knew it was there. I was the only one who knew.

When I scored, I reached in there and got the ball and threw it back out there. Didn't nobody say anything. They didn't see the ball on the ground anywhere, so they must have known it was somewhere on me. They thought I had the ball hidden in my shirt, but I had the ball right in there under my armpit.

When we were not playing league games, we sometimes played the Brooklyn Bushwicks in exhibition games. One day at Dexter Park, in Woodhaven on Long Island, I got a key hit to beat them the first game of a doubleheader, 2–1. And in the second game we were behind, 3–1, and I hit a home run to put us just one run behind. Then Howard Easterling, the next batter, hit one right down the right-field foul line for what we thought was a homerun and had tied the score. But after he rounded the bases, they made him bat over.

The home-plate umpire said it was fair and the first-base umpire said it was foul. And we kicked and a big argument got started. Then the fans started throwing cushions and pop bottles out there on the field, and then *they* came out on the field, too. The riot police had to come out there before they could get it stopped. The Bushwicks were a white team and one bottle almost hit their catcher, and he jumped in the box seats and hit one of the colored fans that he said did it. It was about a half hour before the police could get everything settled down. Then Easterling had to bat over and we lost the game, 3–2.

That was Easterling's first full year with us. I can't remember how we got him, but he was a good ballplayer. He played third base and was good in the field. He was a switch-hitter who hit for average and could hit the long ball, too. He usually batted either third or fifth in the lineup. After Josh came back from Mexico, he and I used to switch around between fourth and fifth depending on who was pitching, but we kept Easterling in third place most of the time.

During World War II, he went to the Army and stayed about two or three years, and when he came back out of the Army, he had slowed down a whole lot. A lot of fellows did that. Major leaguers, too. They'd go in the Army and stay three or four years and do no more than what they want to do, and a lot of times don't even do that. And it slows you down.

But before he left for the Army, Easterling had helped us keep winning when Josh was gone. Another thing that helped us to offset the loss of Josh was, we got Jud Wilson at that time. We called him "Boojum." He stayed with the Grays four or five years. Before he came to us, he was with the old Baltimore Black Sox in his prime, and then when I went up there in 1934, he was with the Philadelphia Stars. And he came to us from there.

He was in the evening of his career at that time, and he had spells—epileptic fits. Sometimes he would be right out on the field when it happened, so we would have to watch out for him. Sometimes he would have one and he would get down on his knees and start to making marks on the ground while the game was going on. We had to call time and go over there and get around him. Then we'd get him off the field and carry him into the clubhouse. Once he was drawing circles in the dirt during the game, and his wife came in the clubhouse after the game and took care of him. And he did things like that.

And sometimes we'd be riding along on the bus and he would have a fit. But his wife had told us how to treat him when he had one. And sometimes we'd have to put a spoon or something in his mouth to keep him from biting his tongue. And his eyes would look glassy and blurry and look like he couldn't see so good. The spells would last about five or ten minutes, and afterward he would be weak. He would just get limp. Then for the next half hour or so he was kind of down. I think he anticipated a weakness. Sometimes we didn't let him play when he would have one on the day before a game. We never knew when he was going to have one.

Once we were on the Jamesville ferry up on the top deck just to look out. And we looked around and he was standing there with his pants off. We had to gather around him and bring him back down to the bus on the lower deck and put his pants back on him. And we had to make him sit down and calm him down. When he had them spells it took something out of him. It took a half hour or so for him to settle down.

We were in a restaurant one morning in Homestead and he had one of those spells. He was strong as hell. When he was in that kind of shape he was even stronger than ordinary. All of us were his friends, but a boy named Robert Gaston, our second-string catcher, was closest to him. He was his friend and his roommate. We called him Rab Roy. Rab Roy Gaston would get on one side and hold his hand and someone else would get on the other side and hold his hand to keep him quiet and try to relax him.

His wife used to tell us to not let him use salt and black pepper in his food, but you can't keep a grown man from putting salt and black pepper in his food. We told him not to, but so far as preventing it, we just couldn't do that.

If those spells bothered him, he didn't show it. I don't know if he had them before he got with us or not. I never did find out. But he was having them from the beginning with us. But other than that, I didn't know of any problem that he had. He wasn't a heavy drinker that I know of. I never did know him to drink, but Jud Wilson played ball a long time before I was with him. I don't know what he did back then.

I do know that he was called one of the "four big bad men" of black baseball. I don't know how he got that reputation, but I would say he earned it. In one game against the Bushwicks, he got mad about the umpire's decision and chased the umpire, and the police had to come out there and chase Jud off the field.

Now, he hit a fellow one time when we were on the road traveling. We went down to Butler, Pennsylvania, to play one night. We were on the bus and a white fellow passed us in a one-seat, two-door Ford, and as soon as he got his front end against us he cut in too soon and ran us off the road. Our bus driver, a fellow named Johnny Maynard, was driving the bus. We got back on the road and tried to catch up with the car but we couldn't overtake him until we started going downhill. Then we outran him and cut over in front of him and ran him off the highway.

And we stopped and three or four of us got out because we didn't know how many were in the other car. Boojum Wilson was one of them that got out with us. We didn't know the other driver was white when he got out, and we went back there and was asking him what did he mean by cutting over in front of us and running us off the road. And he said, well, he was sorry that he cut in front of us. And Boojum knocked him down just with these few words. Boojum didn't say a word. He let us do the talking and he did the hitting. That's why we were so surprised. We didn't intend to do no hitting.

Boojum didn't do anything in the off-season that I knew of. He lived right in the city limits of Washington, D.C., and they said he was originally from a neighborhood in Washington called Foggy Bottom. I don't know what he did after he retired from baseball. He left us before we broke up, and I lost track of him. But he could hit, even then, and he was in the evening of his career. He helped us with his bat. And he liked to win.

When Josh went to Mexico, Boojum's roommate, Rab Roy Gaston, was one of the catchers who played in his place. The year before, Gaston was second-string catcher to Gibson. Sometimes Gibson just didn't want to catch on a given day, but Gaston mostly caught against white teams that were not of major-league caliber. When we played white teams in exhibition games, we played just good enough to win. And we carried some pitchers who only pitched in those games. We called them "sockamyocks."

We had Josh Johnson to help with the catching that year, too. He and Gaston together did most of the catching in 1940. We tried a lot of others to fill Josh's spot, but nobody could really fill his shoes. Some of the others we tried sometime during the year were Ameal Brooks, Walter Perry, Red Bass, and Ziggy Marcell. Marcell was the son of Oliver Marcelle, who had been one of the top third baseman back in the twenties. They spelled their last name different for some reason, but I don't know why.

The next year, when Josh didn't come back, we had Eudie Napier to help Gaston. He was a second-string catcher for us before. The only other time he started for us was after Josh died. He just quit playing and didn't go to another team. He was working at a department store in Pittsburgh, and when the season was over, he'd go back to that department store. And he just decided he wasn't going to play any more ball. He lived in Pittsburgh after he finished playing baseball.

Josh came back and played a doubleheader in Washington, D.C., against the Philly Stars, around the middle of August, but they protested because the league had banned the jumpers for three years. That was the only day he played for us all season.

Most teams provided some stiff opposition at least one or two years during our dynasty period. But the New York Black Yankees were last again in 1940. They were the doormats of our league. I don't think they ever finished in the first division. They had a pretty good team when they were playing as an independent ballclub. When I first started playing against them, they had Eggie Clark as their catcher. Later they got Johnny Hayes. Connie Rector, Bill Holland, Nick Stanley, and Luther Farrell for a while were their four main pitchers. After the war they had Bob Griffith pitching, too.

First base was Showboat Thomas. Second base was George Scales. Shortstop was Bill Yancey. Third base was Rev Cannady. Outfield was Clint Thomas in center field and Fats Jenkins in left. Luther Farrell used to pitch and play right field. They had Rap Dixon there for a while, too. The Black Yankees never kept any players for long. They couldn't keep players because they didn't pay enough. They had some good players pass through there, but they couldn't keep them.

When they got in the league, they still had Clint Thomas. He was a good player. Now, he was in the evening of his career when I saw him, but he could still run and he could still field and he was a fair hitter. Fats Jenkins was a good outfielder, but I saw him when he was in his evening time, too. He was still pretty good, but he had slowed down some from his prime.

Charlie Biot was there in 1940. He was a good fielder, but he was only there one year. Felix McLaurin was another boy they had playing center field for a year or two. Hank Barker was the only one who stayed there. He was there about the whole time that they were in the league. He played outfield and managed some, too.

George Giles was over there with Barker, too, when the Black Yankees first got in the league around 1936. Catching they had Johnny Hayes and Kike Clark. At first base Zack Clayton, who had been a good basketball player, was with them a couple of years during the war. And George Crowe played with them the last few years before the league broke up. He went to the major leagues with the Braves and Reds. Barney Brown pitched with them some years, when he wasn't in Mexico or with the Philly

Stars. But the New York *Black* Yankees were not at all like the New York Yankees.

We finished strong and won the pennant in the last month of the season. I finished the year batting around .376, and Cum Posey selected me to his All-American team again. After the season, I went to the Caribbean to play another winter season of baseball. This time I went to Puerto Rico and played with Mayaguez.

My roommate down there was Chet Bewer, who was a good curveball pitcher. But he got a little extra advantage by "cutting" the ball. He claimed that he didn't, but I know he did. That's one reason why they didn't put him in the Hall of Fame. He threw cut balls and trick pitches.

In the Negro Leagues anything went. They threw a spitball, knuckleball, cut ball, or anything else they could come up with. The last few years I played, they ruled out spitballs. There were several players in our league who scratched the ball. It was supposed to be illegal, but the umpire didn't call it. And then, too, we didn't throw out every ball that had a black place on it. We played with balls that maybe should have been thrown out, and the pitchers in our league would take advantage of that. If a ball had a black place on it or a scuff place on it, they would think of ways and means to make it do tricks. They would make it sail, or break down, or break out or in.

They knew that the umpires weren't going to throw out the ball like they do in the major leagues. And they learned how to throw the scuffed-up ball that was left in play. Our pitchers had been used to doing it, and we had been used to hitting those kind of balls. But the major leaguers had not been used to hitting it, and they complained about it. They wanted a new ball. Sometimes in barnstorming exhibition games, with balls costing what they did, they didn't throw balls out of play as readily as they did in the major leagues.

Satchel was down there in Puerto Rico, too, with another team that winter. He didn't need to cut a ball or do anything else except throw his fastball. Satchel didn't start the season with Guayama, but they sent for and got Satchel a little later. When he got there, the Puerto Rican man who owned the team brought Satchel in the ballpark with a chain around his neck. And lead him in like he was a dog or lion or something. But that was a show, you know. He had been advertising in the paper that he was going to get Satchel, and when he got him, that's how he brought him into the ballpark.

That was the time when Satchel intentionally walked Bus Clarkson with the bases loaded in the first inning and walked in a run. Satchel had only been there about a week when he did that. Some people don't believe that he would do something like that, but I *know* it happened because I was there. I was on Bus Clarkson's team. Bus was a good hitter and led the league in home runs that winter. I was batting third and he was batting fourth. I was on first base—we had three men on base—and Clarkson was at bat.

Satchel told the catcher to get out a little, and Satchel threw one ball and then the catcher got back behind the plate and then Satchel motioned for him to get out again. And Satchel threw another ball. Then the manager came running out there and he said, "No, no, don't walk him." Satchel said, "I know what I'm doing." And he told Satchel, "Don't you know there's three men on base and if you walk this man you're going to walk a man home?" Satchel said, "I'd rather walk one run home than to have that so-and-so hit all three of them home and score himself."

And then Satchel told the catcher to get out there again. And the catcher did, and he went ahead and walked him, and walked in the run. Then Satchel said, "Now, that's all you're going to get today." And that's the only run we *did* get. That was in the first inning, and that's the only run we got that whole day. There was nobody out, and he struck the rest of them out. He beat us, 8–1. We always kidded Satchel about walking that run home. He did things like that, you know. Especially when fellows were coming up to bat that he knew he could get out.

Roy Campanella was also down there that winter, and we were tied for home runs. But Campanella's team got into the playoffs and my team didn't, and he hit a home run or two in the playoffs and went ahead of me. I used to joke him about that and I told him I didn't think it was fair because he had a couple of extra games. And we used to laugh about that. I finished the winter with a .358 batting average and, after a little while back home in Rocky Mount before spring training, I was in pretty good playing shape for the next season.

# Chapter 12

## Good Enough Again (1941)

*Buck is a ballplayer's ballplayer. He's a great competitor and at his best when the chips are down.*

*—Lem Graves, Jr., sportswriter*

Our owners thought Josh was going to come back, but he played in Mexico again in 1941. The Grays offered him six thousand dollars, but they offered him eight thousand in Mexico. So he went to Mexico, and Cum Posey sued him for ten thousand dollars for breach of contract.

Two of our pitchers, Roy Welmaker and Spoon Carter, were down there, too. But two others, Partlow and McDuffie, who went down there in 1940, came back. We had them and Ray Brown, J. C. Hamilton, and Johnny Wright all pitching. The rest of the team was the same as the year before, except for Chester Williams, who we got to play shortstop. But 1941 was not one of our good seasons. We had another year where we were just good enough to win. Other teams were also losing players to Mexico. There was about twenty-five players from the Negro Leagues playing down there.

In our league, we played our regular season from May 1 to

125

September 15, and we tried to play league games on the best days that we could draw a good crowd. Tuesday, Thursday, Saturday, and Sunday were the original times, and we tried to be in a town on those days when we could play a league game. That left Monday, Wednesday, and Friday for exhibitions, but it didn't always happen that way. We could make an exhibition game a league game. If we had a game rained out somewhere and had an exhibition game with the Newark Eagles scheduled in Norfolk, Virginia, we could get together and, with the consent of both teams, decide that was going to be a league game. But we had to have a league umpire to come down there. If it wasn't a league game we could use anybody, any local umpire. But if we declared it a league game, then we had to get one league umpire.

We played around 200 or 210 games that year and traveled about 30,000 or 40,000 miles. Counting winter ball, I guess we played about 300 games year-round. By the middle of the summer it seemed like 3,000. Playing in the Negro Leagues was tough. The traveling was tough. But once you got in condition, it was a little easier. When you're playing, you've got a certain gait you get up to. You play that way all the time, unless the game gets tight. Then you put out a little more.

Sonnyman Jackson bought a bus when he first came in with Cum Posey, and he bought another one later. The first one was a Ford bus and we had a special name for the first bus. We called it the *Blue Goose*. The latter bus was a Dodge bus, and it was light colored with the words "Homestead Grays Baseball Club" on the side of the bus. Our bus had two gasoline tanks carrying forty-five gallons of gas. The bus carried twenty-two people, and we had one regular bus driver and two players who could drive. And we needed them because the scheduling was bad.

We played a different game in a different town every night. That meant a lot of riding, a lot of playing, and a lot of staying in second-rate hotels and eating on the run. We couldn't stay in good hotels, and the meals were bad. Down South, and in some northern cities, we couldn't eat in white restaurants or stay in white hotels. In places where there were not any black hotels or restaurants, we stayed in rooming houses or in the YMCA. And sometimes we slept on the bus. But we didn't care about that. We loved the game and we wanted to play. We played somewhere every day unless it rained, and we were expected to play every day unless we were injured or sick.

Most teams had a player who could pass for white and could go into restaurants and buy sandwiches for the rest of the team. After he joined our team, Wilmer Fields was the one for the Grays who could do that, and I remember one time when he did it in Mississippi.

Sometimes a player from the islands could get served when we couldn't, because he spoke with a foreign accent. One time Luis Marquez, who was about my color, said he was hungry and that he was going to go in a white restaurant and get something to eat. We all laughed and walked on down the block, waiting for him to get put out. After a little while, we went on back down there to the corner and looked in through the window, and he was in there eating. When he came out, we all gave him our orders for him to get us some sandwiches, too. He could do that just because he spoke Spanish, and we couldn't go in there.

See Posey, our business manager, was light-skinned, too. Once in Oklahoma he drove up and registered at a wayside hotel. A few minutes later we drove up on the bus and the hotel clerk said, "No, no, no, you can't stay here." And motioned for us to leave when he saw that we were black. Another time, in Jamestown, New York, a hotel thought we were a white team, and then wouldn't let us stay there when they found out we were black. But even apart from the bad accommodations, the scheduling was bad.

A lot of times we would play three games in one day, and each one in a different town. In a typical tripleheader, we would play a ten-o'clock game in the morning, a three-o'clock game, and a twilight game at six-thirty. In the twilight game we would play until it got too dark to play, about six or seven innings.

In a tripleheader in New York we would play a doubleheader at the Polo Grounds or Yankee Stadium and then go on out to some run-down field on Long Island and play a twilight game against one of the semipro teams out there. When we got through with the Yankee Stadium doubleheader, we changed sweatshirts and got in the bus, and the business manager would have a sandwich for everybody and then we would go on out to Long Island

and play the Barton Nighthawks, the Farmers, or another semipro team out there. They were the semipro teams out on Long Island that you could play Sunday nights. Now, we didn't change clothes, we just changed sweatshirts. We'd keep the uniform on and go out there and start the game. The crowd was already there waiting on us when we got there.

The towns could be 250 miles apart because we'd leave right after the ball game and eat on the run. One Sunday evening, we played a doubleheader in Columbus, Ohio, and after we got through with the games, we played a semipro team at a ballpark in Detroit. From Columbus to Detroit was about 250 miles, and we had one of the players get about twenty sandwiches and we ate on the way to Detroit.

Another time we played Newark a doubleheader in Columbus and we carried Newark on to Detroit and played at Dequender Park. That's a semipro park in the suburbs of Detroit. We didn't go on the same bus, they had their bus and we had ours. We'd keep on our uniforms when we did that.

Once we put on our uniforms at seven o'clock Sunday morning in Philadelphia and rode ninety miles to Meadowbrook, New Jersey, and played a doubleheader. Then we went sixty miles to Hightown, New Jersey, and played a Sunday night game, and arrived back in Philadelphia at four o'clock Monday morning, still wearing our uniforms. Another time, we played a ten-o'clock morning game in Braddock, Pennsylvania, then drove to Dormouth, Pennsylvania, for a three-o'clock game, and came back for an eight-o'clock game in Pittsburgh.

In 1938 we played the Pittsburgh Crawfords six games in three days, July 2–4. We played single games in both Monessen and Greensburg on Saturday, then a Sunday doubleheader in Cleveland, and returned to Pittsburgh for a Labor Day doubleheader on Monday. We won all six games, and in one game I won the game with a home run off Johnny Taylor, who was one of the leading pitchers that year.

Those are just some examples of how we did our scheduling and traveling. Playing in major-league parks on weekends was what we called "getting-even days." The biggest crowd we ever had was thirty thousand in Griffith Stadium in 1942.

If we were going to play in New York or Washington or some-where in some of our best towns where we were going to draw good crowds, we would pitch our ace pitcher. Usually we saved our best pitcher for the first game on Sundays. We knew the first game was going to be nine innings and the second game was going to be seven innings. And since the first game was going to be nine innings we would try to win that first game and wrestle and tussle to win the second game. The next best pitcher would usually pitch the second game, rather than on Saturday. Maybe he was just a little bit better than the Saturday pitcher.

We had some pitchers who wanted to pitch the big games. They liked the big events. We had a pitcher on the team named Terris McDuffie, and every time we went to New York, he wanted to pitch. And sometimes it wouldn't be his time to pitch in New York. Saturday would be his time somewhere else. But he would want us to save him to pitch that big game in New York on Sunday. But we wouldn't do that.

McDuffie was a pretty good pitcher. He was a hardworking pitcher, and he didn't want us to make any errors behind him. If somebody made an error and lost the ball game when he was pitching, he'd say, "You threw this ball game away" or something like that. He was a humdinger. When he was out there on the mound, he was sincere and interested in what he was doing. McDuffie was not mad, but he really wanted to win. And he wanted everybody to keep up their own end when he was pitching.

McDuffie was illiterate and temperamental. One time when we were playing exhibition games and playing on a percentage, we had some bad weather and only made ten dollars apiece for one game. And he bet it all on one roll of the dice and lost. He just shrugged and said, "Today we got rained out." See, when we got rained out, we didn't get any money, and that was what he said because he had lost all his money for that day.

We got off to a good start in 1941, and won two out of three games from the Elites in our first games in Washington. I hit a home run in the first game. About a week later, we hit four home runs in one inning in a game. I hit one, Raymond Brown hit one, and the other two were hit by Rab Roy Gaston, Josh's replace-ment. Even Josh couldn't have done better than that. By the time

June arrived we were in first place, and we won the first half by about two games over the Eagles and Elites.

We didn't do as well the second half of the season, and the New York Cubans won the second half. They had Frank Coimbre and Tetelo Vargas in the outfield, and they were their best hitters. And they had Horacio Martinez at shortstop, and the two Blanco brothers, Carlos and Heberto, also in the infield.

Dave Barnhill was their top pitcher, and he had a good year. Early in the season, he struck me out twice in a game. And he always reminded me about that in later years, and I would ask him about the game when I hit a home run and a triple off him and we won the game in ten innings, 3–2. When I saw him forty years later at the reunion at Ashland, Kentucky, he still asked me about that. And I asked him if he remembered the home runs I hit off him.

We had to beat them in a playoff to win the pennant, and we won four out of five. Barnhill started the final game and we knocked him out and beat them, 20–0. And I always reminded him of that, and that I hit another home run in that game. After we won the league championship, there was not a World Series. The first one would not be played until 1942. Somebody wrote that I finished the season with a batting average of .383. The Grays gave us a big banquet at the end of the season and presented us with radios shaped like a baseball. I've still got that radio and it still works. It might be the only one still around.

In addition to being on the pennant-winning team, I was on the winning All-Star team, too, since our East squad won the All-Star game at Comiskey Park. The score was 8–3, and I knocked in the first run for us in the game. Hilton Smith was pitching, and I got a single to right field and scored Henry Kimbro. I had another hit in the game, and it was a home run off Double Duty Radcliffe.

When I came up in the fourth inning, we had Hoskins on first base and Double Duty was pitching. He said before the game that I couldn't hit a slowball. See, an off-speed pitch was my weakness. So he threw me one, and I hit a home run in the right-field stands that went about 360 feet. That put the game on ice, and they took him out of the game after that. But the last time I batted, Satchel was pitching. He struck out the first two batters he faced before me, and then I hit a high pop fly to the second baseman.

Terris McDuffie, who pitched with the Grays that year, was the winning pitcher. We had over fifty thousand people there to see the game, and some people were turned away at the gate. That was over twice as many as we had the year before, and it was probably because of Satchel being there. The papers said, "Buck Leonard proves brightest star in the East's constellation." They also mentioned my fielding and said, "Throughout, Buck's brilliant big-league fielding was one of the afternoon's highlights."

It had been a good year for me, but during the off-season we all got some news that affected everybody. The Japanese bombed Pearl Harbor. Most people remember where they were when they heard the news, but I don't remember where I was when I heard about that.

# Chapter 13

## Dark Dynasties (1942)

*Buck Leonard had a good glove, but his forte was that bat. He could really hit. He was one of the best hitters I ever saw, and one of the nicest fellows I ever saw.*
*—Buck O'Neill, Kansas City Monarchs*

During the war years we were limited to how far we could go to spring train, so we trained in Dayton, Ohio, and Raleigh, North Carolina. In 1942, Josh Gibson and Sam Bankhead came back from Mexico, and those were the only changes in our starting lineup from the year before. We were the strongest we had been since 1939, but other teams had strengthened themselves, too, and in our spring exhibition games the Newark Eagles beat us most of the time. Our owners, Cum Posey and Sonnyman Jackson, got mad about us getting beat, but when we played them opening day, it was different. We opened the season on May 9, and twelve thousand fans showed up to see us beat the Eagles, 3–2, on Josh's home run.

Monte Irvin says that this team was the best the Eagles ever had, even better than their championship team of 1946. But the Manleys let too many of their good ballplayers get away from

133

them. First they traded Bus Clarkson to Philadelphia, then Monte went to Mexico, and a little later in the season Ray Dandridge jumped back down there again. He had been down there before for a couple of years, and just went back. About that same time, Dick Seay joined the Army. But they still had Leon Day, and he was in his prime and was the best pitcher in our league at that time. One night he struck out eighteen batters against the Baltimore Elites, and Roy Campanella was three of them.

The Elites had a good team that year, too. They had Bill Wright and Sammy T. Hughes back from Mexico. And Campanella was coming into his own and catching. Bill Byrd and Jonas Gaines had good years pitching. Except at first base, it was the same lineup they had in 1939 when they beat us in the postseason tournament. Along about that time we were having some difficulties. We lost three straight to Newark and a little later lost a series to Philadelphia. Then we got back into contention by beating the Elites a doubleheader on the first of August. They had been in first place, but we ended up just barely edging them out.

That was our sixth straight Negro National League pennant, and the Monarchs won over in their league for the fifth time in the same six seasons and for the fourth straight year. That made the World Series that year a matchup of the two dominant teams in black baseball. It was the first time that a World Series had been played between the champions of the two leagues, and we played in a different town every night. Not only that year, but every year after that as well.

We had played the Kansas City Monarchs in three interleague games in 1942, and we won all three of them by one run in extra innings. And we had a good turnout for the games. In Kansas City we had a crowd of thirty thousand fans that came out to see us. Of course, they were rooting for their home team, the Monarchs. Because we had beaten them in those interleague games during the regular season, we were considered the favorites in the World Series. But it didn't turn out that way. They beat us four straight in that first World Series.

There are a few incidents that happened in the World Series that year and, of course, Satchel was involved in all of them. In the game at Griffith Stadium, a policeman was directing traffic coming into the ballpark. Satchel had his own car, and the policeman had told him to go straight ahead and he would tell him when to make his turn. Satchel made his turn anyway before he was directed and ran over the policeman's foot, and the policeman was going to put him in jail. But he didn't when he found out who he was.

Satchel was arrested for speeding on the way to the last game and was late getting there. In that game, Rab Roy Gaston had replaced Josh Gibson in the third inning for some reason and, when Satchel came in to pitch after he got to the ballpark, he struck Gaston out with the bases loaded to save the game.

In the third game, Satchel left early after two innings, claiming a stomach ailment. That was the first game of a doubleheader in Yankee Stadium. The first game was a Series game, but we agreed the second would be an exhibition game. In that game, the Monarchs used a pitcher named Gready McKinnis, who was the same one who pitched for Birmingham.

Then the next game we used a pitcher from another team. That was how it came about that we had to forfeit one game. Now, the team we had going into the World Series was not as strong as we were during the season. There were some injuries, and some players were working at defense jobs and couldn't play. And a little before the Series started, Bankhead had run into a fence and broke his arm. He didn't play much in the Series, and that weakened the team some. Jelly Jackson had to get a defense job, and he had been gone all year. Carlisle got a defense job in Homestead but he couldn't travel with the team. Whatley was our regular right fielder, but he had a charley horse and didn't think he should play any more that season. Sometimes we didn't play him against left-handers, anyway, and he didn't play much in the Series. Roy Partlow had boils under his arm but he had been pitching up until that time, even with the boils.

The thing about it was that if you win with a certain amount of players, then you're supposed to go into the Series with those same players. But we were not at full strength during the Series, so we had asked for and received permission to pick up some players from other league teams to make up for the players who were not able to play. Cum Posey got Leon Day to pitch for us against Satchel in Kansas City. And we got Ed Stone, Lennie Pearson, and Bus Clarkson to play with us.

We didn't think our team was strong enough to play them with the men we had missing, and we got those fellows to play with us, which they said was illegal. Day beat Satchel, 4–1, in Kansas City, but the Monarchs protested that we had used "ringers" and said we had to forfeit that game to Kansas City.

We were calling that one of the regular Series games, and we had classed it as that. But they did away with it, though, and said we couldn't use those fellows. After we found out what they were going to do, we didn't play those players anymore. Satchel beat us the next game to give them the Series. That was the one in Shibe Park in Philadelphia when he was late getting to the game. But the biggest story in the Series was when he struck out Josh Gibson with the bases loaded in the game at Forbes Field.

Now, before that, the same kind of situation had come up in the regular-season game that we played against them in Griffith Stadium. Satchel had a 2–1 lead in the ninth inning with Jerry Benjamin on second base with the tying run and Josh at the plate. Josh hit one over the fence and it went at least 450 feet, but it was just barely foul. Then Satchel ended up walking Josh, and that put the winning run on base. I was the next hitter, and I singled to right field to tie the score. And we went on to win the game, 3–2, in the twelfth inning.

So now we're in the World Series, and we had one man on base just like before. And Satchel walked Vic Harris and Howard Easterling so he could pitch to Josh with the bases loaded. The score was 2–0, so he put the tying and winning runs on base. Then he struck Josh out on three pitches and went on to win the game. That was unusual in a close ball game, even for Satchel. He was just showing off, you know, putting on a show.

Satchel could always get Josh out because he never would throw him a curveball. He'd just throw him fastballs, and Josh was a curveball hitter. And that's how he could get Josh out, throwing his fastball. I was a fastball hitter and he felt like he could get Josh out better than he could get me out. So that's what he did, knowing that Josh could not hit his fastball. See, it was working both ways. Satchel believed he could get Josh out, and Josh didn't believe he could hit Satchel.

The World Series was typical of the kind of year we had. We had things happen all year. Sometime around the middle of the season, we were playing in Washington, D.C., and I broke the third metacarpal bone in my left hand. I'm left-handed, and that was my throwing hand. I was sliding into the base head first and all my fingers went under the base except for my ring finger, and it went up on top of the base, and that's how I broke it. I went to the hospital right after the game was over and they put some splints on it. I came back home and stayed out eight weeks with it.

I had first injured the hand in the spring, in a game against the Black Yankees, and then I hurt it again. I missed a large part of the season from that, but I got back in the lineup in time for the World Series. I was playing with it taped, but I was still playing. I didn't want to miss a game. It didn't hurt too much when I swung. I don't think I was ailing during that time. But later, in 1945, I broke my right hand and I was ailing in that World Series. But this time I had my left hand broken and it didn't bother me too much about playing in the field.

I didn't play in the All-Star game that year because of that broken hand from earlier in the season. It was the first time I hadn't started at first base in the East-West game since 1936. Jim West from the Philadelphia Stars was the starting first baseman that year, and Leon Day was the hero of the All-Star game. He came in with two outs in the seventh inning and the tying run in scoring position, and he saved the game. Out of the seven men he faced, he struck out five of them, and he didn't allow a hit. Dave Barnhill got credit for the victory, and Satchel was the losing pitcher. We beat Satchel in the All-Star game and we beat him in the games we played him in the regular season, but we couldn't beat him in the World Series.

Satchel wasn't the only good pitcher that Kansas City had. They had the best pitching staff I ever saw. They just mostly had ordinary players other than the pitchers. That's what was carrying them, those pitchers. We were a hitting ballclub and they were a pitching ballclub. They had Satchel Paige, Hilton Smith, Jack Matchett, Booker McDaniels, Lefty LaMarque, and Connie Johnson.

That's the Kansas City Monarchs' pitching staff when they were winning. All them guys could pitch. That's what cut teams down so.

After Satchel, Booker McDaniels was the second best on the staff, but he really didn't come into his own until a few years later. Hilton Smith was next, but he couldn't pitch with Satchel. He was a seasoned pitcher and proved himself in ball games time after time. But for my money, I would take Booker McDaniels above him. I might be the only one who would do that, though. Jack Matchett was an underhand pitcher, and LaMarque was a left-handed pitcher. Connie Johnson was just ordinary, we thought. But he went to Baltimore and made good in the major leagues with the Orioles.

Satchel was effective in the Series, but then Satchel was effective *all* the time. We just couldn't hit him. Hilton Smith had a sore arm and only pitched one game. Jack Matchett had pitched pretty good until the last game, when we jumped on him, and Satchel came in to relieve him.

In the infield, the Monarchs had Buck O'Neill. He was a good first baseman all around, except he couldn't run the bases. Newt Allen was playing third base at that time. He was a second baseman in his earlier years, but he played more at third base as he got older. Barney Serrell was playing second base, and he was a good fielder *and* a good hitter. Jesse Williams was the shortstop. He was a good fielder but not one of their good hitters.

Of course, they had Willard Brown in the outfield. He was playing shortstop for a while in earlier years before he finally went to the outfield. He went to the St. Louis Browns later on, but he didn't make it for some reason. Sometimes it's ability. Now, you take Hank Thompson. He had a problem with his drinking, but they went up there at the same time and you see what the heck Thompson did. He went up to the Giants later and stayed there. But Willard Brown just didn't have it. He didn't hustle all the time. In the Negro Leagues, if you couldn't get nobody better, you just had to keep a player. And Kansas City couldn't get nobody better than he was.

Their other outfielders were Willie Sims and Ted Strong. Sims was fast. He could catch fly balls, run the bases, and had good range in the field. Strong was a switch-hitter, but he wasn't too fast and he wasn't such a good outfielder. He was as big as Josh Gibson and hit a long ball every now and then.

Kansas City had a good team, period. And when we got banged up and the team got weaker, then they just could beat us. We tried to play some more games as exhibitions, but when the fans found out that they weren't regular World Series games, they wouldn't come out.

We always tried to make more money by playing some kind of exhibition games after the season was over. We would play among our top league teams, or against white teams or against an independent black ballclub that was not in the league. One of those teams that attracted good crowds was the Ethiopian Clowns. After they moved to Indianapolis they were called the Indianapolis Clowns.

In 1942 the Negro Leagues teams stopped playing against the Clowns because they had an act that was not approved of by some spectators. Whenever we played them in Washington, D.C., Clark Griffith would tell us not to let them have that act. Several ballparks didn't want them to have that act anymore after they had it once. It was an act that some people found objectionable. They might go along with it nowadays. Here's what it was.

King Tut, Bebop, and another boy were out on the pitcher's mound acting like they were rowing a boat, with one sitting up front, one sitting in the back, and all of them acting like they were rowing out into the middle of a lake to fish. And when they got out there to a good place to stop and fish, they would stop rowing. That was an indication that they had gone as far as they wanted to go. And they would look up and while they were looking up one of them would grab his eye and take something out of his eye and act like a bird dropped something in his eye. That was the objectionable act that some people didn't want the Clowns to do.

Another thing was, they had an act where one player would put a funnel at the other one's butt and take his arm and started pumping it up and down and it looked like water was running down through the funnel into a bucket down there.

Those two acts are the ones that people didn't want them to pull during the ball game. They could go on with the other acts.

Now, in Buffalo they could put on that act that I was telling about. But in New York City and in Washington, D.C., they would tell you before the game, "Don't let them have that act."

In one of the Clowns' other acts, King Tut would go out to the pitcher's mound and put a chair down and sit in the chair like he was a dentist. And he had one of them old-timey doctor's bags. And he would open that bag, and he would reach in his bag and get a hammer and a big coal chisel that was about three feet long and he would set them over there on the ground and get a nail puller and three or four more old-fashioned tools.

Now, he's a dentist and he would be sitting in his chair with all of those tools out there on the pitcher's mound. After a while Bebop, the midget, would come out of the dugout with a great big towel nearly as big as a sheet, tied all around his head and tied in a big knot on the side of his face and he was holding his jaw like he had a toothache. When King Tut would look and see him coming he would get up out of his chair and move the tools around and get his hammer and hammer on the bar and get his big chisel and hold that up and knock on that and reach down and get something else like he was getting ready for Bebop.

Then when Bebop would get there he set Bebop down in the chair. And when he got ready to look in Bebop's mouth, he took the towel off and got right up in Bebop's lap with his feet to look in his mouth. Bebop was sitting there with his mouth all open, and King Tut would reach down there and get his chisel. Then he would reach down there and get his hammer and tell Bebop to open his mouth and that he was going to knock on his tooth with that long chisel and big hammer. Then he had a big pair of pliers and he decided that he was going to pull the tooth. He would get all the way right up in Bebop's lap to get ahold of that tooth to pull it out with them long pliers. And that brought the house down. Just to think about a dentist using those kinds of tools to work on a tooth.

I didn't know either King Tut or Bebop's real name. When they was playing with the Clowns all of them had to use African names. Not only were they a good drawing card but they were a good ballclub, too. Anytime that Impo would pitch, it was a good ballgame. "Impo" was Dave Barnhill's Clown name. All the players had made-up names. But Barnhill had left them and was with the New York Cubans in 1942. The next year they let the Clowns in the Negro American League, but they had to stop clowning. They couldn't do that in league games, but they could do it in exhibition games.

In the early part of June 1942 we borrowed Satchel Paige to pitch for us in an exhibition game against Dizzy Dean's all-star major-leaguers. A crowd of twenty-two thousand turned out at Griffith Stadium to see us beat them by a score of 8–1. But Diz was over the hill then and wasn't even in the major leagues anymore. They did have Cecil Travis from the Washington Senators, who had the second-highest batting average in the American League the year before. Only Ted Williams had a higher average, and that was the year he hit over .400.

When whites were playing they had a black section, usually down the right-field line, and segregated seating was required. When we played exhibition games between blacks and whites, many of them continued to sit in the same place. I think it was just a custom, because it wasn't required. Negroes became accustomed to sitting in certain places while the whites were playing, and when we played, sometimes they would go back to that same section. But we sold tickets for anywhere they wanted to sit and they could have sat anywhere they wanted to sit. We sold box seats, too, for those exhibition games, and if blacks had a box seat ticket, then they could sit in the box seats. But it was a custom in Washington, D.C., not a requirement.

The crowd mixture more or less depended on what you were charging. Blacks don't usually go to anything where you charge a lot. We didn't charge but two dollars and, if we had good white major-league ballplayers whenever we were playing, then we had a good white crowd. Most all of the time the crowds would be more white than black when we were playing against whites.

The whites sat where they wanted to and they dressed where they wanted to. Now, if we came to Washington to play them like we did with Dizzy Dean's All-Stars, the white ballplayers went into the home dressing room and we blacks went into the visiting club's dressing room.

I played against Dizzy Dean several times. I remember once he

played with the Bushwicks in Dexter Park and they beat us in
that game. I never really got to know Dizzy and never talked to
him. Neither he nor his brother Paul ever talked to us. I don't
think they were prejudiced as far as that goes. They were there
for the money and they didn't care about anything else. They
didn't care who they were playing. Both of us were just there for
the money.

I did pretty good against Dizzy and his brother Paul, too. I got
a few hits off them. They were still in the major leagues then,
both him and Paul. Some people ask if we ''carried'' Diz later
on, after he hurt his arm. Well, he was billed as the star attraction.
He still knew how to pitch, although he didn't have his stuff, and
for three innings he could get us out by knowing *how* to pitch.
After a seasoned pitcher loses his fastball he knows how to rely
on his other stuff, tricks and everything else, to try to get the
batters out—like Gaylord Perry did.

Dizzy's teams were not the only time I played against major-
leaguers. We used to play exhibition games in Baltimore every
year against major-leaguers after the regular reason closed and the
World Series was over. The games were played on Sundays. The
newspapers said the white major-leaguers would play the black
major-leaguers on a given date, and would feature an important
player like Jimmie Foxx or Al Simmons. Different major-league
players were featured each week. Sometimes Lefty Grove, Bobo
Newsom, or some other player would be with them one Sunday
but not the next, and they didn't have the same major-league all-
stars every week. But we had the same team every Sunday. So
sometimes their strength was stronger one Sunday than it was
another Sunday, but we usually had the same team every time.

I got a hit off Lefty Grove when we barnstormed against him.
If he got behind in the count, I hit him. But he was more or less
a money problem. He was thinking about how much he was going
to make that day rather than who was going to win the ball game.
At that time there was not any fraternizing between blacks and
whites. We came out and played a ball game and they went their
way and we went ours. We didn't talk before the game and didn't
do much talking during the ball game. We blacks had an inferiority
complex. We felt like the only reason they were playing against

us was to make money. And we knew the only reason that we were playing them was to make money. That's the way it was. And they made more than we did because they were the attraction.

We would have about ten thousand people there each week. Baltimore was not in the major leagues then, they were in the International League. I went to Baltimore to play in those exhibitions for two or three years in the late thirties. I would leave Rocky Mount on a train at six o'clock Sunday morning and get in Baltimore about ten o'clock. We would play a doubleheader on Sunday and I would catch the train about eight o'clock that Sunday night and come back here. They ran an excursion up there. The train fare was about eight dollars and we made fifteen or twenty dollars. I earned train fare and change. And next Sunday would be the same thing, I would go back up there again. And we would do that until it got too cold to play.

Some guys had jobs, like in a service station or something, and they wouldn't go to play in these games. One time they called me and wanted me to go to New Orleans to play a series of games, but I was tired and I didn't want to go.

The winter after the 1942 season, I worked at the railroad station, loading and unloading boxcars. That was hard work and I would rather have been playing baseball, but with us being in the war, things were different. The next winter I went to California and played with Satchel Paige's All-Stars against major-leaguers until Judge Landis, the baseball commissioner, made us quit because he thought it looked bad for the major-leaguers to lose to a black team. But then I had to come back here and work at the railroad station for the rest of the winter, and it was that way until the war was over.

# Chapter 14

## World Champions (1943)

*Buck Leonard is one of the greatest clutch hitters in Negro baseball.*
                    *—Cum Posey, Homestead Grays*

In 1943, Josh was beginning to show signs of problems off the field. On New Year's Day he had to go to St. Francis Hospital in Pittsburgh because of a nervous breakdown. They said that he was in a coma when they took him in, but they also said that while he was in there, sometimes he had to be restrained in a straitjacket. I don't know what happened, but from then on he had problems off the field. I really don't know what caused them.

We were close friends but we didn't go around together because he was a beer drinker and I wasn't. He used to go around with Sam Bankhead, our shortstop. I don't know why he was so different so far as our regular life was concerned. He came up there just like I did. I knew his momma and his daddy, too. And they tried to raise him right just like my folks tried to raise me. And I don't know why he went off like he did.

Josh started his slide around the middle of 1942, but he really started going downhill fast in 1943 and got worse about 1944 or '45. Some people say he was involved with drugs, but I don't know anything about that. I have never known him to do that, but I do know that he drank. Beer tastes good to a ballplayer just like anybody else, and he drank a lot of beer. At that time, he had started drinking whiskey, too.

There was always girls that waited for ballplayers outside the clubhouse after games. There still are. One time there was a certain girl who used to wait for me outside after the games, but she quit me for Josh. He could give her more than I could. At least he *did* give her more than me.

But there was one woman that Josh got involved with that might have caused some of his problems. Her name was Grace, and she was a little light-skinned girl. Her husband was in the service and we thought that she might be smoking reefers. That was about the time that he started to go downhill, and we began to notice a change. But we didn't know what it was. I remember one time we saw him standing outside the ladies' restroom, waiting on her, like he was standing guard. But I don't know what was going on. We just thought it didn't look right.

When he took up with Grace, he wasn't with Hattie. Hattie had been his wife and was a nice lady. They might have been still married, but he wasn't living with her at that time. When Grace's husband came back from the service, she dropped Josh. But we always thought that she was the one that got Josh started going downhill.

Once we were playing the Birmingham Black Barons an exhibition game in Norfolk, Virginia. He got started drinking and there were six of us staying at my wife's sister's house there. And he was walking around in the house naked. Of course, we were on the second floor, but women were in the house, too, and the only bathroom in the house was upstairs. And we told him, "Don't be walking around the house naked. What's the matter with you?" And we got him straightened out with that.

Just before that happened, he got on a binge and he had been on it for about a week. And we wouldn't let him play. We sent him to St. Elizabeth Hospital in Washington, D.C. We let him stay there to boil out. He was there about ten or fifteen days. It seems like he was only supposed to stay ten days, but he stayed fifteen. Anyway, he stayed out there a few days and then he came back to the team and he was much better for a while. He had a whiskey problem when he went in. He was drinking liquor, and that was the reason we sent him out there. But he didn't stop drinking, and his problem continued.

We sent him out there to St. Elizabeth Hospital twice. Both times he stayed about fifteen days. I guess that must have been how long they generally kept them for that. And for the rest of the year, he was in and out of there. He had needle marks all in his arm. They were giving him some kind of shots. I don't know what kind of treatments they were giving him, but whatever it was, they were giving it to him in the arm.

We were losing players to World War II, but both Josh and I were classified 4-F. He had bad knees from catching so long, and squatting and getting up and down. Josh always had bad legs. He had bad feet and bad legs, and the older he got, the worse they got. They said I was exempted on account of I had a bad back. I went to the doctor two or three times and he turned me down.

Josh kept hitting good, but his fielding went down some. I started to catch pop flies to help him out. I caught everything I could get to. I ran like the devil from first base to home plate to catch a pop fly. It was when he was going downhill that I did that. Josh had always been a little weak on pop flies, but he had gotten worse at that time. And I tried to help him whenever I could.

Later in the year was when we had to take him to St. Elizabeth Hospital's mental facility. In spite of all his problems, he still hit over .500, according to records that a reporter, Ric Roberts, kept for the home games.

Sam Bankhead had a drinking problem, too. He drank about as much as Josh and they ran around together. We didn't allow no beer to be brought in the bus, but you know the good players are privileged a little more than some of the other guys, and those two would bring bottles of beer on the bus. Well, I don't remember Josh *bringing* them on the bus, but I remember Bankhead bringing them on and Josh would help him empty them. Vic let them get by with it, and other players didn't resent it. When Josh came back to the ballpark, he was ready to play most of the time. But three or four times, he came to the ballfield to catch and he was drunk. When he came like that, Vic wouldn't let him play.

After Candy Jim Taylor became manager, he never let them get by with drinking on the bus. He replaced Vic Harris as manager after Vic took a job in a defense plant after the 1942 season. Candy Jim was there in 1943 and 1944 and we won the pennant and World Series both years. He had been one of the crack players for the ABC's of Indianapolis a long time ago, and had been in the Negro Leagues about forty years. He started as a third baseman back in 1904, and had been playing and managing ever since. So he knew a lot of baseball.

He used to tell a pitcher, a batter's not going to remember the first two pitches he took, he'll remember the last two. He wanted you to *think*. And when he gave you the signals, you had to watch. When we were in the clubhouse before taking the field, everybody put on the uniforms and sat there waiting for him to talk. He would say, "Anything blue I touch is hit and run. The cap's bill is blue, belt loops on the pants is blue, letters across the front of the shirt is blue, and socks is blue. All that is blue." Then he'd say something like this: "If I touch something blue and rub both hands on my pants like this, it's off. If I touch something blue and don't rub my hands on my pants, then it's on." You've got to remember that. And then he'd say, "If I reach down there and pull up my pants like this, then it's a bunt."

Sometimes when players go to bat, they look down there at the third-base coach for a sign. The way Jim Taylor would have it, you get your signals when you're going to the bat, not after you get up there and stand and look at anybody. Everybody is looking at who you're looking at. When you get out of the dugout and you come up there to the batting circle, that's when you get your signals. He was coaching third base and you got the signals on the way up there to the batting circle.

He didn't want you gazing at nobody, and he didn't want the opposition gazing at nobody when he did want you to steal. If you're on first base and he wants you to steal second, every time the batter took a pitch and you came back to first base, you're supposed to look at the coach to see what he wants for you to do on the next pitch. If he sees the first baseman looking, too, he wouldn't give it to you. You're supposed to look at the way he stands. He wouldn't use his hand or nothing. You had to watch the way he was standing. Vic Harris did that the same way.

Now, in Havana, Cuba, where you play all the games in one ballpark, and two teams are playing but the other two teams are sitting there looking, you had to change signals every night. Whatever is hit and run tonight is going to be bunt tomorrow night.

Tom Parker and Raymond Brown had a high leg kick. Jim Taylor would say, "If showing your foot to the batter would confuse him, I would have been the greatest pitcher in the world because I've got a size twelve." He used that approach often. He was more relaxed and a better teacher than Vic. The players responded to Candy Jim better than to Vic. A whole lot better. Candy Jim knew what he was talking about.

His brother Ben Taylor was the one who taught me how to play first base and was the one I was playing for at Baltimore. They had two other older brothers, C. I. and Steel Arm Johnny, but I didn't know either of them. They were all from Anderson, South Carolina, originally.

After he left us, Candy Jim went to a couple of other teams and was with the Baltimore Elites his last year. But the riding was too much for him and he finally just got tired of it. He passed away not long after he retired, in the spring of 1948. That was the same year we won our last pennant.

But in 1943 we had another one of our good teams and we were one of the highest-paid teams in the history of black baseball. There was a lot of jumping around by players. I was an exception. I went to one team and stayed seventeen years. I was better paid than most players, and that contributed to my staying. Josh and I were getting about twice as much money as the rest of the players, not counting Satchel. I don't know what Satchel was getting. I was making a thousand dollars per month and Josh was making about twelve hundred dollars. Other players were making four and five hundred dollars a month.

When the war started is when we really started making money. People couldn't get gasoline to take a pleasure ride and they had to stay in Washington and Pittsburgh because they couldn't get stamps for gasoline and the people couldn't put on a spread and go out on weekends. They had to go to the ball game, so there was more money coming in to the owners. And at the same time, we players were being offered more money to play in other places.

Jorge Pasquel, the president of the Mexican League, sent agents over here to talk to us, and they were passing around money like lemonade. They were giving everybody this kind of money and that kind of money. Pasquel's agent came to talk to the players right at Greenlee Field. He was doing his recruiting and was giving out the money right there at the field. He talked to everybody he could talk to. He talked to Spoon Carter, Josh Gibson, Sam Bankhead, Jerry Benjamin, Howard Easterling, and two or three more fellows.

When Pasquel's agent came right out on the field and talked to us, Sonnyman Jackson got real upset and was going to confront him about bothering his ballplayers. He was trying to use force instead of getting his officers, and that was the wrong approach. Jackson got after the Mexican, and the law got after Jackson. Then somebody got the policeman and he wanted to arrest the Mexican right there at the ballpark, but somehow they didn't arrest him. But Jackson, Posey, and Greenlee ran the Mexican right out of the ballpark. They told him he had to get off the premises and had the policemen put him out of the ballpark.

The Mexicans were paid to come here and talk to us. And when Cum saw them talking to us, it made him mad. But that's how I got my raise. I didn't know one Pasquel from another, but one of them approached me that same day at Greenlee Field and told me that he would give me a thousand dollars a month to come down to play in Mexico. That's the only time that I considered jumping the Grays.

They said, "Do you want it now?" And I said, "No, I don't want it now." I had something else in mind. That's when I asked for more money. We left from Pittsburgh and were playing in Washington, D.C., at Griffith Stadium. I told Sonnyman Jackson, Cum Posey, and See Posey that I had talked to the man from Mexico. I told them the Pasquels had offered me more money to play down there and unless the Grays gave me what Pasquel had offered me, I was going to leave the following Friday to go to Mexico. I said, "Now, I'm giving you time to get somebody else."

That was on a Saturday, and Cum Posey said he would let me know on Sunday night. So on Sunday night he told me that they had agreed to give me a thousand dollars a month and all my expenses at home *and* on the road if I would *not* go to Mexico. So I didn't go, and I didn't have to pay any more expenses. Before that we had to pay expenses at home in Pittsburgh. Of course, I was staying at Jackson's home anyway. I didn't eat there, though, I just slept there, so I had that expense.

That's how I got a good salary. They knew I was going if they didn't match his offer. My salary jumped from four hundred twenty-five dollars a month to a thousand dollars a month. Most of the salaries doubled to keep us from jumping to Mexico. I was scared to get that much money.

That was not the first time that the Mexican League sent agents over here to talk to us. A couple of years earlier they had got Josh Gibson, Ray Dandridge, Sam Bankhead, Spoon Carter, Cool Papa Bell, Willie Wells, and a lot of other players out of our league to go to Mexico to play on the Mexican teams.

And that was not the last time they came over here to recruit players. In 1945 one of the Pasquel brothers came back over here with a lot of money and he was going from city to city during the season getting players to go to Mexico. He would give them seven hundred or eight hundred dollars and, at first, they thought that he was giving them that as a bonus to go to Mexico. But after they got down there and started playing, they found out that he was going to take that money out of their salary. That's why just about all of them came back the next year because he began to take out that money later. Max Lanier and all of the white players who went down there from the major leagues were the same way.

Along about then was when I had to become the traveling secretary for the Grays. I had the job about seven or eight years, until the team broke up in 1950. First Cum Posey handled the money. Then Sonnyman Jackson did. Then See Posey and then me. Me and Vic Harris together were running the team then.

I was captain of the Grays for some time. When Vic Harris was playing left field, I handled the infield. I placed the men in the infield and a few in the outfield, too. I was studying baseball.

I studied the game and studied the hitters and studied the pitchers. Vic took care of the outfield but he just couldn't handle what went on in the infield.

But I didn't want to be the captain of the team and be the traveling secretary, too. I didn't want to be all that, carrying the money and playing. That was too much. Every night after the ball game I had to make out the scoresheet. They had a list of the team with every ballplayer's name on this list. And as they borrowed money from the ball team, I would have to make out a sheet every night and send it back to Homestead, telling how much money I took in that night and how much the fellows borrowed if they borrowed any and how much I spent. I had that sheet to make out every night.

Cum's brother, See Posey, was the traveling secretary, but he didn't go with us everywhere we went. They said that in order for See Posey to book games for us and to be at the office when somebody called to cancel a date or okay a date, he had to be in his place in the home office. Then they started giving me the money to be the business manager. Now, on big days like Sundays in Washington, D.C., or New York or somewhere like that, See Posey or Sonnyman Jackson would be there and collect the money. All the big days when a lot of money was going to be taken in they would show up and I just took care of the small games.

When we got ready to leave Pittsburgh they would give me a hundred dollars or maybe two hundred fifty dollars for the expense money. I had to pay the bridge fare, the toll, and pay for the gas and all like that. And then play, too. I tried to get out of it because I felt like I could play better if I didn't have my mind on anything but playing ball.

My relationship with See Posey was good. I never had any trouble with him and he didn't have any trouble with me. I understood his position and what he was supposed to do. He was supposed to be the traveling secretary, but he wasn't traveling. I was doing his part. I understood him and he understood me. He knew that I was expected to play every game, and I was always going to play. And I was expected to take care of that money, too, which I didn't want to do.

He knew that I didn't want to do it. Sonnyman Jackson, the

owner, knew it, too. Once or twice I wouldn't accept the money to go on the road. It got so they wouldn't give the money to me. They would give it to the bus driver to give to me. Several times I wouldn't take it. The bus driver would say, "Buck, that's the expense money." I said, "I done told them I didn't want to do that." It took my mind off of playing.

I didn't get anything extra for handling the money on the road and I didn't want to take on that extra responsibility. I thought it was too much with me playing, too. So I was kicking on it. I told them that it wasn't my job to be the business manager. But they said it *was* my job, if they told me to do it. And Cum said that if I didn't accept the money, then I could look for another job.

Sometimes I had a thousand dollars in my pocket that belonged to the ball team and I played with it in my hip pocket tied up in a pocket handkerchief. And when I got ready to change clothes after the game, I had to take that money that was in my pocket and carry my pants in the shower and hang them up where I could see them to make sure the money that they gave me wasn't stolen. That's the way it was. Then when I got through with my shower, I'd carry them back in there where I was going to dress.

I had to watch the money in the clubhouse. Some guys, who would never take your watch or clothes, would take your money if you left it even for a second. And that's the way it was. You know, on a baseball team, you've got fellows from everywhere and you don't know what they'll do. So you just didn't trust anybody. Not with money you didn't.

Josh Gibson's son was batboy for us when we were in Pittsburgh, but he didn't travel with us. Later he started playing ball himself, and he told this story about his daddy. He said that while he was batboy, his daddy told him that if he was ever hit in the head by a beanball and knocked out, he wanted his son to be the first one to get to him. His son asked, "Why? To see if you're hurt?" And Josh said, "No, to take my billfold out of my pocket before anyone else gets there."

Now, I don't know whether that story is true or not, but it might have been. It shows the kind of thing I was talking about. But he might have been joking his son. Josh was like that. He liked fun and he liked to tell jokes and fool around. He always kept a smile on his face. Josh was a nice fellow. In all the nine years I played with him, I never saw him get mad.

They sent Josh to Hot Springs, Arkansas, to boil out for four or five weeks and recuperate before spring training. We were still training up North because of the war and we were supposed to train in Akron, Ohio, but the park was condemned and we switched our camp to West Field in Homestead. The weather was bad and we had to stay indoors for a whole week because of snow flurries. We worked out in a junior high school gym until the weather got better. But we finally got outside where we could work into shape.

In 1943 Vic Harris, Ray Brown, and Lick Carlisle were all involved in defense work. Vic worked in the steel mills and played on weekends. Carlisle played some, too, before he went into the Navy at the end of the season. Ray Brown was worried about the draft, and the Mexican promoters were after him, but he played for us until after the war.

Although we had lost a few players, we signed Cool Papa Bell to play with us, and when Cool Papa joined the team, we had the fastest outfield in the league, with Bell, Benjamin, and Bankhead. We still had Howard Easterling and Boojum Wilson in the infield, and we had a boy named Joe Spencer playing some second base, but he wasn't much of a hitter. Vic played in the other outfield spot when he was there, and Bankhead moved to the infield. Pitching, we had Johnny Wright, Raymond Brown, and Edsall Walker, but we didn't have J. C. Hamilton, who still had a bad arm from the year before, or Roy Partlow, who was in Mexico.

When Jim Taylor came over from the Chicago American Giants to manage, some players came with him. The two leagues met to try to settle disputes involving players who had jumped from one league to the other. They ordered us to return some players to the American Giants and gave us a deadline. The others went back, but we kept Cool Papa. He had been in our league before he went to Mexico, so we had a claim on him.

When the season got under way, we got off to a good start. We won a doubleheader on opening day and went on to win our first seven games before we lost one. We were particularly playing good ball in Griffith Stadium and winning most of our games there. In one doubleheader against the New York Cubans, I hit a triple and a home run but Josh hit two home runs. They both went about 450 feet. Then we beat Satchel and the Kansas City Monarchs a doubleheader with about twenty thousand people in the stands. About a month later, Joe Louis was there when we beat the Cleveland Buckeyes in a doubleheader.

There were eight of us from the Grays who played in the All-Star game that year, and five of us were voted to starting positions. That was me, Josh, Cool Papa, Easterling, and Bankhead. Benjamin and Vic Harris pinch hit, and Johnny Wright pitched in relief.

Satchel outpitched Dave Barnhill to get even from the year before, when Barnhill beat Satchel. The game was a real pitchers' duel, with the West beating us, 2–1. Our only run came in the ninth inning on my home run, and I won a suit of clothes for that home run. Before I hit the home run, Jerry Benjamin was on first base and he tried to steal second and got thrown out. And I always told Jerry, if he had stayed at first and I hit the home run, it would have tied the game. But I was just joking him, you know. Who knows what would have happened?

Later in the year we played another All-Star game, at Griffith Stadium. It was called the North-South classic, and I was on the South team. We won the game, 6–4, and that was the only North-South game I played in.

We won both halves of the split season and didn't have to be in a playoff before the World Series. The Birmingham Black Barons were playing the Monarchs in the West for the Negro American League pennant, so while we were waiting to see who won, we played a three-game series against the Negro National League All-Star team and won two of the games.

The Black Barons won their playoff, and we played them for the championship. We played them in the World Series three times during the forties and beat them every time. In 1943 Winfield Welch was their manager, and the Series went seven games. Their pitching wasn't as good as the Monarchs'. The best pitcher for Birmingham was Johnny Markham. He wasn't a fastball pitcher but he had control and could "fish," and he beat us a game in Birmingham in that Series.

Gready McKinnis was a left-hander. He was the one the Mon-

archs borrowed the year before to pitch against us in Yankee
Stadium. He had a pretty good fastball but he didn't have good
control. We carried him down to South America in 1949 and he
pitched good ball for us down there. Alfred Saylor and Bubber
Huber were just average pitchers. Huber didn't pitch a whole lot.
Alonzo Boone was a big fellow and he threw pretty hard, but he
was not as fast as McKinnis. Earl Bumpus was second string, and
I don't think Boone and Bumpus joined the team until the next
year, when we played them again in the World Series.

Most of us carried about three top pitchers for league games
and about three or four second-string pitchers that we used to pitch
against white semipro teams or when one of our main pitchers got
knocked out.

Piper Davis played second base later in his career, but he started
off playing shortstop and first base. In 1943 Tommy Sampson was
playing second base and Piper was playing shortstop. Sampson
had a missing finger on his throwing hand. That finger was cut
off right at the joint, and every time he would throw the ball, it
kind of "took off" a little. He was a pretty good player, both as
a hitter and a fielder. Johnny Britton was their third baseman
that year.

Lester Lockett played left field and was a heck of a player. He
could do everything. He could hit the ball good and he could field,
throw, and run when he wanted to. They had Felix McLaurin in
center field, and Clyde Spearman was the other outfielder. He
was the brother of the one who played third base with us a few
years earlier.

Paul Hardy was the main catcher at that time, and when he
went into the service near the end of the season, we let them pick
up Double Duty Radcliffe to play for them in the Series. We knew
that Radcliffe wasn't going to do no batting because he wasn't a
good hitter, and we knew that he wasn't going to throw anybody
out much because he wasn't that good of a thrower, so we went
ahead and let them use him. We had something to do with who
they used, and we wouldn't let them use a guy who we'd think
was going to help them a whole lot.

Later in the Series Sam Bankhead was injured in a play at first
base and we got a shortstop from the Chicago American Giants,

Ralph Wyatt, to play for us in one game to replace Bankhead. They thought we were going to keep him for good, but we weren't going to keep him. We picked him because they weren't going to let us use one of the top shortstops, like Willie Wells or nobody like that. We had to tell them who we wanted to use and we didn't name any good shortstops because we knew they were going to kick. So we named this fellow.

Bankhead wasn't injury-prone, but he was hurt in both the '42 and '43 World Series. I think he ran into a wall the other time. You know a fellow who's playing hard can't pick any particular time when he's going to get hurt. In that third game when Bankhead was injured, I had two of the first three RBIs, and the next time I came up I was intentionally walked to fill the bases so they could pitch to Josh. But their strategy backfired because Josh singled, and we went on to win the game, 9–0.

We played in Birmingham on that Sunday, and we were playing at Legion Field. That's a football field but we played baseball there, too. I hit a ball to right field, and Goose Curry was playing right field and he jumped up against the fence to catch the ball, and the ball hit in his glove and bounced over into the stands. And I got a home run and that tied the Series.

The next night we went down to Montgomery to play in an exhibition game, and we were going to go to New Orleans Tuesday night to play the deciding game. Birmingham was leading us in the game at Montgomery. The score was 5–2, or something like that. We weren't pitching a good pitcher because we thought it was an exhibition game. Winfield Welch came over and told us that Dr. Martin, the president of the Negro American League, said that this game had to be the final game and there wouldn't be another game.

I don't know whether Dr. Martin was the one who called it or not, but they were leading us by about three runs when they told us that. But we put on a little rally and beat them anyway. But it was a close game and the outcome was in doubt to the end. There were a couple of men on base and Lester Lockett hit a ball to left center field and had that ball fallen, they were going to beat us and win the World Series. All of us had given up on it, but Cool

Papa Bell went across there and caught that ball and we won the game.

And that was the end of it, because that made us winning four games to their three games. Then after we won, they wanted to come back to Birmingham and play another game, but we wouldn't play because he had told us that was going to be the final game. There was a lot of argument about that seventh game and some controversy about the Series, but we were the champions. After the season, Cum Posey selected me on his annual dream team again and also nominated me for the MVP of 1943.

That winter I went out to the West Coast to play with Satchel Paige's All-Star team against the major-league All-Stars. Like the other years when we barnstormed, a fellow named Vernon "Fat" Greene, who was the traveling secretary for the Baltimore Elite Giants, was the one that organized these barnstorming tours and would get the team together. He got us players from the Negro Leagues to go to California to play against Buck Newsom's All-Stars.

As long as we played, Buck Newsom was the featured pitcher for the major-leaguers and Satchel was the featured pitcher for us. The way they had the game arranged was that each Sunday they both had to pitch the first three innings. Then they would come out and we would put in other pitchers to finish the ball game. Our other pitchers were Booker McDaniels, Porter Moss, Raymond Brown, and Jack Matchett.

I was playing first base, and the rest of the infield was Tommy Sampson at second base, Hoss Walker at shortstop, and Howard Easterling at third base. In the outfield was Clyde Spearman in right field, Cool Papa Bell in center field, and Bubba Hyde in left field. Double Duty Radcliffe and Biz Mackey were catching for us. That was the rest of our team.

We learned that if we split the doubleheader the same ten or fifteen thousand fans would come back the next Sunday, but if one team happened to look like they were a lot stronger than the other team, then we wouldn't have that crowd. So the teams were more or less balanced and I can't remember either team winning both games of a doubleheader.

Newsom's best pitch was his fastball, and we knew it. And

that's what we hit. He was going to throw his fastball about every third or fourth pitch, and we were ready for it. One year Newsom said that he wouldn't go to the major leagues until he could beat us, but he was already in the major leagues then and had been for a long time. Everybody on their team was in the major leagues. I don't remember any ballplayers calling us ''niggers.'' That was the word that Newsom was supposed to have used. They might have called us that, but we didn't hear them. At least I didn't.

They had Junior Stephens, Lou Novikoff, Peanuts Lowrey, Jerry Priddy, Wally Moses, Walt Masterson, and all those folks. They didn't want us to beat them and we didn't want them to beat us. We weren't so sure they were putting out 100 percent against us in exhibitions. But I think they were. We won some and they won some. We won a few more than they did because we were playing harder. We needed the money and they were just passing the time. We played three Sundays, and that was when Judge Landis made us quit playing them.

When the commissioner sent the telegram out there was when Newsom said what he did. I know because they showed us the telegram. It was sent to the promoter, Joe Pirrone. He was the fellow who was in charge of both black and white players, although Greene was in charge of us.

There was another team in Los Angeles with Chet Brewer, who was the head of that team. They weren't with us because they would go out there every year. We didn't go out there every year from Pittsburgh after that. After Satchel Paige's All-Stars stopped playing, I played with them one night.

But at that time, Judge Landis had ruled that the major-leaguers had to have one minor-league player with them in the exhibition games. We understood that. It wasn't nothing strange to us. Once in Bradford, Pennsylvania, we had to hold up a game while they rounded up a minor-leaguer. Nobody ever knew why Landis felt like he did. I couldn't say that he was primarily responsible for the color bar. He might have been, but he wasn't the only one.

We made two hundred dollars every Sunday until Judge Landis stopped them from playing us. Then we played the Pacific Coast Stars. Cool Papa Bell was on our team, too, and we both hit .333

for the winter, and I was picked for the All-Star team that they selected that winter.

One Monday morning while we were still playing, the IRS man came out there and he said, "I'm here to get our withholding, and I want it right now." We said, "We're not giving it to you." He said, "Who's in charge here? I want everyone's name and address." And he took everyone's name and address so he could check on it, to see if we would list the income. I added it to my income, but I talked to Cool Papa and some of them later and they didn't.

But I had to come back because of the draft board. I had to get a defense job in the winter when I came home. I couldn't go and spend the entire winter in baseball. I worked at Railway Express and at Southern Express Company handling the express at night. I had been working down there the winter before, too. The man from the draft board here would keep check on me. When I went to California and played with Satchel Paige's All-Stars instead of coming home, they called here and told my wife if I didn't come home I would get drafted. They said if she didn't tell me to come on here and get my job back, that they were going to take some action. I played about two more weeks and then I came home.

After I got back, I hung around here for four or five days before I went back to work. I didn't want to go to work then, but I knew I'd better because if I didn't go back to my job, they would report that I hadn't showed up. It was hard work, I'm telling you. I put express on trains and took express off trains. A lot of trains were running in 1942 and 1943. When you get wet the first part of the night at nine or ten o'clock, you stayed wet all night. I was working at night, and I hurt my back working there. I'm having trouble with my back right now. If it's not trouble with my back, it's trouble with something else. I know we did catch a lot of cold out there that winter, and I was glad when spring training started.

# Chapter 15

## Repeat Champions (1944)

*We played the Grays in three World Series. Buck Leonard and Josh Gibson were their two big hitters.*

*—Piper Davis, Birmingham Black Barons*

In February of 1944 we sent Josh to Hot Springs, Arkansas, again to boil out before spring training. Because of the war we had spring training in Dayton, Ohio, and had to stay in the YMCA dorm. At that time you couldn't go over two hundred fifty miles from your home base, so we couldn't go over two hundred fifty miles from Pittsburgh. So that's why we trained in Dayton, Ohio. That was the same year that the New York Yankees trained in Atlantic City. The year that they wouldn't let the major leagues go South to spring training was the same time that we couldn't go.

The Negro Leagues lost quite a few ballplayers to the service. The Grays had six or seven players gone, in service or holding defense jobs. Some of our good players, too. We lost Howard Easterling and Johnny Wright. Wright was in the Navy and he used to come to pitch every Sunday wherever we would be. He would pitch that game on Sunday and then go back to the service. He was one of our main pitchers. Ray Brown was classified 1-A and didn't go to spring training but, as it turned out, he didn't go into the service. Easterling went into the Army and he got an advance from the team first, even knowing that he wouldn't be playing. We got Rev Cannady to replace him.

Welmaker, Whatley, and Carlisle all missed some time during the war, too. We also lost Garnett Blair, who had been a promising young pitcher. He went into the Army and never was the same when he came out. He hurt his arm and couldn't throw like he had before, so he quit baseball and started playing basketball for a college team. He was tall enough for that, about six-foot-five.

When the war was at its peak, we had to go down in North Carolina and to Atlanta, Georgia, and pick up whatever players we could around there to fill out our roster. The overall play in the leagues was less during the war years. The quality of play was way down because we were using fellows that couldn't have made the team otherwise.

A lot of ballplayers who went into the Army and stayed a couple of years didn't play any ball at all. Or some of them just played "scrap ball." You know, just choose up and play that way. And they got out of practice. We had a shortstop, Jelly Jackson, who was that way. He didn't go to the Army, but he had to get a defense job in D.C., and he stayed out about two years and didn't play any ball during that time. When he came back to the team that year, he was just rusty and never did get straightened out. When he left, Bankhead went to shortstop, and we had Carlisle to play second base. When Jelly came back, Bankhead was doing such a good job that we put Jelly at second base and left Bankhead at shortstop.

During the war, since rubber was rationed, the baseballs were manufactured in a different way, and the balls were dead. We had to play with these balls, even after the war for a little while, until they were all gone. And there were other changes because of wartime restrictions.

We couldn't go but seven hundred miles a month in the bus, because gasoline was rationed. From Pittsburgh to Washington was two hundred sixty-three miles, and back again was another two hundred sixty-three miles. Now, that's over five hundred miles just for one round trip. Then we had to put the bus up for the rest of the month and take the train. One night the conductor told us, "We don't have room for you on the train and we're not going to let you stand up." So we stayed in the baggage car. And played the next night.

Another thing that we did during the war years was to use portable lights generated by a big dynamo located in the outfield. We used to have those portable lights put up during the day to play under them at night. And they had stobs that they put into the ground and guy wires tied to stobs to hold the posts in place that held the lights.

Once there was a white fellow and then there was a black fellow that had some lights. He had a dynamo on a machine and had three or four fellows working for him and they would put up the lights around the infield and part of the outfield. We'd install them on poles all around the ballfield. And he didn't charge but thirty-five dollars for the whole outfit. And we would play that night after he had put them up in the daytime.

Sometimes the lights would dim and then get bright and dim and get bright again. We thought the belt was slipping on the dynamo. We had to stop the game for about five minutes and put some belt dressing on the belt that turned the wheel to keep the belt from slipping. Some people would tell us that they were giving us as much light as we were paying for. They said that we must have owed them some money. They were just teasing us, you know.

We used to have trouble with our outfielders running into poles. Jerry Benjamin broke his leg one night while playing under those portable lights. We were playing in Niagara Falls, New York, under those lights and Benjamin went down to first base and we had a light just a little off from first base. And he stepped on one of those stobs and twisted his ankle. And that's how he broke it.

When the season first started, we beat the New York Black Yankees a doubleheader. In the first game, I hit a home run with two men on base, and Cool Papa Bell had a single, a double, and a triple. In the second game Dave Hoskins pitched a one-hitter. And then we beat them another doubleheader in our home opener in Washington.

Early in the season, we played in Ebbets Field against the Newark Eagles and won another doubleheader, so we got off to a pretty good start. But along about that time we were having some trouble because Josh was breaking training and sometimes would show up and Vic wouldn't let him play because he wasn't in any shape to play. And Boojum Wilson was fined and suspended for tossing a bat and hitting the umpire with it.

Another time we had an incident that year was in the middle of the summer, when we played the Birmingham Black Barons in some exhibition games. I guess it was because we had played in the World Series the year before that there was so much interest in those games. They beat us the first two games that we played, and then we beat them a doubleheader at Griffith Stadium. In the second game I hit a triple to score Cool Papa Bell and tie the score in the last inning. But they had an argument about something and Piper Davis pushed the umpire and hit Jerry Benjamin in the face. And that started a brawl and the riot police had to come on the field to put a stop to the fighting. When they got it stopped, Cool Papa knocked in the winning run in extra innings and we won.

I roomed with Cool Papa for four years when he was with the Grays. He was getting up there in years then. Along toward the last, we wouldn't let him play both games of a doubleheader. If we did let him play both games, then that Monday morning he couldn't hardly get out of bed. One time in Cleveland, we played a Sunday doubleheader and we had to get him out of bed the next morning. Then we ran some hot water in a bathtub and put him in to limber him up some. He had to get good and warm before he could move. I was rooming with him then.

They say a little alcohol is good for the arthritis, and he had it real bad. He would have a pint bottle of gin and would cut up some lemons, the peeling and all, and just mash them in the bottle and put about two teaspoonfuls of sugar in it. Then he would shake it up and take about four or five swallows before he went to bed at night. The next morning, he'd get up and take about three or four swallows. And he was telling me how good it was for arthritis, so I started doing it, too. And both of us had a bottle and both of us took a drink before we went to bed at night. I wouldn't drink anything before a game, but I might drink something after a game.

Another thing about rooming with Cool Papa. He was left-handed and I was left-handed. And a left-handed person likes to sleep on his right arm because he don't want nothing to bother his left arm. That's his throwing arm. And we used to get to arguing about who was going to sleep on the right side of the bed because both of us were left-handed. Before Cool joined the team, I had roomed with Jerry Benjamin for about ten years, but when I was sleeping with him it didn't make any difference because Jerry was right-handed.

Tex Burnette, the fellow that I went out West with when I first joined the Grays, was my first roommate when we were on the road. Then I was rooming with Jelly Jackson, a shortstop, for a while in my early years. I was friends with everybody on the team, but when you get to be a roommate you get closer than otherwise. We chose our own roommates, and Cool Papa and I became good friends and we stayed good friends. The bus driver, Johnny Maynor, was my last roommate, but that was after Cool Papa retired.

Another thing about Cool, he could shave while riding on the bus. We would leave Pittsburgh at four-thirty Sunday morning going to Washington to play a doubleheader at Griffith Stadium. And he would be sitting on the backseat. He carried a little water, some soap, and a cup. And he would lather up and shave right on the backseat. He had a safety razor, but that still took a steady hand.

Cool Papa, Sam Bankhead, Josh, and I were the Grays' representatives in the All-Star game that year. Spoon Carter quit the team for a while because he was mad that he wasn't selected. But he came back a little later. I had a triple in the game, but we lost to the West by a score of 7–4.

There almost was not an All-Star game that year because we East players were going to strike. The West squad got gold watches for playing in the All-Star game. We, the East squad, received money but not gold watches. Now, when I first went to the All-Star game in 1935, we got five dollars apiece after the game. They gave everybody that, not for playing in the game, but just to go to the nightclub at night and spend. Five dollars wouldn't go far now, but you could get some drinks for five dollars back there then, and that's what it was for. They raised it a few years later to ten dollars apiece. And then they raised it to fifty dollars and then, a little later, they raised it to a hundred dollars. That was in 1937. And when they raised it to a hundred dollars they took out withholding, so instead of getting a hundred dollars we didn't get but eighty-five dollars.

So in 1944 we threatened to strike if we didn't get two hundred dollars. Here's what happened. We were going to play the All-Star game on a Sunday in Chicago, and on the Saturday night before the game we usually had a meeting with our East team. And the West squad had a meeting, too. We usually called the meeting at the Grand Hotel in Chicago. Whoever the manager was for that game would go over the rules and regulations and strategies and signals for tomorrow's game. We would also go over them the next day at the ballpark. And the manager would tell who was coaching third base and first base. He would tell who was going to start the ball game, who was going to pitch, and whatever else we were going to do the next day.

Jim Taylor was the manager the year when we struck. After he got through talking and going over with his signals and everything, he said, "Does anybody have anything they want to say?" Ray Dandridge and Harry Williams said, "Yeah, we want more money. We want two hundred dollars." They said, "We understand the West boys are going to get two hundred dollars and we want two hundred dollars." Jim Taylor said, "Well, all right about that, but now I ain't got anything to do with the financial part. Tom Wilson is the one who's supposed to decide about money. I'm just supposed to decide about what happens on the field."

So we said, "Send downstairs and get Tom Wilson." So they went downstairs and Tom Wilson, the owner of the Baltimore team and president of the league, came up there. And Harry Williams said, "Mr. Wilson, we've been talking and discussing it and we want two hundred dollars to play tomorrow." And so Tom Wilson said, "Well, you're not going to get it. You're going to get the same as you've been getting. Anybody who don't want to play for a hundred dollars, they don't have to play."

So they kept on arguing about that and they sent downstairs
and got Rufus Jackson, our owner, and Ed Bolden, who owned
the Philadelphia Stars. All three of them said, "If you don't want
to play for a hundred dollars, you all don't have to play. If enough
of you don't want to play we can't have a team out there, and
we'll just call off the game."

We didn't believe they were going to call off the game. We
believed they were going to play it, and they were going to prom-
ise us two hundred dollars and not give it to us. We thought that
when they got ready to pay us off, they were just going to give
us a hundred dollars. We said, "We're not going to start the game
if you don't pay us the two hundred dollars." They said, "All
right, we'll give it to you." And then they left and that's when
we discussed whether they were going to fool us or not. Harry
Williams was the ringleader at that time. He was the first one who
spoke. But all of us were in favor of it. We had already talked it
over among ourselves.

When we first started playing the All-Star game, blacks used to
keep the money and count the money at the ballpark around ten
o'clock at night. And we would get paid off the next morning.
Then they got this company and, when the game was over, Brinks
just took the money from the ballpark and carried it to the bank.
They didn't trust us to carry it and they didn't give the money to
owners until the next day. And the next day we got paid off. The
owners would pay us the money, but sometimes we had already
gone back up to our team Sunday night or Monday. So they promised to pay us, and they did when we got back to our teams.

Now that year, we had some controversy about who won each
half of the split season. On the last day of the first half, we played
a doubleheader against the Newark Eagles at Ruppert Stadium and
had to win one of the games to win the first half. I hit two home
runs in each game, but we lost the first game when McDuffie hit
a grand slam in the bottom of the tenth inning. Then in the second
game, we knocked Don Newcombe out in the first inning and won
by a big score, but we used Roy Partlow, who was pitching for
the Philadelphia Stars.

Our manager, Jim Taylor, said that the Stars' manager, Goose
Curry, had given him permission to use Partlow in the game. But

Ed Bolden, the owner of the Philadelphia Stars, said that he hadn't given the permission. And when Effa Manley, the owner of the Eagles, protested the game, Tom Wilson said that we had to play it over. He was the league president, and he ruled that Partlow was an ineligible player and that we had to replay the game because of the dispute.

So we played it over about a month later and won it again. But we had to come from behind twice to do it. Josh hit a home run and a double and I hit a triple off McDuffie, who was pitching for them. Johnny Wright was on leave from Fort Huachuca and pitched for us. Earlier in the year he had pitched a no-hitter for the Great Lakes Naval Station team.

So we finally officially won the first half, but then the Philadelphia Stars claimed that they won the second half. We had lost a doubleheader to the New York Cubans on Labor Day, but those were not supposed to be league games. When we were rained out in a game against the Cubans, then we declared the first one of those to count as a league game. Ed Bolden, the owner of the Philly Stars, said that they both should be counted as league games and he contested the decision not to count the second game, too. That would have given them the second half, but when the league officials got together, they ruled that we won.

Now, the Philadelphia Stars claimed that we stole the pennant from them that year. They had a pretty good team but they were not as strong as we were. In the outfield they had Gene Benson, Goose Curry, and Ed Stone, who went over there from the Eagles. They had Pee Wee Austin, a rookie from Panama, at shortstop. And they had Marvin Williams and Mahlon Duckett at second base. Jim West was at first base, and catching then was Bill Cash. Their top pitcher that year was a spitballer named Ricks, because two of their best pitchers, Barney Brown and Henry McHenry, were not there during the war.

The Philly Stars' best years were when Boojum Wilson was still with the team. They played at Forty-fourth and Parkside, and the Pennsylvania Railroad had a roundhouse right across from the park. Some nights when they were firing up the engines over there, so much smoke would come over on the field they had to stop the game. It was just a little rinky-dink grandstand, but we played there at night. Some of the Stars' players still say that we bought the pennant because the owners thought that we would draw better crowds since we were better known.

The 1944 season was almost a repeat of 1943. Since we won both halves, there was no play off, and we went straight to the World Series against Birmingham in a rematch from the year before. This time we won in five games, and I hit an even .500 in the Series.

The first game was played at Rickwood Field in Birmingham, and I had three hits. Both Josh and I hit home runs, and we won the game, 8–3. Roy Welmaker won both the first and last games. Edsall Walker won the second game, 6–1, in New Orleans, and Raymond Brown pitched a shutout in the third game. Double Duty Radcliffe got a little bloop hit, and that was their only base runner for the day. The only game they managed to win was the fourth game, which was played in Pittsburgh. The next day we wrapped it up in front of the home fans in Washington.

But Birmingham was not at full strength for the Series. They had a car wreck near the end of the season, and Tommy Sampson broke both of his legs. Some other players were hurt, too, but Sampson missed the entire Series, and he was one of their best players.

After we won the World Series, our two teams played some exhibition games at Yankee Stadium and at Shibe Park in Philadelphia, but I went home right after the Series and didn't play in those games. After the season ended, the draft board would not let me play ball, and I took a job with the Southern Express Company again, handling express at night.

# Chapter 16

## Ninth Straight Pennant (1945)

*Buck Leonard is one of greatest first sackers of all time, white or colored.*
*—Lem Graves, Jr., sportswriter*

In 1945 Vic Harris came back to manage the Grays, replacing Candy Jim Taylor after we had won two straight World Series championships. Since about the middle of the previous year there had been stories that Candy Jim was going to be replaced. Some said he was too strict in his discipline, and others said he was too conservative in his managing and they said that he had favorites on the team.

Vic had been with the Grays for a long time and he knew our ways and we knew his ways. Josh was on the way downhill and I broke my right hand and missed some games, but we still managed to win both halves of the split season again. That made us nine straight pennants. No other team in baseball has ever done that, and I don't think any other team in any sport has ever done that.

For the third straight year, Josh was sent to Hot Springs to boil out before the season started. He was there for about a month before spring training. Because of the wartime travel restrictions, we trained in Raleigh, North Carolina, not too far from my home in Rocky Mount.

I had broken the metacarpal bone in my left hand in 1942, and in 1945 I broke the same metacarpal bone in my right hand. I tagged a guy coming back into first base and he fell on my fingers and bent my hand back. I stayed out eight weeks with the left one and I stayed out seven weeks with the right one. The first year when I broke my hand, I went home, but the second time, I still went around with the team. I broke it before the World Series in September, and it bothered me in the World Series because it was still tender.

I never had any other serious injury in my career. I had a cut place where I was spiked on my leg and I needed three stitches in it, but they wouldn't let the doctor stitch it because I wouldn't be able to play if he did. So I just kept on playing. That's why this thin skin came back. It would have knitted back together if it had a couple of stitches in it. Had I been in the major leagues, I would have had proper attention.

But we didn't have a trainer. We rubbed each other. If I had a sore back or a sore arm or something, I'd get another player to rub it. And we had to tape ourselves as best as we could. One time I missed about a week with an injured thumb. Another time I had trouble with a hernia and I had to wear a truss for about a month when I played. But the only serious injuries were the two broken hands.

Vic Harris filled in for me when I broke my hand. I was the only first baseman we had during the time I was with the Grays. We had one backup first baseman one time, but he didn't stay. He came there as a first baseman, but they thought that I was going to be there forever, I reckon. So they tried to turn him into a pitcher but he wasn't good at pitching and it didn't work out.

Before my injury, we had got off to a good start. In the month of June, we were in first place. One game we rallied to score six runs in the ninth inning to beat the Elites. I had a triple, and Cool Papa had a double and a home run. In another game, I hit a home run off Jimmy Hill that went over a thirty-two-foot wall in deep right field and helped us win a doubleheader against the Eagles.

That was two of the teams that we had to beat to win another pennant.

In exhibition games against the Kansas City Monarchs, we knocked Satchel out of the game, and beat them a doubleheader at Griffith Stadium. But Jackie Robinson had seven straight hits for the Monarchs. In another game against a Negro American League team during the season, Ray Brown pitched a no-hitter against the Chicago American Giants, and I helped him with two doubles for us.

We won the first-half title without too much trouble, and then took the second-half title when we beat the Eagles a doubleheader in September. In the East-West contest, Welmaker, Benjamin, and myself were the players from our team that played in the All-Star game. Roy Campanella beat out Josh in the voting for catcher. Josh was still hitting for a good average, but he didn't have the power he used to have. By the end of the season, Josh hit .393 to lead the league in batting, and I finished third with a .375 average.

The Cleveland Buckeyes won the Negro American League pennant that year, and after we won the pennant, we played them in the World Series. Quincy Trouppe was their manager and catcher, but their best player was Sam Jethroe. I saw him coming and going. He went to the Boston Braves and was rookie of the year with them in 1950.

Parnell Woods was a pretty good ballplayer for the Cleveland Buckeyes. He played third base when they won the pennant. They had two Jefferson brothers who pitched, Willie and George. Willie was the older one. And they had Gene Bremmer pitching for them that year, too. We were confident that we could beat them in the World Series, but we lost in four straight games. They caught us in a slump and we only scored a total of three runs in the four games.

Before the Series started, we "ragged" them some before the first game. Josh, especially, called them a bunch of names, and told them what we were going to do to them. But after they beat us the first two games, we got quiet. We still thought we could beat them, but we never did play like we could.

They beat us the first game in Cleveland, 2–1, when Quincy Trouppe hit a home run over Benjamin's head in center field.

They didn't have that little fence in Municipal Stadium then. The older Jefferson brother, Willie, pitched that night. The next night we played in Pittsburgh and they beat us, 4–2. Gene Bremmer pitched that game. The third game we played was in Washington, D.C., and George Jefferson shut us out that game, 3–0. The fourth game we played in Philadelphia and we pitched Raymond Brown, but a boy named Carswell beat us, 4–0. That was the final game.

After the World Series was over, we played some exhibition games against them and we beat the Buckeyes all of them. But the fans wouldn't turn out after they found out they were just exhibition games and not World Series games. We only played a few more games before we quit.

That winter we took an American All-Star team to Venezuela to play the local teams. The team I went with to Caracas included Jackie Robinson. A man named Chataing Blanco, who was one of the local cats down there, was in charge of putting the team together. He talked to us in the summer and organized the team.

Felton Snow was the manager, and other players on the team, besides me and Jackie Robinson, were Roy Campanella, Sam Jethroe, Quincy Trouppe, Gene Benson, Marvin Barker, and Parnell Woods. Pitching, we had Roy Welmaker from the Grays, and George Jefferson, who had pitched for the Buckeyes in the World Series. Jethroe, Trouppe, and Woods also played for the Buckeyes. Verdell Mathis, a little left-hander from Memphis who had started and won the All-Star game for the West both of the last two years, was on that team we took to Venezuela, too. And we had a pitcher named Bill Anderson. There's two more boys we carried on the team, Marvin Williams, who had a tryout with the Boston Red Sox, and a boy named Ncal. We loaned them to the local team to play to try to strengthen them.

Off of that team, Robinson, Campanella, Jethroe, and Trouppe all later played in the major leagues. And there are three of us on the team who are in the Hall of Fame. We had a real good team and I don't think we lost a game that winter. When we got down there, they asked us what kind of ball we wanted to use and we told them Wilson 97 because we knew that ball will ride. We used them for about three weeks and then we started using another ball. We won the first nine games and they told us we had to lose some to make it interesting. We said, "We didn't come down here to lose."

During that barnstorming tour, George Jefferson almost choked Chataing Blanco to death. He had his hands around his neck and was choking him. I was a witness to that. They got in a fight but I forget what it was about. They were arguing about something. Maybe it was money. Jefferson was choking Chataing until we got Jefferson off of him. In helping him, we may have saved his life. But there were no hard feelings afterward. They forgot it.

After our exhibition series was over, I didn't stay down there. I was sick of baseball. You know, if you play all summer and then go down there in the winter, you just get tired of playing and you want to go home.

When we went down there, we were supposed to leave New York on the fifteenth of October. But there was some kind of revolution going on down there and we had to delay our departure, and we didn't leave until about the fifteenth of November. When we got down there we could see where some shooting had been done, and we couldn't go out just anywhere we wanted.

Jackie Robinson had signed with the Dodgers the day before we left, but we didn't know it. That was the big story about our trip that winter. Before we were on the same team in Venezuela, I had played against him during the season.

He came up in 1945 with Kansas City and we had played them and we looked at him play, but we didn't have any idea that he would be taken into the majors. We just thought that he was a big ol' college boy coming into the league. He was running and ripping and we just said, "Well, soon as he gets tired, he's going to calm down like the rest of us." But we didn't have any idea at that time, in the summer of 1945, that he would soon be going to the major leagues.

When we got ready to go to Caracas, we all met in New York City and we didn't know Jackie was even on the trip until we got to New York and saw him. That's when we found out he was going to South America with us. We would rather have had Willie Wells as shortstop instead of Jackie Robinson.

When Branch Rickey came to the hotel and talked to Jackie, we thought Rickey was going to try to organize a black team to put into the Negro Leagues and he wanted Jackie to help him get some players. We thought he was going to try to have one of the best teams in our league, or maybe start another team in the new league—the United States League—and put Jackie in charge of it. That's what we thought it was, and we asked Jackie if that was what Branch Rickey was talking to him about. Jackie said, "No, that's not what it was. He was just talking to me about some business."

We had seen him talking to Branch Rickey at the hotel, and Rickey came down there to the airport to talk to Jackie again, but we still didn't know what they were talking about. That was before we left New York, when we were getting ready to catch the plane to go to South America. So when we got down to Caracas we asked Jackie again. We said, "What was Branch Rickey talking to you about?" He said, "We were just talking about some things. He had something that he wanted me to do."

We didn't have any idea what Rickey had in mind. We didn't have any idea they were trying to get Jackie to go to the white leagues, and *that* was in the making. Then about Christmastime, it came out in *The New York Times* that Branch Rickey had signed Jackie Robinson. We were down in South America then, when we found out. And we asked Jackie about it and he said, "Yeah, that's what it was. That's what we were talking about." And Rickey had told Jackie not to say anything about it, and to let him make the announcement.

When we got the paper, it was four or five days old. And it said, it was thought that Jackie was going to be sent to play with Montreal in the International League. So we asked him about going to Montreal. We felt like up there in Canada he had a better chance of not being called "nigger" than he would down South. And it finally came out afterward, that was the case and he was going to play in Montreal.

At that time we didn't think too much of him as a ballplayer. He was a hustler, but he wasn't a top shortstop. He didn't look too good when we got down there, and we noticed that he couldn't hit the inside pitch. He hadn't been playing as long as we had and we didn't think he was so good. Not at that time. So we said, "We don't see how he can make it."

We talked among ourselves about Jackie and realized the impor-tance of the situation. We knew that he was an example and that the way he acted was going to have a bearing on who else might be selected. And we thought that if he didn't make it, they would be through with us for the next five or ten years. And if he did make it, we thought they would keep him in the minors for a long time. But we were wrong.

While Jackie Robinson was not the best ballplayer we had in the Negro Leagues, he was what we needed. He was a college man and he knew how to take charge of his weaknesses. I was glad to see him go to the Dodgers. He was the best one for that role. We think Branch Rickey made a good selection and we felt that Jackie was the best one to handle that condition.

I think Rickey looked at his ability first. Jackie was big, fast, strong, a fair hitter, had a good arm, but he wasn't the best of hitters. Of course, he was only in his first year in the organized Negro Leagues. And he was intelligent. He had been to college and we felt like a fellow who'd been to college and was intelligent could cope with things better than the average fellow. Situations come up, and he was more able to handle them than some of us who had not been to college. We thought that he was the best man to pick for that particular time and for that situation. And which turned out to be right.

At UCLA, he had played *with* white players and had played *against* white players. And his reactions might have been better than someone else who hadn't played under those circumstances. He grew up with it, so he knew how to cope with the condition. I think Jackie was the right man—the ideal man.

I don't know anybody that would have been a better pick for the first one. We thought if they had picked some other ones, there might have been a big mess. I think some of them might have done just as good in playing as he did, but they wouldn't have took what Jackie took. Sometimes people will try to excite you so that you say something or do something. He took it all. I don't know anybody else who would have.

I would say we had some others that they took later, like Larry Doby, who might have been able to do what Jackie did. But if they had taken him first, knowing Doby like I do, I don't think he would have stayed. I don't think even Campanella would have taken it at first. I know when they took Campanella and Doby and those guys the heat had died down somewhat, and the pressure wasn't as intense as it was when Jackie first went in. Maybe some more would have taken the pressure, but I don't think so. We felt like Jackie took more than most of us would have.

As far as ability was concerned, some players could have gone straight to the major leagues. We already knew how to play base-ball. What we needed mostly was to learn to play *with* white boys. It's a little different in playing *against* a fellow and playing *with* them. You don't know their actions and they don't know yours. Some lot of folks thought you're not going to have blacks in the majors right off the bat, and you have to send them down for orientation. I don't think that was it so much as there being a need to play *with* whites.

I don't know if anybody else could have taken the pressure that Jackie Robinson did. I don't think I *could* have withstood the pressures of being the first black player. And I *know* I *wouldn't* have. Not like that. I don't know anybody else that could have taken it. To stay there and take what he took, day after day.

Jackie had trouble *off* the field and *on* the field. We heard that Dixie Walker didn't want to cooperate with him, and probably would have done the rest of us the same way if we had been on the field. Of course, all of us would have liked to have been in the major leagues, even though the conditions turned out to be like they were. We still wanted to play in the major leagues re-gardless of the conditions.

They were signing the younger players. At first they didn't want anybody over twenty-five. Most of our good players, who were good enough to go up to the major leagues, were thirty years old or older. So at that rate, we felt like they said they didn't want to take the fellows who really could make it. Jackie was right on the edge of it. But they finally started taking them over that age, and they took Monte Irvin, Bob Thurman, and a whole lot more of the fellows over twenty-five.

They knew they couldn't count on us older players to play for four or five years. We were a poor risk to play for that long, and an injury would stay with us longer. A lot of players shaved years off their ages, like Ray Dandridge and Dave Barnhill. Both of them could have gone right into the majors.

Another thing, in the major leagues there was one requirement that we didn't have, and that was your character. If you don't have good character, you don't stay in the major leagues long. But if you could play ball, regardless of your character, you could play in our league. Some of the good ballplayers in our league couldn't have met the major-league requirements. Maybe some players' conduct could have been better, but as a rule our conduct wasn't so bad. Because playing under the conditions we did, we were too tired to do anything bad.

All of us in the Negro Leagues wanted to play in the major leagues, but we never tried to do anything about it. We just felt like it was beyond us, and we just contented ourselves to keep playing in our own league. We didn't have time to worry about it, anyway.

After Jackie Robinson signed with the Dodgers, he became a role model for blacks, especially our young people. During the time that I was playing with the Homestead Grays, we felt like Joe Louis, Jesse Owens, and Jackie Robinson were our top people. Jesse Owens' track records were outstanding, and he did a lot of good with what he accomplished. Just like Joe Louis with his boxing and Jackie with his baseball.

We felt like they represented what the Negro really is and not what some folks think. When you don't deal with intelligent people, you don't know what intelligence is. But we felt like they had had enough contact, especially Jackie Robinson and Jesse Owens. And Joe, being quiet like he was, he could take care of the situations that would come up. Joe didn't talk much and he was a good fighter. And he didn't claim that he knew a whole lot about something when he didn't, like about finances. About boxing, we felt like he was just gifted. But with Jesse Owens and Jackie Robinson, we felt like they were good symbols, and that they could show whites that Negroes could be intelligent, too.

I think kids looked up to Louis and Robinson more than others. They were getting a lot of publicity, and kids had a chance to read about it. Blacks followed Louis's fights. He inspired them and lifted the spirits of the blacks. One thing was, it showed that he could take care of himself in boxing and in behavior. He wasn't rowdy like some might have thought. He could have been and maybe he could have got swellheaded. But success didn't go to his head.

Sometimes people think that if a black is successful that it's going to his head and he's going to show it. When I went into the Hall of Fame in 1972, some folks called and wanted to know if I had "cut back to the ground." I said, "What do you mean?" They expect blacks to be affected by success or achievements. With some of them, they may be right about it going to their head. Not only blacks, but whites as well. Some whites are the same way about success. It goes to their head. But a person has to more or less adjust for that and try to cope with it as best as he can.

# Chapter 17

## End of the Long Gray Line (1946)

*Buck Leonard was the equal of any first baseman who ever lived. He was a terrific fielder and a great hitter. If he'd gotten the chance to play in the major leagues, they might have called Lou Gehrig the white Buck Leonard. He was that good.*
*—Monte Irvin, Newark Eagles*

Cum Posey passed away on March 28, 1946, at the age of fifty-five, but I didn't go to his funeral. He had two daughters, and one had married Raymond Brown. Cum had been with the Grays from the beginning, and maybe his passing was the end of an era. In a way his death marked the end of black baseball as it had been, because the big story that year was Jackie Robinson and Johnny Wright going to spring training with the Dodger organization.

Wright was a good pitcher. He had a good curveball and everything and could throw the ball over the plate. He was as good as Joe Black, or maybe even better. Right after the Dodgers signed Jackie Robinson, they got Johnny Wright from us, and both of them went to spring training at the same time in 1946 with Montreal.

When they reported to camp, they weren't allowed to rest in

the clubhouse with the other players. We were training in Jacksonville that year, and the Dodgers came to town to play the Jacksonville team an exhibition game. Since they couldn't take part in the
game with the Dodgers, Johnny Wright and Jackie Robinson came
over where we were playing on the other side of town. They were
not angry, they knew before they got there that they wouldn't be
able to go in and change clothes in the clubhouse. It wasn't one
of those things where it was sudden, or anything like that. They
understood the conditions and we understood the conditions, too.

Johnny Wright had the ability to play in the major leagues, but
that was only one part of it. There was something else, too. Robinson stood up under the pressure and Wright didn't. He just
wasn't able to stand the pressure and couldn't take the things he
had to take. I don't think many people *could* have or *would* have.
So he didn't stick with Montreal, and later, when they signed
Partlow, he didn't stick either. I think that at that time they didn't
want but one black player.

Everybody gives Branch Rickey credit for being the one who
broke the color barrier, but Happy Chandler deserves some of the
credit, too, because he was the first commissioner to stand up for
black ballplayers' rights to play in the major leagues. One Sunday
night at Cooperstown when we had our banquet for that year's
inductees, he told all of us how he stood up for us when everybody
else was against Negroes coming into the major leagues.

After he became commissioner, Rickey asked him about signing
Jackie, and Happy Chandler told Rickey that he had been afraid
to even ask Judge Landis about it when he was commissioner. It
took some backbone for Happy Chandler to stand up for blacks
against the fifteen other owners. He was always a politician, so
he knew he was taking an unpopular stand.

When he approved Rickey's signing Robinson to a Dodgers
contract, that marked the end of the Negro Leagues, even though
we still played a good brand of baseball for two or three more
years. Robinson's signing changed baseball forever, in more ways
than one.

Another change that was taking place was that, after nine
straight years, the Grays didn't win the pennant in 1946. The
Newark Eagles, with Monte Irvin and Larry Doby playing for

them, beat us out. That was the end of a dynasty, although we did come back a couple of years later with some new young ballplayers for the last pennant.

The Eagles were owned by the Manleys. Abe owned the team but his wife, Effa, ran the team. She was the business manager. I didn't know her until one night in Trenton, New Jersey. We had played a doubleheader in Newark that Sunday evening, and we went down to Trenton to play that Sunday night. And we beat them all three games and we were joking them. And she came out there and was talking about how we ought not to joke the boys and said, "You all are a lot older than my boys." We told her, "They're out there on the ballfield, so we're going to joke them, too." Now, that's the first time that I knew her.

She would tell them who to play. We were in Brooklyn one day, and she was there and had her little group, a women's club, with her. Terris McDuffie was one of their best pitchers, and she told Mule Suttles, who was managing the team at that time, to pitch McDuffie. So he pitched McDuffie and we killed him. She did have favorites on the team. Among the players that she liked best, McDuffie was one and Lennie Pearson was another.

Pearson played first base for Newark in 1946. He had pretty good power and he was good defensively, but he wasn't fast. He could have played in the major leagues. Monte Irvin and Larry Doby were both on the team. Larry Doby was the first black player in the American League, and Monte Irvin made it to the major leagues, too.

Doby played second base and we knew what he could do. Irvin played shortstop that year. Doby and Irvin were regular infielders from the beginning and then went to the outfield later. Pat Patterson and Pint Israel were the third basemen in 1946. Patterson was a good player. He was from Wiley College, out in Texas. He was big and strong, and he could hit the ball. He was a little older and wasn't too fast, but he was a good defensive man. He was with the Pittsburgh Crawfords when they had that good team in 1935. Pint Israel was pretty good. He was fast and a pretty fair defensive man, but he wasn't much of a hitter. He was what we called an ordinary player. We picked him up the next year after he left the Newark Eagles.

Johnny Davis played left field, and he was a humdinger. He had good size, but his speed on the bases wasn't anything to write home about. He went to the Pacific Coast League and played triple-A ball. He tried to pitch some and we used to tell him, although we weren't on his team, that he was just good for out-fielding and hitting, rather than trying to pitch. He'd be a better ballplayer if he didn't try to do both. But you know a lot of us ballplayers try to pitch. I tried to pitch myself for a while in semipro ball. And a lot of times, that's a mistake. A good ballplay-er's trying to pitch, and then he messes up his arm and he's just through, as far as throwing. He still might be able to hit, but his throwing is impaired somewhat.

The other two outfielders were Bob Harvey and Jimmy Wilkes. Harvey played right field and was just an average ballplayer. Their center fielder, Wilkes, was fast, but he was a weak hitter and he was a small fellow. He didn't stay with Newark long.

Catching they had Leon Ruffin and Charlie Parks. Defensively Ruffin was good, but offensively he wasn't so good. He could throw and he could catch, but he couldn't hit and he couldn't run. Parks was a pretty good catcher and a fair hitter. He was a backup to Ruffin.

Willie Wells played with Newark for several years. He was the manager part of the 1945 season but had a run-in with Manley, and Biz Mackey took over as manager at that time. I don't know what caused their problem, but Abe Manley said he would have traded Wells for a broken bat. Mackey was about over the hill as a player, but he caught a little that year. As far as I know, he was all right as a manager. He knew the game and he could teach it.

Leon Day, Max Manning, and Rufus Lewis were their best pitchers. Day was a veteran and was their ace again that year. Manning was right behind him, and then Lewis. All three of them had been in the Army during the war. When he was out there pitching, Rufus Lewis was interested in what he was doing and he didn't like for somebody to make an error behind him. And he would get mad, too. Lewis was a good pitcher, but in my judgment he was not quite as good as Manning. Another pitcher was Len Hooker. He was right-handed and was a pretty good knuckleballer.

Jimmy Hill was a left-hander and had been one of their best pitchers for several years, but he had already left and was not with the team that year.

In 1946 we had lost Johnny Wright to the Dodgers and Ray Brown went to Mexico. That weakened our pitching quite a bit. But we got Easterling and Red Fields back from the service, and Fields took over from Brown as our top pitcher. Josh and Cool Papa were in their last season, and we got Double Duty Radcliffe to help with the pitching *and* catching.

During the previous two years I could see a change taking place in Josh's defense. I don't know exactly when he got so bad off, but in 1946 he couldn't hardly get down behind the plate. He caught kind of standing up and stooping over. Easterling took over for Boojum Wilson, who had retired.

We lost one Wilson but gained another one, when Dan Wilson joined our team. Dan Wilson did all right with us. He could hit pretty good. He was a singles hitter and he was fast. He could steal bases but he didn't have such a powerful arm. He played both third base and outfield, and he was with us after we had our good teams.

That year, we got off to a good start. Early in the season we won four straight games, beating the Black Yankees and somebody else, and moved into first place. In one of those games Josh hit a home run that went about 450 feet in Yankee Stadium. We stayed in contention for a few more weeks, in a four-team race.

In one game Double Duty Radcliffe lived up to his nickname, when he shed his catching gear and took the mound to relieve Wilmer Fields, and retired the side with five pitches. Near the end of the first half, we beat the Black Yankees a doubleheader at Griffith Stadium. Josh hit a home run, two doubles, a single, and had six RBIs. That's not a bad day's work. And he only had six more months to live.

The Newark Eagles won the first half, while we finished at an even .500. The next half, we did even worse, and the Eagles won the second half, too. Even though 1946 was not a good year for the Homestead Grays, it was a memorable season for baseball.

We had two All-Star games that year and split even. In the first one, in Comiskey Park, we lost to the West 4–1, but we played a second game, at Griffith Stadium in Washington, D.C. and won, 6–3. And after Jackie Robinson played in the white leagues, the Cleveland Buckeyes signed a white player named Eddie Klepp. We always said that Wilmer Fields had integrated the Homestead Grays a long time before that.

# Chapter 18

## A Season After Josh (1947)

*Buck Leonard is one of the finest hitters we have ever watched in action. His play at first base is graceful and steady. For slugging ability he reminds one of the late Lou Gehrig. But for poetry of motion, he is a closer counterpart afield of onetime kingpin George Sisler. Leonard is the perfect gentleman on and off the field.*

*—Bill Burk, sportswriter*

Josh Gibson died in January of 1947, and I was a pallbearer at his funeral. There was not a big crowd there, just family and close friends mostly. He was still a young man, only thirty-five years old. There are a lot of stories about what was the cause of his death. I heard about somebody who said he died of a broken heart because he was frustrated about not being the one to go into the major leagues. I played with him nine years and I never heard about no frustration.

When I went to the funeral, they told me he had some drinks Saturday night and they carried him home. Sunday he had a headache and they thought it was a hangover, but the doctor gave him some pills. They told me he had a stroke of the brain.

187

The newspapers called us the "Thunder Twins" and the "Dynamite Twins" and it seems like everybody remembers us together. We even went into the Hall of Fame together. For nine years we were on the same team. If a left-handed pitcher was pitching, he batted third and I batted fourth. Usually, if a right-handed pitcher was pitching, I batted third and he batted fourth. We changed around like that in the batting order.

There's no telling what he could have done in the major leagues in his prime. He counted home runs in the league and also in nonleague exhibition games and all like that. One year he counted all of them and he hit seventy-two. But you've got to remember all that wasn't on good pitching. Some of the pitching was just mediocre pitching that he was batting against. We didn't face good pitching day in and day out. My best home-run total was forty-two in 1948, but that was for all the games we played. We played 84 league games that year, and that was about the same as half a season in the major leagues, but we played around 210 ball games during the entire year.

I didn't claim to hit the ball as far as Josh Gibson. Nobody hit the ball as far as he did *and* as often as he did. They used to say our baseballs were more lively than major-league baseballs, but they weren't. It was just that Josh hit the ball farther.

I didn't see the one that he was supposed to have hit out of Yankee Stadium. But I saw him hit a ball one night in the Polo Grounds that went between the upper deck and the lower deck and out of the stadium. Later the night watchman came in and said, "Who hit the damned ball out there?" He said it landed on the "el." It must have gone six hundred feet.

The longest home run I ever hit was in Newark, New Jersey, against the Newark Eagles off Rufus Lewis. I had borrowed a bat from a fellow and the bat was a little heavier than the one I usually used. And I was using that bat when I hit the home run. But I know I couldn't handle that heavier bat over an entire season. I pulled everything, and it went over the right-field fence. Some tanks was behind right field, and it hit up against those tanks. I'd say it was about four or five hundred feet, or something like that. They didn't have any way to measure it. Some fellow sitting high up in the stands said it just kept on going.

Another thing, we were playing without batting helmets. The pitchers were bad about throwing at you. And there wasn't a penalty for dusting you off. He could dust you off just as often as he wanted and hit you maybe. If you were hitting the ball they would knock you down. And hitting behind Josh with all the home runs he hit, if you was the next batter you got knocked down. You know how that happens. You had to learn to hit *and* to duck. When I batted behind Josh, I got dusted off but I was never hit.

I played twenty-three years as a professional, not counting my sandlot days, and I was only hit by a pitched ball three times. I was hit on the elbow once, hit right on the back of my shoulder once, and hit on my hand against the bat. That was in Baltimore, and Jonas Gaines, a left-hander, was the pitcher. It busted my thumb and I was out eight or ten days. I might not have been out that long if something else hadn't happened afterward.

On the way back to Pittsburgh that same night, we stopped at a service station to get some gas, and a white man at the filling station called me over and asked me what was wrong with my thumb. I told him and he said, "Stick it down in this kerosene." And I stuck it down in some kerosene that he had there. I thought he was trying to help me. And I don't know whether it irritated it or not. Some of them around there said that if I hadn't done that, I wouldn't have stayed out that long, but they didn't know what they were talking about. And I didn't know whether they were telling the truth or not. But I stayed out about ten days. I couldn't grip the bat.

I have been thrown at a lot of times, but that's the only three times that I was ever hit. The thing about it was, I could bat standing away from the plate. I didn't stand close to the plate. One time a left-hander threw me a curve and I bailed out. The next batter asked me about how far his curve broke and I said, "I don't know, I wasn't there to see it."

In spring training, after Josh passed away, we knew we were going to miss him, but we felt like we had enough batters in the lineup to take care of the slack. We had Luke Easter, Jerry Benjamin, Sam Bankhead, and Bob Thurman. We started spring drills in Jacksonville the first week of March, and we also played some in Daytona Beach. That spring they touted Luke Easter as the new Josh Gibson, but he wasn't anywhere near the player that Josh was.

But in late July, at Yankee Stadium, myself, Easter, and Bob Thurman hit three consecutive home runs. Thurman was first. He hit a ball that went about 360 feet into the right-field stands. And I hit one in about the same spot. Then Easter hit one about 450 feet to center field and got an inside-the-park home run.

Josh Gibson had played primarily because of his hitting. He wasn't as good defensively as Biz Mackey or Campanella. Not even in his prime. He was a catcher, not a receiver. Now, the difference in the two is a receiver works a pitcher, and he calls for certain pitchers, inside and outside, high and low, and all like that. That's what Mackey and Campanella did.

Josh more or less was just a catcher, and with him gone, Eudie Napier did most of the catching, along with Rab Roy Gaston. The only other new player in the starting lineup was Clarence Israel. We called him "Pint." He was from Rockville, Maryland, and came to us from the Newark Eagles.

After breaking camp in the spring, we divided the squad up into "A" and "B" teams like the major-leaguers did, when we played exhibitions. We played exhibitions all through Georgia, North Carolina, Mississippi, Louisiana, Alabama, Kentucky, and Virginia before getting back home for our opening game at Forbes Field.

But when Jackie Robinson began playing with the Dodgers, everybody forgot about us. Some of us got good salaries right on to '49 and '50, but most of them ended after the war in 1945. Salaries wasn't the only thing that went down. So did attendance at black baseball games. We couldn't draw flies. Then, when they started taking blacks into organized baseball, that was just the end of it. Cleveland signed Larry Doby, and he went directly into the major leagues. And Willard Brown and Hank Thompson went to the St. Louis Browns. All that was in 1947.

Partlow was released by Montreal. Neither he nor Wright had showed the same form that they had demonstrated in the Negro Leagues. They suffered from a lack of control. Wright just couldn't take the pressure, and Partlow didn't have the temperament. Partlow was the kind that would go to pieces if the umpire called a ball that he thought was a strike, or if the shortstop made an error behind him.

At the beginning of the season, I missed about three weeks with injuries, and we didn't get off to a good start. I didn't play in the opening-day doubleheader at Forbes Field against the Cubans because I was out with a fractured hand. Howard Easterling also missed the games because he was holding out. Jerry Benjamin got a hit in the ninth inning, which was the only one we got off of Lino Donoso, a Puerto Rican who later signed with the Pittsburgh Pirates in the major leagues. He was a left-handed pitcher and he talked a lot, but he threw the ball almost as hard as Barnhill.

We won the second game to split with them on Saturday, but the Cubans beat us both games the next day in Washington. Pat Scantlebury, who later pitched with the Cincinnatti Reds, and Luis Tiant, Sr., the father of the one who played for the Boston Red Sox and Cleveland Indians, were the winning pitchers.

Scantlebury was from Panama, and he was a pretty good pitcher. He was a left-hander and had a good curveball. He went to the minor leagues and then to the major leagues. He could hit, too. Tiant was also left-handed. I didn't see him when he started, back in the 1920s. The first time I saw him was when he came over here with the Cubans in 1935. When I saw Tiant, he was about through. He had been pitching fifteen years or so, and he was forty years old. He was old, but he could still throw the ball when he felt like it. He was 10–0 in 1947, when they won the championship.

Tiant had one of the best moves to first base I ever saw. One time he struck out a batter while trying to pick off a runner. When he threw the ball to first base, the batter, Goose Curry, swung, and the umpire called him out. When Goose argued about it, the ump said, "If you're dumb enough to swing at it, I'm dumb enough to call it." That's the only time I ever heard of anybody striking out on a pickoff throw to first base. Now, I didn't see that, I only heard about it.

But Tiant had a good move to first base and used to pick us off first base all the time, until we went to Cuba and played on the same team with him. Then we learned to watch his feet. When he was on the mound and came to a rest after his stretch, if his feet were together, he was going to throw to home plate, but if his front foot was a little toward first base, he was going to throw over there. But we didn't find that out until we went down there to play in Cuba.

Dave Barnhill was another one of their leading pitchers that season. I think Barnhill threw harder than Day or Byrd. He was right up there with Slim Jones and Satchel Paige. Right next to them. I don't know why he didn't go to the All-Star game more often. He threw just as hard as any other human being. He went to white baseball with Minneapolis in 1949.

Barney Morris had a good knuckleball, and he threw it harder than any knuckleball pitcher you ever saw. Most of them knuckleball pitchers float the ball, but he didn't. He just fired it, and when it got up there, it would go right down. But he wasn't trustworthy because he didn't stay in condition.

The New York Cubans got off to a good start, and they went on to win the pennant that year. They also had Minnie Minoso, who later went up to the Cleveland Indians and Chicago White Sox. He played third base for the Cubans. The rest of their infield included Chinquitin Cabrera, a big left-handed fellow, at first base. Bicho Diaz was the second baseman. He was kind of a wild guy. He hit the ball and scattered it around. And he would run wild, but he wasn't a finished ballplayer.

Silvio Garcia played shortstop. He was a big fellow and he had a good arm. He was a right-handed hitter, but he hit the ball to right field and was one of the best hitters to come out of the Caribbean. He was kind of mean. What we call mean is, he stayed evil all the time. But he was a good baseball player. He was from Cuba and the other shortstop, Horacio Martinez, was from Santo Domingo. Martinez was a better fielder than Garcia and was a pretty good hitter, too, but he couldn't hit the ball as far as Garcia.

In the outfield they had Tetelo Vargas, and he was just like a deer. He was a hustling ballplayer and was good all around, as a hitter, runner, and fielder. And he had a good arm. The first time I saw him was in San Juan, Puerto Rico, in 1935. He was playing for the Puerto Rican teams and he came to New York and played for the Cubans for a couple of games. I think the play was too tough for him up here. We played every day, and down in Puerto

Rico they didn't play every day. He was good enough to play, but he just couldn't stand playing every day.

Claro Duany was a big fellow and could hit the ball. He was left-handed and he wasn't fast. He was an ordinary fielder and wasn't nothing to really brag about in the outfield. Pedro Pages was the other outfielder, and he was another left-hander all the way. He wasn't a top-notch fellow and was only an ordinary outfielder. A few years earlier, they had an outfielder named Coimbre. He was good. He wasn't such a fast man and he didn't have such a good arm but he was a pretty fair hitter. But he got fat and couldn't move.

Another outfielder from earlier years with the Cubans was Alex Crespo. He was an extra-base hitter but he wasn't a home-run hitter. He hit doubles and triples and all like that and he was fast. He'd hit a double and use a head-first slide and stretch it into three bases. He was a rough-and-tumble player. He didn't play too long in the league. Some fellows just can't play every day. Not like we could. He couldn't take the wear and tear.

Louis Louden was the catcher, and he was just ordinary all way around. He and Barnhill were roomies up there. Their manager, José Fernandez, was an old-time catcher, too, and he knew baseball.

I didn't play in the All-Star game that year. John Washington started at first base because he had a better year than I did. The West won, 5–2, at Comiskey Park, and they had a second All-Star game, at the Polo Grounds, and the West won again, 8–2.

We played an exhibition game against the Cleveland Buckeyes in Cleveland on the same Sunday that the East-West game was being played in Chicago. I was sitting the game out, but when we got the bases loaded against Sam Jones they put me up to pinch hit and he walked me and walked in the only run of the game. And we won, 1–0.

Later in the year, we played a game at Forbes Field in August against a team called Dormont in what was called the Cum Posey Memorial Game. They were a semipro team and we beat them, 10–1. Along about that time we beat Satchel and the Kansas City Monarchs in a doubleheader. And in another game after I got back in the lineup, we beat the Cubans, 6–5, and I went three for four and had two home runs.

But we didn't have a good year and, for the second straight year, we didn't win the pennant. When a reporter asked Vic Harris about it, he said, "We didn't have Leonard." I had missed a lot of games because of the injury, but I still hit .410. My teammate Luis Marquez hit .414 to lead the league. The Newark Eagles had been doing good before Doby left in the middle of the year, but then the New York Cubans edged out Newark and went on to beat the Cleveland Buckeyes in the World Series.

At the end of the season I barnstormed with Dan Bankhead's All-Stars. When the season closed he asked some of us to go around with his All-Star team. We asked how he was going to pay us. So he said, "Well, we've got to see what we make." But I bargained with him for twenty-five dollars a game. It made no difference what was made, he would pay me twenty-five dollars every game that I played.

Bankhead was just a mediocre pitcher in our league. He wasn't one of our aces. But he was in demand around blacks at that time because he had been with the Dodgers, and everybody had heard of him and wanted to see him pitch. He was using the Homestead Grays' bus for the players and he had a big car that he and his wife rode around in. I think it was a LaSalle. And he had a maid going around with him.

The first game we played was in Roanoke, Virginia, and we had a pretty good crowd, but it was getting chilly there. Then we went on down into Florida, around Jacksonville and Pensacola and all around there. Then we got to Mobile and played one Sunday. We had a good crowd of a couple of thousand people and he gave the boys about forty or fifty dollars apiece, and I kicked because I wasn't getting but twenty-five dollars. But that was my bargain.

So we got to Jackson, Mississippi, and the weather got bad. And it stayed bad in Lake Charles, Louisiana, and Alexandria, Louisiana, and in the place where they made Hadacol. I remember seeing that sign up there where it said "Future Home of Hadacol." And we got rained out all those nights. At some places that we played, the grounds were minor-league ballparks and the grass had grown real high. And they had cut off the hot-water system in the ballparks and there was a lot of other bad conditions.

When we got to Jackson, Mississippi, and played, Bankhead had lost some money because he was paying out board and lodging, and he said that he was going to keep all the money that we made in Jackson that Sunday. It was about four or five hundred dollars. He said that he was going to keep that day's receipts because he was losing money. We kicked but decided to let him go. And so we went back to Mobile to play and that's when I left them. He was supposed to pay me twenty-five dollars and he didn't pay me. Of course, I kicked but he kept it. He didn't pay me what he said he would, so I left and went back home after Mobile.

I was going to leave that night after I got my twenty-five dollars. I already had my suitcase packed. The business manager said, "Come over here where I'm staying, and we're going to settle up this evening." So I carried my suitcase over to where the business manager was staying, and I set my suitcase down on the porch.

He said, "All right, I'm going to take you one at a time." He didn't want any of us to see what he was paying the others. When he came to me, he said, "Whose suitcase is that out there?" I said, "Mine." He said, "What you going to do with it?" I said, "Well, I think I'm going to leave tonight." So he said, "Well, you're not getting anything." I said, "What about my twenty-five dollars?" He said, "You're not getting anything. You promised to make the entire trip. We still have to go to Texarkana." And he didn't pay me. Not one nickel, and he owed me twenty-five dollars.

I always kept railroad fare home in my pocket just in case of something like that. I had a little over twenty dollars, so I went down to the railroad station and bought a ticket and came home to Rocky Mount.

Later I found out that none of the players got paid anything from that time on. I saw them the next spring and they said that the bus broke down and the water pump and air brakes went bad, and they had to buy another water pump and have something done to the airbrakes. And Dan Bankhead kept all the money for that. And a lot of fellows had to send back home and get money to go home from Texarkana, where they broke up. So I made the right decision not finishing the trip.

# Chapter 19

## The Last Hurrah (1948)

*When I joined the Grays, Buck was one who took
me under his wing and was always encouraging
me. And I tried to imitate what he did. Everybody
respected him and looked to him for leadership,
guidance, and stability. Not only on the playing
field but also in the dugout, too.*

—Wilmer Fields, Homestead Grays

The next spring, Vic Harris was optimistic and we had a successful preseason exhibition tour. This was the last quality year
of black baseball and was also my best earning year. I made ten
thousand dollars, and half of it in Cuba. And it was personally
gratifying, since we won the World Series and I won the batting
title with a .391 average, tied for the lead in home runs, and
played in my twelfth All-Star game.

We had five players in the lineup for our East All-Star squad
who later went to the major leagues—Monte Irvin, Minnie Minoso, Luke Easter, Junior Gilliam, and Luis Marquez. I had a
double, but we only got three hits and lost the game, 3–0. I didn't
know it then, but that was my last All-Star game.

Another thing that made the year special was, the fans gave me

197

a "Buck Leonard Day" along toward the end of the season. I don't know why they did that because I never said that I was going to retire or said that was going to be my last game or anything. The special day was scheduled and postponed and then rescheduled. They finally had "Buck Leonard Day" in Griffith Stadium in Washington, D.C., and they said that was my last game. They had a big crowd there and had a big celebration. They gave me a suit of clothes, a citation, a couple of shirts, and they put a barrel out there at the gate for the folks to put in money. And I picked up two hundred and some dollars. Everybody thought that was going to be my last season, but I played seven more years after that. That was the only time I had a special day for me while I was playing.

In 1948 I was playing first base and Bankhead was playing shortstop. We were the only two left from the earlier years when we won the nine straight pennants. And Bankhead didn't come with us until we had already won the first two pennants, and then he left to play in Mexico for two more of those years. I was the only one who had been there the whole time.

Luke Easter, Luis Marquez, and Bob Thurman were in the outfield. All three of them later played in the major leagues. Easter tied with me for the league in home runs with 13. That was in 59 league games, and he had 58 more at-bats than I did.

Vic Harris wasn't playing too often then, and Howard Easterling and Jerry Benjamin were gone. Marquez never could do much with a good curveball that the pitcher could get over the plate. And that was his main trouble. He was an outfielder and played second base for a while, and was a good fielder. He was fast and could run bases and all that, but he was just weak on curveballs and his average dropped a whole lot from the year before.

Wilmer Fields was our top pitcher that year. He was a good pitcher, and he lives in Manassas, Virginia, now. We had high hopes for him. At first, in 1949, when the major leagues were taking players from the Negro Leagues, they wanted to send him out on the West Coast. But he didn't want to go, and didn't go. Then he went to Toronto in the International League, but I'm not sure how that came about.

Raymond Brown didn't play with us the last couple of years.

He was in South America during that time. Somebody offered him more money and he went down to Caracas to play. And he also played in Mexico sometime. He would leave us when he was offered more money by another team. We just didn't worry about him after his daddy-in-law died. I don't know how long he stayed down there but I never did see him anymore. He went up to Canada for a while and then died in Dayton, Ohio, a few years later with a heart attack.

There were five Bankhead brothers that played in Negro Leagues. The best one was the oldest one, Sam. He was our short-stop and we also had the youngest brother, Garnett, with us for a little while. He was brief, and was not so good a player. Dan was with the Dodgers in the major leagues. He and Sam were the best-known ones. Fred played second base for the Memphis Red Sox, and Joe played with Birmingham briefly.

After Johnny Wright tried out with the Dodgers, he came back to the Grays and pitched for us in 1948. Partlow left us and went somewhere in triple-A ball. Dave Hoskins was an outfielder and pitched, too. He was best known with us for his pitching, but he played right field some, too. We had some good-hitting pitchers, so he fit in. He went to the Indians as a pitcher, but he went to some team in Texas for a while before he went up to Cleveland.

We also had R. T. Walker, Willie Pope, and Cecil Kaiser on the pitching staff. And Groundhog Thompson was still with us in 1948. We got him from Birmingham and he was a little left-hander, only a little bit over five feet tall. He had a pretty good curveball and a fair fastball for that size. He was walleyed and had a harelip and a chipped tooth. Josh used to joke him all the time and make fun of him because of his looks. Josh put him on his "all-ugly" team and things like that.

One time Groundhog pulled a knife on Luke Easter on the team bus when they were gambling. Easter was a card sharp and Thompson claimed he was cheating and pulled a switchblade and threatened to cut Easter down to his size.

Luke Easter later played in the major leagues with the Cleveland Indians and had some good years. Then he got hurt and went down to the minors and played several more years. After he quit playing ball, he was given a good job at some plant in Cleveland.

Every payday he would go down to the bank and get the payroll and carry it back to the plant. There were some fellows who knew that he did that. So one day, when he went down to get the money for the employees from the bank, they waited out there in the parking lot when he came back to the car. And they told him, "Give us that money." When he refused, they shot him. Right there in the parking lot.

While they were getting away, they went on the underpass and they had a wreck. They hit another car on the underpass and couldn't go any farther and the policemen got them. They only gave them fifteen years apiece. For killing a man! That was around 1979. They might even already be out of prison by now.

Easter was one of the young players we had on the team, and we had a lot of young players that year. Playing in the infield with Bankhead and me, we had Clarence Bruce at second base and Charles Gary at third base. Gary was just a so-so hitter, and I've seen a lot better fielders. The only reason that they had Gary was that Howard Easterling, our regular third baseman, was gone, and we were using Gary when they couldn't get better players.

We lost the opening game of the season to the New York Cubans, who had won the pennant the year before. About a month later, we played them in a doubleheader in the Polo Grounds and I hit back-to-back home runs. I liked batting in the Polo Grounds, since I was a pull hitter.

We played a split season, and on the last day of the first half we were a half game behind the Baltimore Elites and were playing them a doubleheader. We beat them the first game but lost the second game and they won the first-half title.

The second half started as a four-team race. There was one game when we scored seven runs in the ninth inning to win. I had a single, double, and home run. Then with about a week to go, we beat the Philly Stars five straight games to knock them out of contention, and went on to win the second half over Newark and Baltimore.

Then we had a playoff against the Baltimore Elites for the pennant. That year the Elites had a good double-play combination of Pee Wee Butts and Junior Gilliam, the one that went to the Brooklyn Dodgers. Pitching, they had Joe Black, who also went to the

Dodgers. They also had Henry Kimbro, Lester Lockett, and Johnny
Washington. And Bill Byrd was still pitching. Their other pitchers
were Juan Guilbe, Enrique Figueroa, Al Wilmore, and Bob
Romby.

We had a best three-of-five playoff and were playing them in
Baltimore. We won the first two games, and we were playing
them the third game on Friday night. The score was tied, and we
scored four runs in the ninth inning and we had three men on
base and two out and the game was called off because of a curfew.

The next game we played, on a Sunday, we wanted to finish
the suspended game before we started the regular game for that
day. They didn't want to do that. They wanted to play the regular
game first. So we played the regular game first, and they beat us.
Then we put the men back on the bases and had the situation just
like it was when the Friday game was called off. And they
wouldn't come out there and play. They walked off the field and
the game was forfeited to us. And that gave us the pennant.

Then we beat the Birmingham Black Barons four games to one
in the World Series. I think that Birmingham had their best team
that year. Piper Davis managed their team, and Artie Wilson was
the shortstop. He led their league in batting that year and he was
a good player defensively. A few years later, he got to the major
leagues up with the Giants, but he didn't stay long. Art said that
the reason he didn't stay was that they had too many blacks on
the team. When he was there in 1951, Willie Mays was there.
And Monte Irvin and Hank Thompson were there, too. Three
blacks was about the limit for a major-league team at that time,
and he said they wanted to send him somewhere else.

Now, that was his side of it. But he was a left-handed hitter
and he hit the ball to left field. He was one of those late hitters
and we thought that was the reason why they didn't keep him.
He never could pull the ball and they could gang up on him over
there in the third-base area and get him out. And that's what we
thought was why they let him go.

In 1948, the Black Barons also had Willie Mays playing center
field. I remember that because he threw me out in one game when
I was trying to go from first to third on a hit. I was on first and
somebody singled to center field. I said to myself, ''That young

boy's out there and he ain't going to throw true to third base. I'm
going on to third base.'' And I went on to third base and he threw
me out. He still remembers that, and he talks about it even now.
Willie Mays wasn't but about seventeen then, and he was still
going to high school. But I remember that throw when he got me
out at third base in the '48 Negro World Series.

In the only game they beat us, he lined a hit through the pitcher's legs to knock in the winning run. That made three times that
we beat Birmingham in the World Series. We won in '43, '44,
and '48. And that was the last World Series. The Negro National
League folded after the end of the season. There were seven World
Series played from 1942 through 1948, and we had played in the
first four, and we played in the last one. We were the last Negro
World Series champions.

That winter I went back to Cuba for another winter season on
the island. Outside of the United States, they played a better brand
of baseball there than anywhere else. Conditions were better in
Cuba than in Puerto Rico. Puerto Ricans demand more of publicized baseball players. Whereas Cubans consider an error just to
be another part of the game, the Puerto Ricans never cease riding
a player for making one. The Cubans knew baseball. They knew
an error was going to happen. The major-leaguers had been down
there. Even Babe Ruth went down there a long time ago. And the
Cuban players had been over here and they understood baseball.
Puerto Ricans didn't understand baseball then and still don't understand it.

I played with Marianao in Cuba that winter, and some fan gave
me a diamond ring for hitting a grand-slam home run to win a
ball game. It happened one Sunday when we were playing Al-
mendares in Havana. And on Monday this guy came to the hotel
and gave me a diamond ring. It wasn't the owner of the team, it
was some other guy. I never had seen him before. He might have
been betting on the game. In fact, I'll bet he did win some money
on the game. The ring had twenty-one diamonds and was worth
five hundred dollars then. The stones got slack in it and I carried
it to a man here in town to tighten the stones and he said it was
worth about a thousand dollars and that was about seven years
ago. I haven't had it appraised since then.

You won't hit many home runs down there in Havana. They had a big ballpark called Tropical Stadium. I never hit a ball out of Tropical Stadium. I don't know anybody who ever hit a home run out of there. Bobby Estalella, a white Cuban who played in the major leagues for nine seasons, hit some of the longest flys I ever had seen, but they didn't go out of that ballpark.

Dave Barnhill, Don Newcombe and I were on the same team, and they let Newcombe go to play with the Dodgers. That left Barnhill and myself as the only blacks on the team, and the only two players that hadn't played in the major leagues. Everybody else had been to the major leagues. But I was older than most of them and had more experience. That was the last time I went down there. I was half sick and I wasn't worth a dime. I had an injured back, and in one game Chiquitin Cabrera had to pinch hit for me. That was the only time anyone ever pinch hit for me. During my whole career there were two things that only happened one time. I was only pinch hit for once, and I only bunted once.

When I was down there I had never heard of Castro. I liked it fine before Castro took over the country. But before Castro took over, America was running just about everything down there. They had two hotels that blacks couldn't stay in, the Presidential Hotel in Havana and another hotel there that was run by Americans. Ordinary blacks and some dark-colored Cubans couldn't stay in the second hotel. But a black celebrity could stay in the hotel. Joe Louis and Jessie Owens were the only two blacks that stayed in the hotel.

In Cuba the conditions were about the same as they were later when I played in Mexico. They would put us in second-rate hotels and if we wanted better conditions we had to pay the difference. And it was the same way in Puerto Rico and in Venezuela. There was not any racial discrimination at all in those two countries.

There was a language problem, though, because Spanish was the native tongue and we didn't know Spanish. We learned a little Spanish, enough to get by. About the first thing we learned was how to ask for food. And we learned a few baseball terms. And that was just about all. I didn't learn to speak Spanish too good.

When we would leave in the early spring around February to come back to the United States, that Spanish would get away from us. After playing over here all summer, we would forget it. Then when we went back down there in the fall of the year, we had to try to learn it all over again. We had books that we used to study, but we couldn't pronounce it just exactly like they pronounced it. And some areas used different words for certain things. For instance, in Puerto Rico they called beans *habichuela,* and in Mexico they called them *frijoles,* and in Cuba they called them something, I'm not sure what. Whatever they were using for certain things in certain countries, that's what you had to learn how to use.

I was always glad to get back to Rocky Mount, where I could understand everybody and they could understand me.

# Chapter 20

## Scufflin' (1949)

*Buck Leonard was outstanding as a ballplayer and as a man. He was respected by everybody, and was sort of a father image for the younger players on the team.*

*—Josh Gibson, Jr., Homestead Grays*

After the Negro National League broke up, they said we were in the Negro American Association, but we really weren't. We started the season in '49 but we found out that we didn't have the same quality of team. The major league franchises took nine of our best players, and that just about shot our team. All our best players were gone, and our team was so weak, we just decided to cancel the rest of the games and got out of the league.

We managed to finish the season by going down to North Carolina and Georgia and getting some replacements. But they weren't the same caliber as the players that had been taken from us, and we knew that we would never be able to field a strong team again like we had before the major leagues started taking black players. So we played against lesser teams and kept playing for two more years.

When Sonnyman Jackson died March 6, 1949, his wife had to

take over the team and that caused a lot of uncertainty among the players and started a lot of rumors. The newspapers had stories about us going to make a tour of Hawaii, but that never happened.

We had spring training in Danville, Virginia and then got in the league with those southern teams like Richmond, Raleigh and Winston-Salem. We won the first half championship with a 24–2 record becuse the competition was not as strong down there as we had been used to playing. We just couldn't play at the same level as we had before because we had lost so many players.

One of the players the major leagues signed was Luke Easter. But Easter was older than he said he was, even then. When Easter signed, Rufus Jackson was dead and his wife was in charge. At first the major leagues didn't want to take anybody who was over twenty-five. Then they finally decided that they would take whoever they thought could make the major-league teams.

Vic Harris quit us and went to the Baltimore Elite Giants in 1949–50. He was not managing there, but he was coaching. Bankhead managed us those last two years. He was a pretty fair manager and then, when the Grays broke up, he went up in Canada and managed a white team. He was the first black manager ever to manage a white team.

In the Negro Leagues, our equipment was not of major-league quality. We had to buy our own baseball shoes, and they were not of the highest quality. And our uniforms were not of major-league quality. We had one set of home uniforms and one set of road uniforms. We had to use bats off the rack. We got them from major-league teams. I used a Lou Gehrig-style bat at first. Then I found a bat that I liked better. It was a *Louisville Slugger,* Okrie-style bat. Glenn Okrie was a catcher for the Washington Senators, and he only played for a short time. Somebody asked me if I ever used a black bat, and I can only remember using a black bat once.

And we didn't play with major-league baseballs. The major leagues used a Spalding ball, which cost about twenty-four dollars a dozen. We used a Wilson 150 cc, which cost about seventeen dollars a dozen. We had to buy our own sanitary hose, sliding pads, and sweatshirt. And, of course, we had to buy our own gloves. When I bought a new first baseman's mitt, it would take about half a season to break it in.

I worked on my fielding because I took pride in being a team man. I was pretty agile around first base and had a strong throwing arm. I played a little deeper at first base than the ordinary first baseman did. I played farther back and there was a lot of balls that would go by for hits for other first basemen, but I could come up with them because I played deeper. Of course, that made me run harder to get to first base to take the throws. I was good at taking low throws, and I didn't have any trouble on pop flies. I never used sunglasses, but I never lost a ball in the sun. My weakness in the field was throwing balls to the pitcher covering first base. I would toss the ball too high or too low, in front of them or behind them, or something like that.

Some writers compared me to Hal Chase as a fielder. I didn't see Hal Chase and I didn't know how he played. I would rather be compared to Lou Gehrig because that's who I used to pattern my play after. I saw him play several times, and saw how he played and how he batted. And I wasn't that good. I considered it an honor to be called the Black Lou Gehrig, but I didn't ever think I measured up to it.

After the season in 1949, I joined a team called the New York Stars. Felton Snow was the manager of the Stars. In the infield we had Ray Neil at second base, Bus Clarkson at shortstop, Howard Easterling at third base, and I was at first base. Our outfielders were Ducky Davenport, Felix McLaurin, and Art Pennington. Chico Renfroe and Stanley Glenn were the catchers, and we had Andy Porter, Gready McKinnis, Pat Scantlebury, Bob Griffin, and Emory Long pitching.

The way they got the team together was, they went around in the summer and wanted to know if you would go with the team to South America. Somebody came by and asked me if I would go, and I told them I would. We played some games around New York and then we left, playing our way South until the weather got too cold, and then we went to Venezuela.

We started in New York City and went all the way to Wichita Falls, Texas. We played en route one night on an open field and we played on cow pastures or anywhere else as long as there was

a crowd. We tried to play every day and sometimes we played
two times in a day. We played a game in Richmond, and that is
our area. When we play around here, we wanted to win the game,
so we pitched our best pitcher. Carl Furillo, who played with the
Dodgers, was on their team. They had him leading off and he hit
the first pitch out of the park. But we won the game, 3–2.

The weather was getting too cold here, and we went on down
to South America. After we got to Venezuela, we won the first
four or five games down there, and they wanted to break us up.
They took three players from us, our shortstop, second baseman,
and another player, and they put them with the Mexican League
team. And still we beat them. We were down there about two
months, and when we came back, I was ready to begin my last
year with the Grays.

# Chapter 21

## Demise of the Grays (1950)

*I was talking with Sam Bankhead and Buck Leonard about Robinson, Campy, and Newk making it with Brooklyn. I'll never forget Buck's eyes filling with tears when he said, "But it's too late for me."*
—*Elwood Parsons, Dodger scout*

I played with the Grays again in 1950. We started out again with a weak team and we managed to finish the season even with a weak team. After we got so we couldn't play the caliber of ball that we had been playing in previous seasons, we went down around here in North Carolina and played in a southern league with all of those teams.

Traveling was tough in the Negro Leagues, but when we got down there to that southern league, it was really tough. But I remember one time during the late forties, we were staying in the same hotel as some Frenchmen. They had about six girls and they tried to get those girls to get us. Of course we would have to pay, you know.

I don't remember what kind of record we had during the last season. They tried to get me to stay on as business manager, but I told them I didn't want to have anything to do with the management or the money. I didn't want to handle the money because I thought they were going to break up. Cum Posey and Sonnyman Jackson had both passed, and Sonnyman's wife said she wan't going to have anything to do with the team. Bankhead was the manager and he handled it all.

Josh Gibson, Jr., played with us in 1950. Bankhead and his daddy had been good friends, and Bankhead took an interest in him, but I wouldn't say a special interest.

It had been rumored since the previous year that the Washington Senators would sign me, but I was still with the Grays until they broke up after the last game of the 1950 season. The way it happend was, the team met and decided that they didn't want to play anymore. Nobody wanted to assume the management of the team. And that included me because I didn't see any future for the team. I felt like they couldn't continue. So they decided not to try to operate anymore.

Some of us were playing on a percentage. They promised us a salary but you might get it and you might not get it. I was still one of the highest-paid players, but I was kinda glad the Grays broke up because the money was getting kinda scarce. We were playing weaker teams and not making any money because we couldn't draw a crowd. As I said before, we couldn't draw flies.

After the Grays broke up, I came back home to Rocky Mount. Then somebody called and I went to Mexico. The Memphis Red Sox called, too, but I didn't want to go with them. They had called me before, in 1948. After the Negro National League broke up that year, they put all the players' names in a hat and the Negro American League teams drew to see who they would get. The Memphis Red Sox drew my name, but I didn't want to go with them then either. I didn't go because I didn't think they were going to operate the full season. That made me want to quit black baseball, and I just decided to go to Mexico.

I don't know what everybody else did after the team broke up. Me and Bankhead were the only ones who had been with the Grays a long time. After I had been to Mexico for several years and had quit baseball and was back here for four or five years, I heard that Bankhead was killed in a fight.

# Part III

# Latter Years (1951–94)

# Chapter 22

## Mexico (1951–55)

*Buck Leonard was a star with the Homestead Grays for a long time until they broke up. When I got him to go to Mexico, I knew he could still hit even then.*

*—Chico Renfroe, Kansas City Monarchs*

After the Grays broke up in 1950 I went to Mexico and played in the Mexican League for about five years, but I didn't shave any years off my age when I went down there. Now, they may have thought that I was younger than I was, and I wasn't going to tell them any different. I liked it all right down there. It was a good place to live, and baseball was easier down there because we didn't play every day. We played three games a week, and I could still play like the devil for them three days. But I couldn't have played every day. And we were a little better ballplayers than the Mexicans. They could run and field, but they weren't good hitters. They couldn't hit the long ball like we could.

Sometimes the team on which we were playing would pay our board and lodging, pay our way down there, and pay our salary. Sometimes the hotel that they had for us to stay in wasn't as nice as we wanted and we would move to a better hotel. But we had to pay the difference in the cost. Once they were paying twelve pesos a day for me to stay there and I got a room at another place.

The first time I went to Mexico, I stayed about three months until the league ended. Chico Renfroe was the one who got me to go to Mexico, and the first year I hit fourteen home runs. That was the fourth best in the league. When I went back the next time, they asked me to name some other players to come down there and play certain positions and I would name players. I was the main one to put them in touch with the fellows from the Homestead Grays.

In Mexico they had baseball parks in Mexico City, Monterrey, Puerto Rico, Vera Cruz, Xalapa, Pueblo, Tampico, and Torreón. There were two teams in Mexico City, the Mexico City Reds and the Mexico City Tigers, and all other towns just had one team. Every year, when we would go down there, that water would give you dysentery. That was one thing I didn't like. It would last a couple of weeks and then get all right. I was forty-four years old and baseball wasn't too tough down there, but I would rather live in the States.

I played in Mexico from 1951 on through 1955, both in winter and summer leagues. I would come back here to Rocky Mount about three weeks and then go back down there for the summer. And when summer was over, about September, I'd come here again and stay three or four weeks and go back down there for another winter season.

I played the first three summers with Torreón. That was in the main Mexican league, the one that's considered triple-A. In the three years with them, I hit .322, .325 and .332. The next two summers, I played with Durango, in a different league, the Mexican Central League. That league wasn't the number one Mexican league and wasn't as strong as the one that Torreón was in.

In the winters, I played in 1951 with Obregón. That's in Mexico over near the Gulf of California. And then I played the next two winters in a place called Xalapa on a Mexican team. We were named after hot peppers, like you put in chili and everything. That was our name, the "Hot Peppers." While I was there I had a knee injury and a German doctor fixed me in a knee brace to play in, and I was the team MVP the last winter I was there. I didn't play winters the last two years. I came back home and worked at an automobile garage in Rocky Mount, washing cars and doing things like that.

At Torreón, a fellow named Guillermo Garibay, a white Mexican born in San Antonio, was about the best manager I had down there. He spoke English and Spanish. With Torreón, I played with a player named Charolito Orta. He had a young son, Jorge, and I used to hold him in my lap and carry him around. When he was grown, he played for the Chicago White Sox in the American League.

During my career, I also played with the fathers of other major-league ballplayers. I played against Luis Aparicio's father in Venezuela and against Orlando Cepeda's father in Puerto Rico. Both fathers were shortstops. Cepeda's father's name was Perucho. Later in his career he played first base, but he was best known as a shortstop while we were down there. His son was a little bigger than he was and had a little more power, but Perucho could hit the long ball, too.

He didn't play in the States. Pompez tried to get him to come to play with the New York Cubans, but he just wouldn't come. I don't know why. For a lot of those fellows, it was the kind of food they ate. And they didn't like our food over here too much. He was good enough to have played here. He was a good fielder, a good shortstop, and he was fast for a big man. He was just as good all-around as our shortstop with the Homestead Grays, Sam Bankhead. And he could hit the long ball better than Bankhead.

At Torreón, the team's nickname was the "Peas." Barney Brown was pitching on the same team I was on. We called ourselves the "black-eyed peas." Our team broke up in Torreón in 1953. We were way down in the standings, and we couldn't win anything. The owner said he was going to let the foreign ballplayers go home. They would agree how many foreigners each team could have every year. Usually each team could have three foreigners. Anyone other than a Mexican was considered a foreigner. He could be from Santo Domingo, or Cuba, or wherever. One year each team could have three foreigners, then maybe a couple of years later, they'd let you have four foreigners. We had three of us on the team. We had a boy from Panama and two of us from the United States, and they sent us all home. Martin Dihigo was fired one week and I was the next.

Most of the rest of the time in Mexico after that I played with Dihigo. He was my manager, both at Xalapa and also for two years at Durango. He was a good manager, and spoke both English and Spanish. He knew more about baseball than any of them down there and could play more. He could do all of it. He was a good teacher of baseball and could tell you all about playing. He told me things I never heard of, and I had been playing over here.

He had played on the Homestead Grays, but that was before I started playing with them. As a pitcher he had just about everything. He had a slider, a curveball, and a fastball. And he could throw the ball over the plate. He was a seasoned ballplayer at any position you wanted to play him.

As a manager he was a strict disciplinarian. Players knew they were going to have to play because they knew that he knew the game. He knew when you were playing and when you weren't playing. So you just couldn't fool him, and the fellows knew that. They knew that they were going to have to put out at the beginning of the season, or else they wouldn't play for him.

When the '52 winter season opened, Dihigo was the manager of the team in Xalapa. He called me and wanted to know if I would come down there and play for the team. He needed someone who could hit the ball out of the park, and he felt that I was the one who could do it. I told him, "Yeah, what will you pay me?" He said, "Four hundred and fifty dollars." I said, "All right, send me a ticket up here."

At that time, especially in foreign countries, they didn't want to send you money. Western Union would call and say, "Are you expecting money from somewhere?" I'd say, "Yeah." They'd say, "Where?" I'd say, "Mexico." They'd say, "Who are you expecting it from?" Those Western Union people used to do like that. I'd tell them, "I'm expecting some money from Martin Dihigo." They'd say, "Where is Martin Dihigo?" I'd say, "Mexico." And they'd say, "Well, you come down here. We've got that money for you." Then I'd have to go down there and show them my identification and they'd give me the money. That's how they used to operate down there in the foreign countries, because they had sent so much money over here to ballplayers who didn't go. And they didn't never hear any more from them. So that's how we started operating.

In Mexico, everybody went out and sat in the plaza and watched people walking around and that's how people passed the days and nights. And I spent a lot of leisure time watching bullfights and cockfights. We would play ball games in Mexico City on Thursday night, Saturday evening, and at ten-thirty Sunday morning. Sunday afternoon at four o'clock everybody went to the bullfights. The big bullfights were in Mexico City, and the bullfight ring there would hold about fifty thousand. They had these bulls that were trained for that purpose and some of them came from Spain. And most of the top matadors were from Spain.

At the bullfight, at first a guy would blow a trumpet. They called it the fight call. Then they would turn a bull out of a gate and when that bull got ready to come out they would stick him in the back with a little short thing and that would make him mad. There would be three or four fellows out there in the bullring, and the bull would run all of them around behind a little fence there inside the ring. They would gather and hold the rails up in front of him and run him behind that little fence. For the first five minutes that's what happened.

Then one guy would come out there with two little things that looked a little longer than a spear. He would get in front of the bull and motion in front of the bull. And when the bull passed by him real close he would stick them two things in his back and that would make the bull madder. And the bull would run him and the others out of the ring.

Then a guy would come out on horseback with the horse padded on one side. He would get the attention of the bull and the bull would be snorting and scratching in the ground. Then all at once the bull would charge against the padded side of the horse. And the horsemen had a long spear like they used to fight with in ancient times and he would be pushing it into the bull right up on top of the back, trying to keep him off of the horse but also deliberately weakening the bull's neck muscles. The bull wasn't hurting the horse because the horse was padded on that side and he had turned that padded side to the bull. He would keep pushing the bull and after a while he would get the bull off the padded side of the horse with no damage. Then he would meander around and turn that padded side to the bull again and the bull would charge again into the padding. And he would push the bull with that spear, trying to push him off the horse. Then they would open the gate and that fellow on the horse would go out.

The bull's getting more tired all the time. Then a couple of more fellows would come out there and wave in front of the bull and stick two or three more things in his back. Then the matador who was going to kill the bull would come out there. He waved three or four things in front of the bull and the bull would pass by him real close. The crowd would holler *"¡Olé!"* Then he would go around on the side of the bull, getting the bull's attention by waving that red thing in front of him.

The matador would get down on his knees, hold the red cape up there, and let the bull go just that close right by, right under his arms. And the crowd would holler *"¡Olé!"* That was the crowning point. He's getting ready to kill the bull now. Sometimes the crowd would holler "No! No! No! No!" That meant that they wanted him to *"olé"* the bull a little while longer and not kill him right now. So he would *"olé"* the bull. Wave that thing right in front of him and let the bull go by. And the closer the bull goes to him, the louder the crowd would holler. And sometimes he would cross his legs and let the bull go right by him.

That's why we said the bull always shuts his eyes when he charges. Because if not, he would have snagged his clothes or something like that. I have seen the times that he did hit him right on the leg. But when the bull would happen to hit him on the legs to get him down, the other matadors would come out and wave all in front of the bull, waving him off of the matador. Sometimes he would be rolling over as the bull was trying to horn him. And the matador would keep rolling over to keep from being gored. I have seen bulls pick up a matador and drop him right back on the ground unhurt. And I have seen times when they would have to go out there and get him. Because he was bleeding on the side.

After being able to have the bull pass close a couple of times, he's getting ready to kill the bull. He would go back over there on the side and they hand him a sword about so long and he would hold that thing up, sighting down it like he's going to stick that thing right in a certain spot. He waved that cape in front of the bull. The bull was snorting and the matador would keep waving that thing in front of the bull. He was just waiting for the bull to charge.

Then, all at once, the bull would charge. When he stuck the bull, the sword would go right above the bull's neck. Then the other man would come out there and wave all around the bull and let him run this way and run that way. And then after a while the bull, weakening now, would get down on his front knees. And he was so weak then that the matador wouldn't do anything but wave his hand and the bull would fall over. When he fell over, one of those guys would stick him right in the back of his head, in his brains, just that quick, and he's dead.

Then they would come out there with two mules and drag him out of the ring. That was the first one. And then they would kill five more. They killed six every Sunday afternoon and evening. We understood that during the week, the beef would be given to the poor.

They had the bullfights on Sunday afternoon and evening, and the cockfights were at night. They had a little ring, not big like for the bullfight, but just a little ring. And they had seats all around it. And they would charge you to go into the ring. We'd go out there and they had a sign up there about the first two fights between two roosters and fellows were going around selling tickets. This rooster is number one and that rooster is number two, and people would bet a dollar or two that the rooster of their choice would win.

After they got up all the money that they thought was going to be bet, one fellow would put down his rooster and the other fellow would put down his rooster. The owners would put them in the ring and then they'd start fighting to let everybody see how much spirit each rooster had and how aggressive he was. And then each owner would pick up his rooster and try to get some more bets. And after they got a few more bets up they would put metal spurs that were real sharp on each rooster's legs.

Then they would put them back in the ring. The owners of the roosters were in the ring, but when they put down the roosters, they got out. The roosters would fly over the top of each other, and every time one would fly over, he would hit the other up the side of the head or somewhere. If one rooster got the other rooster down, they would stop it and the owners would take up their roosters and revive him by putting the rooster's mouth in their mouth and blowing in his face.

When they thought they had him straightened out, maybe somebody wanted to put down another bet. Then they put them back down on the ground and the other rooster would kill the rooster that was about out of it. The losing rooster would lay down and they would stop the fight and wring that dead rooster's head off. They had a poor section in the grandstand and they would throw that rooster with his head off over into the poor section. And the people there would wrestle and fight over it like the devil. And then the owner of the rooster who had won would take his rooster up and they would pay off the bets. That was the first fight, and they had six fights a night. Sometimes it didn't take over fifteen or twenty minutes per fight.

We have cockfights in North Carolina. Of course, it's not legal. They'd clean off a place down in the woods where they'd think the sheriff wouldn't come. The fellows who owned roosters would bring them down there and they'd put them down and let them fight. And they used to bet on them. Somebody would say, "I'll bet on this rooster" and somebody else would say, "I'll bet on the other rooster." They put them down just like they did in Mexico, and let them hop around awhile and then pick them up and put some more bets up. The same thing would go on just like they did it in Mexico.

When the sheriff came down there, such running through the woods you never seen in your life. But they would always get the man who owned the farm who was in charge of it. They didn't have any poor people there because everybody was standing up, and everybody who was standing around usually was interested in the fight. So they would just wring the losing rooster's neck off and throw him over in a pile. We didn't never know who they gave them to.

In Mexico they also play a game called jai alai. Most of the better jai alai players played in Mexico City. They threw a ball up against a wall. We used to go to see just how they could catch that ball in things that looked like baskets and sling it back up there and the other one catch it when it came off that board and sling it back up there. Now, they bet on that, but we didn't know just exactly how they bet. But we knew that if one threw it up there and the other one couldn't return it, then you lost a point. Just how the score was counted we didn't ever know. They used to pass out leaflets about just who was playing and a little update on his record so you'd be more encouraged to bet again before-hand. They have jai alai over here now. They've got it in Boston and of course they've got it down in Florida now.

And in Mexico they had picture shows, too. Down there they had our pictures from the United States. Now, the talking was in English, but the reading under the pictures was in Spanish. While I was playing in Durango in 1955, they were filming a Western movie, *White Feather,* down there. Two of the main actors were Robert Wagner and Jeffrey Hunter. I was staying in the same hotel where they were staying, and they came to watch us play. We talked a little about baseball and had some pictures taken and all like that. They put a picture of us in the paper. It said, "Bob Wagner talks with Durango's Babe Ruth." That's what they called me down there in those days.

I went down to Latin American countries twelve years alto-gether. In addition to Mexico, I played winter ball in Puerto Rico in 1935 and 1940, in Venezuela in 1945 and 1949, and in Cuba in 1936–38 and again in 1948. Playing in Mexico, Cuba, and Puerto Rico was all right. Mexico and Cuba was a little better than Puerto Rico. South America was a little better than all of them, on and off the field. They were better developed.

Playing winter baseball helps a lot because you can improve things that you're weak on. When you go to play in Cuba, Puerto Rico, South America, or Mexico in the winter, you can practice. In Cuba we played Tuesday, Thursday, Saturday, and Sunday. But in other countries, three games a week was just about all we played. In Mexico at Torreón, we played Thursday night, Saturday evening, and Sunday morning. And the last two places in Mexico where I played, in Durango and Xalapa, we played Saturday evening, Sunday morning at ten o'clock, and Sunday evening. In Caracas we played the same days as in Durango.

And you practiced on your off-days. You go out in the morning about ten or eleven o'clock and you practice until about one or two o'clock. You can go to the ballpark and they'll send somebody out there with you. And to improve your batting, you can go out there and bat a half day if you want to. Playing winter baseball improves a fellow a whole lot. Of course, about the middle of the season in the summer, you get tired and you slow down if you have to play all the games.

One time I had a chance to play in the major leagues. This was after I had been to Mexico and played during the winter of 1951. Bill Veeck owned the St. Louis Browns, and he called my home and wanted to know if I would come to play with the Browns. I told him, "Well, I don't know anything about you. And I'm too old to even try to play any major-league baseball." He said, "Well, come on out here and we'll see."

Then about two or three days later a colored fellow named Winfield Welch, who was managing Birmingham, called me and said, "Buck, we want you to come out here to California where the St. Louis Browns are training. We just want you to come out here and we're going to send you the money. You go down and ask for a job just like you're walking in. And Bill Veeck's going to ask you some questions and he's going to decide to use you." But I told him, "No." I didn't want to do that, and I didn't go. I told him I was too old to play major-league baseball. I was almost forty-five years old. My legs were gone and I knew I couldn't play ball every day. I didn't even want to try it. He didn't mention my salary if I had played with them.

But I would have liked to have played in my prime. Bill Veeck was planning on buying the Philadelphia Phillies in 1944 and stocking it with black ballplayers. There was some speculation about who he had in mind. Some people thought that if it happened, I would go with them. That would have been different, then but, in 1952, I knew I was over the hill. I didn't try to fool myself.

When Jackie went to the major leagues in 1947, I was forty. I think I could have played in any league, even then. When Luke

Easter went to the major leagues he said that the main trouble he had was that he faced good pitching every day. That was the basic difference in the majors and our leagues. In the major leagues you faced good pitching every day, but in our leagues you didn't. I know that good pitching will check good hitting. And I know that five years is a long time when you're already past forty.

In 1953 I played with Portsmouth, Virginia, in the Piedmont League at the end of the season. That was a Class B league. They had lost their first baseman, and after I got back from Mexico, the owner of the Portsmouth Merrimacs, Frank Lawrence, wanted me to finish the season with them to try to help win the pennant. There was about a month left in the season, and I hit .333 while I was there.

Two other black players, Brooks Lawrence and Charlie Peete, were on the team. I was a veteran and they were younger players. Lawrence was a pretty good pitcher when he was with Portsmouth, and I knew him pretty well. He went up to St. Louis the next year and won fifteen games, and then pitched some more years with Cincinnati. Peete was a young prospect on his way up, and two or three years later he played in the major leagues, too. He was going to Venezuela to play winter ball when he was killed in a plane crash. He was only about twenty-five years old and would have been a star if he had lived.

# Chapter 23

## After Baseball (1956–75)

*I remember hearing about Buck Leonard being a good ballplayer, but I never saw him play. When I managed at Rocky Mount, we had a pretty good ballclub. I think there were two or three players who later went up to the major leagues for a while.*
*—Max Lanier, New York Giants*

I quit playing baseball in 1955 after I had been in Mexico five years. I came back home and decided I wouldn't play any more. I was forty-eight years old and I had slowed down to a walk. My back was hurting and I had the arthritis and I just didn't think I could play another year.

After I stayed around Rocky Mount the rest of 1955, I decided that I wanted to work again. So I went down to the Watson Company. They sold cigars and cigarettes as well as several other items such as Cocoa cola syrup, candy, and snuff. But the main things they sold were cigarettes, cigars, and chewing tobacco, and they were called a tobacco company.

I went down there in 1958 and worked there about a year delivering cigars. The salesman used to come around with some sample cigars and I started smoking his samples until I found one cigar that I liked, which was Robert Burns. And I smoked that awhile. Then I decided that since I was getting cigars free, I would smoke Dutch Masters, and I smoked them for a long time until I stopped working there. When I got out where I had to buy my cigars I went back to little Robert Burns because I couldn't pay for Dutch Masters. I've been smoking cigars ever since and enjoying them.

After I left the tobacco company I worked with the schools for twelve years. I was a truant officer for ten years and I helped with recreation the last two years. That was before integration. They had a white truant officer and a black truant officer. He had an office and I had an office. I looked after the black children and he took care of the white children. But I had to report to him because he was really the truant officer and I was his assistant.

The way that I worked the truant officer job was to go to two schools a day and ask if they had any children out of school who they thought should be in school. They would tell me how many children they had out that they believed was being truant or else they didn't know what was wrong with them. They would give me the name, address, and grade of each one and I would go to his house to find out why the child was not in school. I wanted to talk to the parent, but most black parents were working.

A lot of times the child would be sitting there in the house or maybe they would be gone somewhere else. If I couldn't see somebody at the house to talk to, I would go back to the house at night and talk to the parent when they came home from work and tell them that the child was out of school and find out what seemed to be the reason. Sometimes they would tell you that they didn't have sufficient clothes, or the weather was too bad and the child couldn't be sent out without a raincoat or didn't have sufficient shoes or rainwear.

We had that trouble often. Sometimes we would try to help the mother get things for them. We would go down to the welfare or the family service office and tell the head lady there that we needed a pair of shoes for a certain little girl who was in the third grade and couldn't go to school because her shoes were not sufficient. Sometimes they would give us a slip and we would go to the shoestore and take the little girl and buy her some shoes. Other times I would beg shoes from people I knew around the neighborhood who had a child about that size, and they would give me shoes and dresses and other clothes for that child.

They stopped me from doing that because they said it was unsanitary. I couldn't just go to a house and have somebody give me a dress or a pair of pants or some other piece of clothing for a child. I would have that stuff cleaned before I could carry it to the other child. The hardest part of the job was going around at night after I had been around during the day. That was tough because sometimes after working all day, I felt like going home and sitting down. Especially on those nights when it was rainy, or was sleeting or snowing.

I hated to carry them to the training school when the weather was bad. They didn't want you to carry a child to training school handcuffed, and I had to do that three or four times. They said a child shouldn't have to be handcuffed. That being a man I ought to be able to subdue him without handcuffing him.

One day I stopped at a stoplight in Raleigh, North Carolina, and the child jumped out of the car and ran. By the time that I found somewhere to park, the child was out of sight and I didn't know where he was. I just had to wait and hope that I would be able to locate him and report it to the police there.

Another time I was carrying a child to training school and I had a flat tire. I changed tires and the spare tire was also flat. So I had to catch a ride and go about five or six miles down the road to put some air in that spare tire and come back. It just happened that the child was still there when I got back.

Today's children have more freedom than when I was growing up. And the parents more or less let the child do what he wants to do. If he doesn't want to do anything, they don't make him do it. If he wakes up in the morning and doesn't want to go to school, he says, "Momma, I don't feel like going to school today," and they just let him stay home. Now, when I was that age, we had to give a reason why we didn't go to school. We had to tell Momma, "My stomach is hurting," or something like that. And if we told her that, she would give us a dose of castor oil. We couldn't get by with things like children can now.

In 1968 they took the truant officer job away from me. They changed the name of truant officer to attendance officer, and they said that I wasn't qualified for the job because I had never had any social work. I didn't know anything about that kind of work, so they told me they were going to hire somebody else.

Of course, they gave me plenty of notice. They gave me about a year's notice that they were going to put that job under another head and whoever was going to have the job was going to have a diploma in social work. I didn't have that, and I wasn't about to get it. So they took the job and gave it to the welfare department for somebody to have. When they took the job away from me, they took the job away from the white truant officer, too, because he wasn't qualified either. They got rid of both of us at the same time.

That's when I started working with the children at the playground. I worked out there for two years, from 1968 until 1970. I would go to school and take the first, second, or third grade out on the schoolground and give them exercises. And then I'd leave there around eleven o'clock and go to another school until twelve o'clock, and at one o'clock I'd go to another school. I had certain schools that I went to on certain days, and I had to go to a school about twice a week.

I already had my real-estate brokerage license from the self-extension university in Chicago. I saw in the paper where they were offering a real-estate correspondence course. So I wrote to the company and they sent a representative around to talk to me. In order to take a brokerage course at that time you had to have a high school diploma, and I had my high school diploma. Therefore I was eligible to take the course. At that time the course cost four hundred dollars and they would send you a set of real-estate law books from the state of Illinois. They were a little bit different from the real-estate laws of North Carolina, and I had to compare them to what they were in those books to see the difference.

I finished the American Correspondence School in 1959, and after I finished the real-estate course I had to pass a test to get my real-estate license. The brokers took the course in the morning and the real-estate salesmen took the license test in the afternoon. Taking the course from the extension university helped me a lot in taking the examination. But the first time I went to take my real-estate board in Raleigh, North Carolina, I didn't pass. At that time it took twenty-five dollars to take the test, and if you failed the first time you would have another trial free. But if you failed a second time, you had to pay another twenty-five dollars. So when I took the test the second time, I passed.

I got my real-estate license in September and announced it in the paper, and just went right on to work then. That was in 1966, and I only worked part time. I went full time in real estate in 1970 after I finished working for the city, and I stayed with it until I had my stroke. If I was doing it over, I wish I would have saved more money while I was making good money. But I bought real estate instead, and it paid off later. I built nine houses from the ground up. I paid sixty thousand dollars for them and I sold them for a hundred thousand dollars in 1984.

While I was working with the city and in real estate, I was also the vice president of the Rocky Mount baseball team in the Carolina League. That's Class A ball. There was a fellow named Frank Walker who used to be a baseball player in Rocky Mount. I had been knowing him ever since 1921, before I ever started to go off to play ball. I must have been about fourteen years old, and he was a center fielder, manager, and owner of the Rocky Mount baseball team.

He sold himself to a major league team and he stayed up there in the major leagues with the Detroit Tigers, the Philadelphia Athletics, and the New York Giants over a period of five seasons. Then he came back here and was still managing until he let the team go. Some other guy was here as owner for a while, and Walker had a bowling alley and a dry cleaning plant. Then Walker took the team back in 1962.

He decided to organize a baseball team in Rocky Mount, and since I was back home, he wanted to know if I would help him sell shares in the team to blacks. I told him, "Yeah, I'd be glad to." So I went around to the blacks in the area and asked them to buy shares, and I got fifty-nine blacks to buy shares in the baseball team. Some of them didn't buy but one share, and some bought three or four. A share was worth five dollars at that time and it was not that much money, but after I showed quite a lot of interest in the team by selling shares, he said he was going to make me a vice president of the team. We got a rich fellow from

Durham, named Mr. Criffin, to come to Rocky Mount, and he
decided that he would put in most of the money.

I was with the team for fourteen years, from 1962 to 1975. We
were in the Carolina League. At first we worked with Cincinnati
for two years, and next was the Detroit Tigers and finally with
the Philadelphia Phillies. We had some good players come through
Rocky Mount, including Tony Perez, Lee Maye, and Jake Wood.

Max Lanier, who had pitched for the St. Louis Cardinals and
was one of the players who jumped to Mexico in 1946, was our
manager for a while. But he didn't do so well. I was vice president
and I used to talk to him a lot. He was easygoing and, with some
fellows, that didn't work. With some ballplayers, you've got to
shut down on them.

Now, we had a fellow down here named Rufus Anderson, a
second baseman. He was a black fellow and he used to carouse
around on the day of the ball game. He was supposed to have
been there at five-thirty and he'd show around seven-thirty with
the smell of drinking on him. You take a guy like that and you've
got to shut down on him. Max wasn't doing that. He stayed with
us about two years. Max had a son, Hal, that played baseball, too.
He was an infielder and played in the major leagues for a while,
and then he managed the Houston Astros.

During the time that I was still affiliated with the Rocky Mount
baseball team, I had the biggest loss in my personal life. My wife
had a heart attack and died on the fifteenth of February in 1966.
That was the hardest thing in my life I ever had to deal with. It
was the worst time of my life. We were married for over twenty-
seven years, and adjustment after my wife's death was hard. It's
about a six-month process. Most people have to wail, but for the
first four or five months it is really tough.

I reckon if I'd had children at home or somebody with me, it
wouldn't have been as tough. But we never had any children.
That's just the way it worked out. Every man wants a son, but I
would have liked to have at least two children. One of each, a
boy and a girl. But I never had any choice. So my being there by
myself and staying in a big nine-room house made it kind of tough
on me. And my mother died two years later, in 1968.

Talking about children, a few years later, there was a ballplayer named Bernie Leonard, who was claiming to be my son. He had played in Japan and was playing in Monterrey, Mexico, in 1972. I had to go and have a talk with him about that. I told him he was going to have to stop telling everybody that. He said that he was just trying to get more recognition and to get somebody to notice him, and to maybe help his baseball career. But we got that straightened out and I never did hear any more about it.

# Chapter 24

## Smelling the Roses (1970–94)

*Buck was a dead pull hitter. I remembered one time when a pitcher tried to pick a runner off third base and Buck pulled the ball down the right-field line.*

—*Bowie Kuhn, baseball commissioner*

After the Negro Leagues folded, all of us black players were forgotten until about 1970. Since then there has been a growing interest in the kind of baseball we played. At first it was just a little attention, but it's getting bigger all the time. We have reunions, educational forums, recognitions at ball games, and all kinds of other appearances to make. And now there are books, movies, television programs, and radio shows. And there are baseball cards, posters, calendars, statues and all kinds of memorabilia. They keep coming up with new things.

A few years ago, we players from the Negro Leagues were talking and, you know, they've got Babe Ruth, Roberto Clemente, and Jackie Robinson on postage stamps and all of them come from the major leagues and we don't have anybody from the black leagues on a postage stamp. When we went to Cooperstown that year, we had thought about asking the new commissioner, Peter

Ueberroth, if he would be in favor of asking that Satchel Paige's picture be put on a postage stamp.

But we didn't know Ueberroth. We hadn't ever heard of him until the Olympics, and we didn't know just what to think about him. We were going to ask him if he would advocate it somehow, since Satchel was our star, but we decided not to ask him, since we didn't know him. Since then, they've got stamps for Jim Thorpe and Joe Louis, too. I believe Satchel still deserves a stamp, and maybe someday he will get one.

Now, all of us knew Bowie Kuhn, and he knew us. And we wouldn't have hesitated to ask him. I hated to see Bowie leaving the commissioner's office. He had helped us players from the black leagues. We never asked him for nothing that he didn't do. We told him that we needed a better display in the museum and he got us a bigger display. And we told him that we needed more light on our display there at the museum and he got us more light.

We told Bowie Kuhn one time up there in Cooperstown, "Say, Commissioner, it's being talked around here that you all have put five or six of us into the Hall of Fame and now you have slammed the door. It's being talked around here that you all are not going to elect anybody else from the Negro Leagues." He said, "Well, we're going to add some more. Keep sending me names of ones who you recommend and we'll see what can be done."

But ever since they got a new commissioner, Bowie Kuhn don't have any influence because he don't have any money. That's the reason they kicked him around like they did. If he was a millionaire before he got the job and was still a millionaire, he'd have some influence. If you've got some money you can be outspoken. That's one thing about Bowie Kuhn, he ain't got a quarter out of the fifteen years he was commissioner. The more you make, the more it takes. And he never had nothing to start with. He used to put scores on the scoreboard for us in Griffith Stadium when he was about fifteen years old.

You get a guy like Steinbrenner and all those other owners who are millionaires, they're not going to listen to Bowie Kuhn. No one else would do it either. Anybody that had a million dollars in an undertaking wouldn't let somebody with only three quarters, so to speak, tell them what to do with any team that they had influence over. Them fellows don't care about nothing but what you got. You can have all kinds of education, but if you ain't got some bread, then you can forget it. Just like Bowie Kuhn.

If a man has money, he's got all kinds of influence. Look how they tolerate Steinbrenner. If he didn't have so much money, they wouldn't have let him bring Billy Martin in and out like he did, to save your life. They say that you don't make money by being a damn fool—you get money by being smart. It's not that Steinbrenner is so intelligent, but he's being smart to get that money. But it's true, too, that most of them inherited their money. But, however you got it, if you got it, they're going to listen to you. I would rather see Steinbrenner out of baseball because he depends on his money. He thinks that money will get him what he wants—which it will. I don't think that him coming back after his suspension will help the game.

I believe Peter Ueberroth's decision regarding reinstating Mickey Mantle and Willie Mays to good standing in organized baseball was a good one. I'm not for gambling, but we all know that they are a help to baseball. Of course, now, I don't go along with where they were working. But since all of us have done some things that some folks didn't like, I think that was a good move to bring them back. They mean so much to baseball.

Everybody's still talking about Pete Rose and the Hall of Fame. I think that they ought to let Pete Rose back into baseball. After all, he was a help with baseball. They say his gambling was a hindrance, but his playing overshadowed all of that. It would be a shame to keep him out. He did so much for the game. I never did get to know either Bart Giamatti or Faye Vincent, and I don't know the details about what proof they had about Rose's betting on baseball.

Gambling and drugs are two of the biggest problems in sports today. When I played ball, I went to bed and stayed at home and stayed out of trouble. I never used any kind of drugs, but they were not the problem back then that they are now. I would advise youngsters to stay off drugs. If an athlete will behave himself and stay off drugs, he will be better off. Players who use drugs should be suspended. I think that's what it takes. They're making so much money that they can pay any fine you put on them. Some athletes shouldn't be held up as role models. Those who played for the love of the game—and a little money—should be considered as role models.

The athletes are making even more money now than ever. A million dollars looked like the password about ten years ago. Now they're making about twenty or thirty million just for a few years. About everybody who can do anything is making millions of dollars in athletics. The multimillion-dollar contracts today are all out of reason to me. It's too much money for that kind of activity. Until lately, I never heard of some of those ballplayers who are making big money. If it had not been for television, I don't think salaries would have been what they are. Radio and other things also helped, but television was the main reason. It looks to me like it's gotten out of hand as far as salary is concerned. The average cost of salaries is out of sight. But if the owners will pay it, the players are going to take it.

A few years ago, Steve Carlton wanted to be the highest-paid pitcher. He felt that he was as good as that boy with the Dodgers, Fernando Valenzuela, who was making a million. And Carlton felt like he ought to make a million point two or something like that. We were the same way when I played. We would hear what somebody else was making and we used it. If I heard that somebody else was making more than me and not playing near the ball I was playing, I'd think, "I'm behind." And I'd start wanting more money.

But I would like to be playing now, I know that. I'd only ask for about a million. But you've got to remember that I'm eighty-seven years old and have had a stroke. I'm talking about the kind of shape I'm in *now*. If I was playing ball today and was in my *prime,* I'd be asking for the same things these fellows are asking for. I would ask for as much as the other top players were making. But I don't really give that too much thought, because I think that it's unfortunate in some ways. It's just different times than when I played. We went to the ballpark with our gloves, and nowadays ballplayers go to the ballpark with their lawyers and agents. Now, the players today still love to play, but they want to be paid. We really didn't care if we got paid or not.

But I may not have felt the same if back then I had to pay

what prices are today. Back then, a good meal would cost thirty-five cents, a haircut would cost twenty-five cents, and a shave was fifteen cents. Now a haircut cost you about ten dollars, and it costs about five dollars to eat a good breakfast, and I don't know what a shave costs now because I always shave myself. Maybe I would have asked for as much if the prices were like they are today.

Not only did we not get much money back then, we never got any recognition to speak of either. But we players from the Negro Leagues are getting more recognition now. There have been a lot more books, movies, and television programs about those of us in the Negro Leagues. Some of them are good and some of them are not so good.

*Only the Ball Was White* was the first book about Negro baseball that was put out. Bob Peterson, the author, really went to a lot of trouble getting the material together, and I would say it is mostly accurate. He came and talked to me and he talked to several other fellows. Now, he can talk to me and Cool Papa Bell about the same incident and I'll tell him one thing and Cool Papa will tell him another thing. Cool Papa is telling what he can remember about it and I'm telling what I can remember about it. And sometimes it's not together. We don't have any official record that says just exactly how it was. We're talking from memory and just tell how we remember it.

I think that was the best book about the Negro Leagues until 1994, when *The Biographical Encyclopedia of the Negro Baseball Leagues* came out. That's a real big, thick book and the best one ever written about the *players* in the Negro Leagues. All the fellows say that it is the best. There's a lot of information in there that can't be found anywhere else. I know a lot of years went into putting all that together, and a lot of what I know went into it, too. Now people can read about us and learn about our contributions to baseball.

I don't have much to say about Art Rust's book because I didn't like that from the beginning. And we didn't like the name he gave his book, *Get that Nigger off The Field*. He said he gave it that name because when Jackie Robinson played the New York Giants at the Polo Grounds, a chant went throughout the grandstand, "Get that nigger off the field." Art Rust borrowed a lot of my pictures

and never returned them. He did the same thing to Monte and
Cool Papa. After we asked for them back and he wouldn't return
them, we got a lawyer and told the lawyer to go there and tell
him that we wanted them back. We didn't want to take any legal
action, we just wanted our pictures back. But we never got them
back. He owns a bar on Riverside Drive in New York and he had
all our pictures up on the wall. I told *Sports Illustrated,* "Don't
let Art Rust have anything because he's not reliable."

I didn't care too much for the movie *Bingo Long's Traveling
All-Stars and Motor Kings* either. I never did read the book, but
they sent us a script of the movie. And the script was all right,
but when they made the movie, it was different from what the
script read. We talked to them about it and they said that the only
way they could get the movie to sell was to arrange it like they
did. Now, we didn't like the rearrangement because there was
some things in the film that might have happened, but we didn't
think they should have been put in the movie. And there's some
things that's in the movie that we know didn't happen in Negro
baseball.

Specifically we didn't go into a town and parade before the ball
games. They show where we went to town to play and got on
wagons and all and rode through town and strutting and "yah-
yahing" with their uniforms on and with the band playing. And
we didn't do that.

And some nightlife in the film might have happened but we
had rather for it not to have been put in the movie. The characters
in the movie were patterned after certain black players, and they
were supposed to act just like we acted when we were playing.
For a man to really act as a ballplayer, he's got to have been a
ballplayer in his actions and in his talk. He's got to talk the language of the ballplayers. Now, they had some of those characters
that didn't act or talk like baseball players. They had fellows in
the picture who were supposed to represent Satchel Paige, Josh
Gibson, and myself. I think the character named Leon Wagner
was supposed to have been patterned after me.

I like it better when they show us more like the way it really
was. The white people coming up now don't understand segregation. And some black people now don't understand segregation

either. They don't understand what we went through. They don't know what black baseball was, and when I tell them I played on a colored team, they don't know what I'm talking about. They say, "Why don't they have colored teams now?" I say, "They did away with segregation." And they did.

After I retired from baseball and before I was elected to the Hall of Fame, I would get some recognition at hot stove leagues. A hot stove league is something you go to around February and start talking about baseball. A long time ago, old-timers used to meet at the country store and they had those great big potbellied stoves sitting in the middle of the floor. And everybody would sit around the stove and talk about the prospects of baseball for the coming season. That was the beginning of calling it the "hot stove league."

Almost every small town then had a baseball team, and that's where the main discussions went on about the coming season. In North Carolina, we've got hot stove leagues in Raleigh and Wilson and several other towns. They have a banquet and a lot of discussion about baseball in their area. The president of their league and owners of some of the teams in the league are there. They have just a grand time and it gets the baseball spirit to rolling.

Most people in the hot stove league are businessmen in the community and are responsible citizens. At the meetings they introduce us, and we just stand up and wave and take a bow for everybody. Everybody is glad to see us and we're glad to see the folks and the other old ballplayers. We don't even have to say nothing, but sometimes they call on us to say something about what we think of major-league games and baseball players now.

Enos Slaughter, Al Hibbing, Ray Scarborough, and all of us players who were living in North Carolina used to go around to them. Gaylord Perry and Jim Perry were at the one in Wilson one of the times I went there. Almost everybody is there every year, but they can't get Catfish Hunter to go. They also want us to sign autographs, and all of us autographed for them.

Catfish Hunter and I were inducted into the North Carolina Sports Hall of Fame in 1974, and we were both there for the ceremonies one year. Catfish was one of the top baseball players and he was one of the first players to get a good salary and folks wanted his autograph but he didn't sign. Catfish had his wife signing for him.

I can't understand things like that. Everybody has heard about you and little children and grown people, too, saying, "Autograph this for me." Somebody came out there with a baseball and he wouldn't do it. There's some fellows who don't like to autograph, but there's some of us who don't mind autographing. I reckon it's better than being forgotten. Now, if it was an autograph show, that would be different.

I still spend a lot of time answering my mail. I'm getting more now than I've ever got. I wasn't getting any mail until I was inducted into the Hall of Fame. There wasn't anybody asking me for autographs until then. Now I'm constantly bombarded by requests. People wanting autographs has changed a lot since I got in the Hall of Fame. I still sign autographs at certain functions, but now autographs and memorabilia has gotten to be such big business that I don't do it like I used to do. I used to give autographs free, but now I charge. The reason why I changed is because it *has* become such a big business. People ask for your autograph and they don't really want it. They are just going to sell it, but they don't tell you they're going to sell it.

When we go to Cooperstown, we know folks are going to ask for an autograph. We know that and we ought to be prepared and willing to autograph. It doesn't happen but once a year, and all of us ought to make a sacrifice to accommodate the people to autograph while we are there. It doesn't cost nothing, and sometimes we're in a hurry to go somewhere, but we ought to always stop and autograph some and come back later and autograph some more. It's just the people come there for that and we ought to oblige them.

A few years ago, Bobby Richardson autographed for two hours right here in Rocky Mount. He's active in the Fellowship of Christian Athletes and goes around talking about how athletes should be Christians. He was speaking at one of the churches in town and they had a nice banquet. And the pastor of the church asked me to come over there so he would have somebody to talk to while he was waiting to speak. So I went over there and met Bobby Richardson, and I had a nice time with him.

But sometimes people will take advantage of you. In 1984, a promoter from Miami was putting on some kind of exhibition on black baseball. He called me and I said, "If it's a black function, then I won't charge anything, I'll just come for the expenses." So I went down there. We sat there at the University of Miami from two o'clock until five-thirty and not one person showed up. Nobody. And he called me again and asked me to come back and promised to pay me a thousand dollars. I didn't believe he was going to give me a thousand dollars, and I didn't go. When I go to a card show now, they pay more than that and all expenses for three people. Since I had my stroke, I've had to have my wife and her son to go with me. The last card show tired me out so much that I don't think I'll do any more.

But at certain kinds of functions, like the North Carolina Sports Hall of Fame induction, I think it's more like it used to be before autographing got to be such big business. Other blacks who have been elected to our state Sports Hall of Fame are Jethro Pugh from the Dallas Cowboys; Meadowlark Lemon from the Harlem Globetrotters; John Baker from the Pittsburgh Steelers; Sam Jones from the Boston Celtics; "Big House" Gaines, a coach at Winston-Salem State College; and a track man named Walker, who got Olympic runners from Africa to come over here and run in the Olympic Games for him.

They were going to put former heavyweight boxing champion Floyd Patterson in there, but although he was born in North Carolina, they said he had neither gained his fame nor lived most of his life in North Carolina. Seems like he left the state kind of early and grew up in New Jersey and New York and went on to boxing and became famous. But they said they were going to pull some strings and try to get him in there a little bit later on. We had an induction in Shelby in 1982, and Floyd Patterson was there with his mother and father, who live right around Shelby.

All the towns want the Sports Hall of Fame to be located in their place. The state of North Carolina is going to give the Sports Hall of Fame a building in Raleigh to display the memorabilia, since they are centrally located.

It seems like everybody is asking for memorabilia. I gave my shoes and my cap to the Baseball Hall of Fame in Cooperstown.

They wanted my uniform, but a fellow from New Jersey named Hapler gave me two thousand dollars for that uniform. I could have sent that uniform away for nothing, and here's a guy going to give me two thousand dollars. It's probably worth a lot more than that now. He wanted my pants, shirt, cap, and socks. And he wanted to write my name inside the pants and shirt to authenticate them. He's also got Bob Feller's uniform, Joe DiMaggio's uniform, Mickey Mantle's uniform, and a whole lot more.

I sent one uniform to the Smithsonian Institution to display. That was the one that the team in Mayagüez, Puerto Rico, gave to me. I got it back from the Smithsonian, but it got away from me somehow. Rawlings gave me another pair of shoes to wear in old-timers' games to replace the ones I gave to Cooperstown. I've got the last glove I used and the last bat I used, and I signed some home-run balls I hit.

They dedicated the Negro Baseball Hall of History in Ashland, Kentucky, in 1982, but it didn't last. That was a beautiful site, but there was nothing inside, and we had to send some stuff up there to put into it. We found it difficult to find something to send to go in that Hall of History. Ordinarily we baseball players from the Negro Leagues don't have anything to donate. When we left the ball team every year we had to turn in our uniform. The owners took up the uniforms before they gave you your last pay. You couldn't keep a uniform, but I finally did keep one. Of course, I told a lie about it. I said I didn't have it. I told them I left it downstairs, but I carried it on home with me.

And as far as bats and balls, they belong to the club, and they take that up at the end of the season, too. So the only things we had left to take home was the shoes, the sliding pads, and your gloves. Of course, that belongs to you. A lot of the players disposed of the gloves and shoes over the years since 1950. And we just didn't have much that we could put into the Hall of History to be shown. I sent some photographs and clippings from my scrapbook to Ashland. That's about all I had left to give them. Most of the things that they asked for to be displayed in the Hall of History, the memorabilia such as bats and gloves and uniforms, we just didn't have the stuff to send up there to put in the museum.

We tried to open a year earlier but we just didn't have enough stuff in the museum to make a good showing.

Ashland is off the path anyway, so to speak. You've got to be going *to* Ashland. You can't be going through there to be going anywhere else, and it is out of the way from the large black population centers. I think that was a hindrance. If the museum had been put on the East Coast somewhere like Washington, Philadelphia, Baltimore, or somewhere out that way, then people could have stopped by there to see it and then go on to New York or somewhere. It would have been a whole lot better that way.

Folks who talked about it said that it was too far out of the way, and they want to know why it was established out there. We say, "Well, that's the only way we could establish it." And Cooperstown is out of the way, too, just like Canton, Ohio, where the Football Hall of Fame is located. And they have the Basketball Hall of Fame up in Springfield, Massachusetts. It's just whoever decides to do it.

The idea of the Hall of History grew out of a birthday party. A fellow named Bob Stutz organized the first reunion. He was a newspaperman in a little town in Kentucky called Greenup. He knew Clint Thomas, a fellow who used to play with the New York Black Yankees. Clint was born up there, and Clint's folks worked for Bob Stutz's daddy. That's how it was back then, with a big white man having Negroes working for him around the house. Clint was retiring at the age of eighty-five from New York, and he went back out there to live. Stutz decided to give something for him, and he invited thirteen of us out there the first year, 1979.

Stutz left up there after he had this reunion and he's preaching now, down in South Carolina. The people in Ashland looked at the reunion and said that it could be something bigger, so they took it away from Stutz and brought it to Ashland in 1980 and 1981. They asked us in 1979 if we wanted to make a bigger thing out of it and if we would be in favor of them having a bigger affair than what Stutz could give us. We told them, "Yeah, we would appreciate anything that anybody could do for us." Because there wasn't anybody else doing anything for us. And we agreed that they could have it.

Now a little conflict came up at that time. The black ballplayers said that we fellows who are in Cooperstown were not going to take part in it. But we did. All of us went out there every year and took part in the ceremonies just like everybody else. Now we fellows who are in the National Baseball Hall of Fame in Cooperstown didn't accept any offices in the Hall of History. There was not but five of us that were living then, and now there are only two of us—me and Monte. Judy Johnson, Cool Papa Bell, Monte Irvin, and myself were the four Hall of Famers who took an active part. Satchel helped some, but he was erratic. We didn't do any directing because they thought that we were trying to take it over. We were only working to show people other players.

They wanted Monte Irvin to work with them because Monte knew a lot of the ballplayers and I knew a lot of them. Cool Papa had been playing in the black leagues from 1922 until 1950, and he knew a whole lot of guys that played in the twenties that I didn't know. Just about anybody you name, he could tell you about him. Judy Johnson was also active, and he would remember certain players that others would not. Anybody Judy didn't know out East, we contacted Chet Brewer out West. He was with the Kansas City Monarchs, and he lived in Los Angeles.

Bob Feller and former commissioner Happy Chandler came to the reunions. And Bowie Kuhn came once, too. Three of the networks—NBC, CBS, and ABC—were there in 1981, and they put it on live. A whole lot of folks saw that telecast because it was on national TV. I thought we were going to get more recognition after we were on national TV. It had been on local television news before, but that is not the same as national exposure. I still think it helped the black ballplayers a whole lot. Several folks called me afterward and told me they saw it. During the reunions, we went to the ballpark in Ashland. In 1980 we put on our uniforms, but in 1981 we didn't wear them.

At the reunion that year, all of us got in Ashland by six o'clock Monday evening and we had a jam session. We met in a big room and all of us were talking and shaking hands with people we hadn't seen in thirty years. Then the next morning we went down to the auditorium with the press and TV people.

Somebody was talking to Satchel Paige, somebody was talking to me, somebody was talking to Cool Papa, and there was somebody talking to everybody else. After they got through with that, they had a question-and-answer session. There were four or five hundred folks down there. Then, about eleven-thirty, we had a luncheon. And they had things for us to do in the afternoon. Then we took about an hour to rest.

Then they came and got us and took us to the banquet. At the banquet they called on a few of us to say something. Then the mayor talked. Then they moved all the dishes off the table in front of us and we started to autographing and got through about eleven o'clock that night and we got ready to go back to the motel. The next morning at six o'clock they took us to the airport.

Now, when I got to Kentucky, there was a couple of fellows who said they played with the Grays but if they played with the Grays, they played before I got there. I know they didn't play after I left, because I stayed with the team until it broke up. I couldn't remember them ever being with the Grays. And I was the traveling secretary and used to keep everybody's name. I used to give everybody his eating money every day, and if he was there anytime after I got there, I would remember.

Over seventeen years, we had so many ballplayers coming and going until I can't hardly think of one unless somebody mentions a name. Now if a fellow comes to me and says, "Look, I played with the Grays," I say, "When?" And he tells me when he played, and if he did, I can remember. I mean, from the time that I was there. But just for me to call their names right now, I just can't call them.

They paid all those folks away out there on the plane, and that took quite a bit of money to finance. Ashland Oil Company financed it in 1980, and Joseph Schlitz Brewing Company did it in 1981. I don't know who financed it in the other years. Rufus Lewis had to pay his own way one year. He lives in Detroit, and somebody told him about it and he came. A lot of players don't have the means to come to reunions.

But the reunions were a good thing because we had been out of touch with each other since the Negro Leagues broke up. When a guy quits playing ball and goes off somewhere, you don't know where he is. It's hard to keep track of him. Since the breakup of the Negro Leagues and before the first reunion, I had only kept in touch with Jerry Benjamin, Sam Bankhead, Cool Papa Bell and Vic Harris until they died. We used to write and send each other Christmas cards.

They quit having reunions at Ashland and closed the Hall of History and sent all our things to Cooperstown. In Cooperstown somebody will see it, but they said some of it got lost carrying it there. Now they've got the Negro Leagues Museum trying to start out in Kansas City, but I don't think they've got much either. After a few years, they had another reunion in Atlanta and another one in Cooperstown. They may not be able to have any more anyplace.

I don't know what course this growing interest in the Negro Leagues is going to take. I would like for it to take a money course, with fellows getting a chance to endorse certain products, because blacks were playing pretty good baseball back then, too. I would like to see us be recognized as playing the game, too. We had an organization an we had two leagues, the Negro National League and the Negro American League. And we did have a World Series every year and we were playing baseball, too. A lot of folks didn't know anything about the black leagues. I would just like to let them know that we were playing baseball and people were going to see us play.

I used to go to Cooperstown every year, and some of the fellows from the Negro Leagues come to Cooperstown to be with us. Now it's getting harder to travel, and I think I'll go every other year. I went to Ashland every year when they had the reunions and I used to go to Florida in the spring for the governor's banquet and to see some games. And I used to go to old-timers' games, but I don't go to old-timers' games anymore. They used to take in all the old-timers and invite the Hall of Famers but then they just used ten-year periods. And they said anybody who was over sixty-five, they'd rather have them not play.

One year in Chicago it was really hot. It was ninety-five that day. And they said anybody who has a heart condition or who suffers from high blood pressure, we'd rather they didn't play. But Lloyd Waner said, "I'm going to play. I don't care what they say." And he played two innings. But they don't want anybody to get hurt. Luke Appling played one year and hit a home run and he was seventy then. But they tried to keep it so that they don't want anything to happen to anyone out there on the field.

I was down in Atlanta playing in an old-timers' game and Mickey Vernon was playing. Mickey hit a ball down to first base and, man, I tell you, I just kind of swiped at it. The ball could have hit me right then with my reflexes all slowed down and my eyesight not what it used to be. Somebody might get hurt out there. They could pinch hit or just make an appearance, but the old-timers want to play. Just like Lloyd Waner, they want to go out there.

Now you take a guy like Luke Appling, who was a batting instructor for Atlanta and was around the game a whole lot. He taught fellows how to bat in spring training and went all around to the farm teams to teach them how to bat. He had the use of the ball right on, while fellows who don't even touch a ball for four or five years, their reflexes are slow and they don't want to be out there.

I was down to Puerto Rico in 1976, when they had an old-timers' game down there. All of us from the United States played the old-timers from down there. We played a game in San Juan and then went to Ponce. But that's been over fifteen years ago.

In the last few years, some of the major-league baseball clubs have had special nights where they recognize all of us from the Negro Leagues. They've had special ceremonies in Pittsburgh, Chicago, New York, Atlanta, and in Baltimore, at Camden Yards, during the 1993 All-Star game.

# Chapter 25

## The Hall of Fame (1972)

*Buck was the best first baseman we had in the Negro Leagues, and one of the best hitters. Nobody deserves to be in the Hall of Fame more than he does.*

*—Cool Papa Bell, Homestead Grays*

The biggest thrill I ever got was when I went into the Hall of Fame. I can't say what my biggest thrill was on the ballfield. There's so many things. Maybe the home run I hit that won a ball game or a good stop that I made and cut off two big runs or something like that. But going into the Hall of Fame was something that I dreamed of. That is the high point of baseball. I had no idea that would ever happen to me. Especially since I had got so old.

The official announcement of my selection was made in February of 1972 at the Americana Hotel in New York. Monte Irvin kind of tricked me into coming up there. Monte, who worked in the commissioner's office, called here one evening and asked me if I could come to New York. I said, "To do what?" He said, "We're going to pick an All-Star team from the old Negro Leagues and try to get the names of that team into the Hall of

249

Fame on a plaque.'' And they were going to put a photo of the team in the Hall of Fame, too.

They had already put Satchel Paige in there the year before, in 1971. And Monte said, ''Since it looks like we're not going to get anybody else in there, let's see if we can get some All-Star names put on this plaque and put this plaque into the Hall of Fame.'' He said, ''Will you come up here and help us select it?'' I said, ''Yeah, I'll come up there. I'd be happy to.'' He said, ''All right, you come to the Americana Hotel in New York and I'll call and see if you're over there. And then I'll come over there and talk to you.'' I said, ''All right.''

He told me, ''I want you to get here the day before,'' and he gave me the date. He said, ''You'll get there about five or six o'clock in the evening and you stay in the hotel and don't come out until I come over there and get you the next morning. And I'll take you where you're supposed to go.''

So I arrived in New York on a Monday afternoon and went to the Americana Hotel. Monte called over there and said, ''I'll be there in a few minutes.'' He came over and said, ''Buck, tomorrow morning about nine o'clock, I'm going to come over here and get you and we're going over and start selecting names.''

So the next morning, we went over there to his room across the hall where I thought there was going to be some fellows sitting down and discussing black baseball players. I thought we were going to a meeting place where they were going to ask us who did we think should be named on an All-Star team from the Negro Leagues.

Then in the hall on the way over there we saw Bowie Kuhn, the commissioner of baseball, going in. When I saw the commissioner, I said, ''This is going to be bigger than I thought.'' I asked Monte, ''Monte, what is the commissioner doing here? Is he going to sit in on this?'' he said, ''Well, he might, I don't know. He just wants to sit in on the meeting and hear who is named for the All-Star team from the Negro Leagues. Come on, let's go over there.''

So we went over there to the other room and went in. And there was Frank Gifford and about fifty to seventy-five folks sitting down there, and all those lights around. And I said, ''Monte, what are they going to do now? What are you getting ready to do?'' he said,

"Well, they're going to see what they can do about this issue. You know how they have been talking about how they're going to put blacks into another room at the Hall of Fame, back there in the back somewhere. They just want to hear what's said and make a record of who you all want to go into the Hall of Fame. We're going to name Josh Gibson to the Hall of Fame." That's what I thought they were going to discuss, that part of it, too.

So they kept on getting everything ready and had the platform up there. The commissioner was up there on the platform. Frank Gifford was up there, too. Then they told me, "Hey, Buck, you come on up here a minute. We want you to sit up here on the rostrum." I was sitting down there with Monte. They said, "Monte, you come on up here, too." I asked Monte, "Why do they want me to sit up there on the rostrum?" He said, "Well, go on up there, and we'll straighten that out a little later. They want to ask you some questions about Josh Gibson. You played with him for nine years and you ought to know a few things about him."

So I went up on the rostrum with Monte and we sat down. I looked and there's Roy Campanella up there. They said, "We need Roy Campanella up there." Then they called Larry Doby. They told him to come up there. So they got all of us up there on the rostrum. After the commissioner got everybody kind of quiet and got the TV lights straightened out, he said, "We have met here for a very important announcement. The induction committee has seen fit to name Josh Gibson to the Baseball Hall of Fame in Cooperstown, New York." And everybody clapped. Then the commissioner said, "The committee has also seen fit . . ."

And I started sweating. I had a new shirt, and sweat was meeting right under my chin and dropping down on my shirt. And when he said, "The committee has also seen fit to nominate Buck Leonard for the Baseball Hall of Fame," I was speechless. All the cameras started clicking and all the lights went on and I was already sweating. Everybody gathered around to shake my hand. The lights were getting brighter and I was sweating a little harder and everybody congratulated me. So Frank Gifford said, "Buck, aren't you going to say something?" I said, "Well, I don't have anything to say. I just want to thank everybody, and that's all. Somebody ask me a question and maybe I can answer that." Then they began to ask questions. They asked me things like, "How do you feel?" And questions like that. So that's the way it was at the announcement ceremony in New York City.

I told Larry Doby, "I don't want to wake up and realize I just dreamed this." It was the most uplifting feeling I've ever had. It was the greatest moment of my life, at that time, being selected to the Hall of Fame.

On February 17, 1972, I sent a letter to the members of the Hall of Fame Selection Committee, saying, "I wish to thank each member of the selection committee for selecting me along with Josh Gibson to be enshrined in the Baseball Hall of Fame for 1972. This honor will be cherished by me for the rest of my life. Again I thank you."

The actual induction ceremonies took place about six months later, at Cooperstown, New York, on August 7, 1972. In my acceptance speech I told about how Monte tricked me and said some other things. I don't remember all I said, but I talked about the contributions that we in the Negro League had made, and what a thrill it was to be inducted into the Hall of Fame. And I closed my speech by saying, "It is nice to receive praise and honor from men, but the greatest praise and honor comes from our Lord and Savior Jesus Christ."

There were so many great players from the Negro Leagues who deserve Hall of Fame recognition. Satchel was the first one, inducted in 1971. Recently, Leon Day missed by one vote, and we're hoping that he makes it next year. We haven't had but two inducted since 1977.

The last ones going in were Rube Foster in 1981 and Ray Dandridge in 1987. I think they deserved it. I played against Dandridge, and I know about him. But Rube Foster is different. I didn't know him and I didn't ever see him play. When I got in the Negro Leagues, he was dead. All I know is what I heard said about him. When I started, a fellow named Cole, an undertaker, had the Chicago American Giants. So I heard all them fellows talk about how good Foster was as a player and as a manager and everything.

There are some blacks in there that I didn't see play. I didn't see John Henry Lloyd. I saw Oscar Charleston play, but he was over the hill when I saw him. He was still playing around first base when I came in, and he could still hit. But I saw Satchel Paige play, and Josh Gibson and I were on the same team together. I played with Coal Papa Bell for four or five years. I played *with* Martin Dihigo and I played *against* him. And I played *for* him in Cuba and in Mexico, when he was managing. Judy Johnson was with the Crawfords when I first came into the league, and he was still one of the better players at that time.

They say that they have not closed the Hall of Fame to players from the Negro Leagues. I'm not on the Hall of Fame committee for old-timers, but Monte Irvin and Buck O'Neill are on the Veterans Committee. Roy Campanella was on there, too, before he died. They don't remember the real old-timers, and they ask us to recommend somebody. Monte Irvin asks us every year what old-timers should be in the Hall of Fame. Each year he asks who you would recommend for nomination.

In 1981 I sent twenty-five names. That was the year Rube Foster went in. I put down first, second, third, fourth best, right on down the line. Campanella, Judy Johnson, and Cool Papa all did the same thing. Satchel didn't cooperate much. We send Monte ten or fifteen names that we think ought to be recommended for the Hall of Fame each year. In 1982 and 1983 I sent Monte about fifteen names that I thought were deserving, ranked in order from one right on down the line.

And Monte called me and said, "Look, you better get some western players on there because those guys are raising sand out there. Because we're not naming somebody from the Negro American League." And I sent him another list with two or three of them names. And there's something else, you can't pick all the same position. They want you to mix them up. That's what we try to do. And when we send the names to Monte, he and Campanella and O'Neill select who they think deserves it out of that group.

Smokey Joe Williams, Willie Wells, Dick Redding, Biz Mackey, and Bullet Rogan. Those are the top five that I think should be in the Hall of Fame. Maybe not in that order. If the living players were elected, they would have a greater impact than the dead ones. Once you name a dead player, that's the end of it. But if you name a living one, then you will have a new one every year. That's what they told us up there in Cooperstown in 1981.

We finally got Ray Dandridge in there. That was in 1987, and we haven't had another one since then. Leon Day deserves it, and I think he's going to be the next one.

Before he passed away, Willie Wells was at the top of the list of the living prospects. Wells died in 1989 in Austin, Texas. Mackey's dead. Redding is dead. Turkey Stearnes died in 1979. He's another one who's supposed to be good. But I think a lot ought to be put in before him. Some of them old-timers like Rogan. When I saw Rogan he was in his forties and over the hill, but he was still out on the field. He had quit pitching, but he was a good hitter and was playing right field then. I never did see him pitch. I just know what they said about how he could play.

Another pitcher that a lot of people think should be in the Hall of Fame is Willie Foster. I batted against him and he was a good left hander, but not as good as Slim Jones. But Foster is dead now, too. He died in 1978 down in Lorman, Mississippi.

In picking an all-time team from the Negro Leagues, I lean toward the best players during my time, the ones I saw play myself, not just those I heard about. Catching is Josh Gibson. Biz Mackey was second and Campanella third. I pick Gibson for his bat and his catching, and Mackey for his brain. Mackey had seen his good days before I saw him. His best years were back in the twenties.

Most people put me on the team at first base, but I won't talk about myself here except to stay that I always had confidence in my ability. I'll pick Piper Davis and Buck O'Neill for second and third place. Mule Suttles and Ben Taylor were both good first basemen, Suttles for his hitting and Taylor for his hitting *and* fielding. I never saw Taylor until he was through, but he could still hit even then. Mule could hit the ball as far as anybody, but he wasn't such a good fielder.

I would say Sammy T. Hughes was the best second baseman I ever saw. Sammy T. could field and hit, and I would take him over anyone else. I'll put George Scales on the second team. Martin Dihigo has to go somewhere and, although it's not his best position, I'll pick him next. Now, they talk about Bingo DeMoss, but I never did see him play. He was through when I played. Dick Seay was a good fielder but he had no bat. The Kansas City

Monarchs had Newt Allen, and he was a good ballplayer, but I never saw him in his prime.

At shortstop I would take Willie Wells. He could field and run and hit. They talk about John Henry Lloyd, and I never saw him play, but I have to put him next. Dick Lundy was another great shortstop, who could hit and field. But I would take Wells and Lloyd over him and put him third. Now, Beckwith played shortstop some, and he was a good hitter, but I never saw him that much.

I would have to take Dandridge at third base. Judy Johnson was a good third baseman, and they say that Oliver Marcelle was, too, but I never did see him play. I'll take Judy for the second team. Boojum Wilson could hit, but his defensive play didn't compare to these others I named. I think the Radcliffe brothers were all right, but I wouldn't consider them as top-notch ballplayers, either one of them. Alex was a third baseman, and he played mostly in the West. I'll put Howard Easterling of the Grays on the third team over the others I named.

In the outfield, I would have to put Oscar Charleston. Everybody knew Charleston, of course. Everybody I hear talk anytime says that Charleston was the greatest. He was playing first base when I saw him, but he could still hit, and they say when he was in his prime, he was as good as Willie Mays in center field. And I have to put Cool Papa in there somewhere. They were both center fielders, but I can't leave out Cool Papa. I'll put him in left field.

The other outfielder would be Turkey Stearnes, who played for the Detroit Stars, or Bill Wright of the Baltimore Elite Giants. They both could hit, field, and run. I saw more of Wright than I did of Stearnes, but I think I would have to go with Stearnes, because he had more home-run power, so I'll put Stearnes in right field.

I would put Sam Jethroe in the second outfield with Wright and Rap Dixon. When I saw Rap, he was past his peak, but he could still play ball. The same is true for Fats Jenkins. They were good ballplayers, but they were really in their prime in the twenties. I never saw them play in their prime.

I'll still put Jenkins on the third team. Some other outfielders who go back farther were Chaney White and Clint Thomas. And I only heard about Cristobal Torriente and Pete Hill, who both played in Chicago for Rube Foster's teams. Everybody said that they were great, and I'm going to put Hill on the third team, too. Now, Monte Irvin and Willard Brown were both good and they deserve consideration, but I don't think I can take any of the first three I named off the team. I'll pick Monte for the last spot in the third outfield.

We all go along with Satchel Paige being our best pitcher. I'll take a teammate on the Grays, Raymond Brown, as the second pitcher, and I'll pick Leon Day for the third pitcher. Other good pitchers when I was playing were Hilton Smith and Bill Byrd. That's from when I was playing. Any of them could go in the Hall of Fame. Day is the only one still living.

There were others who were good pitchers. When I saw Smokey Joe Williams and Dick Redding, they were over the hill. Those fellows were really pitching back in the twenties, and I don't know about them. Smokey Joe Williams quit the year before I entered the Negro Leagues, and Dick Redding was over the hill when I played with him. So was Bullet Rogan, who played out West and who was already gone when I came in.

Slim Jones didn't pitch long enough to be included. Both Willie Foster and Rube Foster were star pitchers, and I saw Willie, although he played mostly out West. He was better than Hilton Smith. They say José Mendez was good, but I never saw him. He pitched from 1908 to 1926. Now they talk about a left-hander named Luis Padron, a Cuban, and they say he was a good pitcher, but I never did see him either. He played from 1909 to 1926.

Everybody said that Rube Foster and C. I. Taylor were great managers, but I never saw them. I would have to take Oscar Charleston as the manager for my team.

As long as the rules governing the Veterans Committee remain the same, it will be hard to get the deserving players from the Negro Leagues into the Hall of Fame. A whole lot of them should be in the Hall of Fame or should get more recognition than they do get. I think more players from the Negro Leagues should be nominated than have been in the past.

There are a lot of good white ballplayers that deserve to be in the Hall of Fame, too, and who have been overlooked. Before he was inducted in 1985, Enos Slaughter had been overlooked. Enos is from Roxbury, North Carolina, and I know him pretty well, now. I never played against him and didn't know him until one day several years ago, when we rode the same plane to Atlanta for an old-timers' game and rode back.

That was before he went into the Hall of Fame, and there was only two things he talked about, his tobacco and those SOBs in Cooperstown won't put him in the Hall of Fame. He'd be going along all right and everybody just joshing and him autographing and somebody would say something about the Hall of Fame. That was just like spitting in his face. Somebody would just ask, "Hey Enos, when do you think they're going to put you in the Hall of Fame?" And that started it. He'd say, "I don't give a damn about those SOBs and I don't care if they won't ever put me into the Hall of Fame. I'm just forgetting about it."

After he was elected to the Hall of Fame we were on the same plane again going somewhere, and he was getting handshakes and everything. He used a few cusswords about these so-and-sos, saying it took them a hell of a long time to make up their minds about him. You know, he had been pestered about it so much and so long, I guess he was just in a habit of saying those things. His personality might have had something to do with it taking so long to get into the Hall of Fame. I was glad to see him get elected.

The same year Enos went in, Arky Vaughan went in, too. I saw Arky Vaughan play a lot of times because he was playing with the Pirates when I was with the Grays, and both of our teams were based in Pittsburgh. He was one of the better shortstops in the league and could hit, too. I saw him play in the All-Star game in 1939. We were going to play that night, so I had the day off and went out to Yankee Stadium to see the All-Star game. In the sixth inning of the game, the bases were loaded and Bob Feller was pitching, and Arky Vaughan came up and hit a solid ground ball to Charlie Gehringer at second base, and he threw the ball to Joe Cronin, who was playing shortstop for the American League All-Stars, and they made a double play and the game was over. The American league won, 3–1. I kidded Joe Cronin about that before he passed away, and he always laughed right back.

That year both of the players selected by the Veterans Committee deserved it, but some people say that there is too much politics involved in their choices. I know there are many players from the Negro Leagues who keep getting overlooked for some reason. And there are others who don't deserve to be considered for various reasons.

There was one player who was a good pitcher, but they say he cheated. He would throw a cut ball or some other illegal pitches. Now, whether he did or not I don't know. I have played on the same team with him, and if he threw it I didn't know anything about it. If he *did* throw a cut ball, then he shouldn't be considered for the Hall of Fame. The fellows in the Negro Leagues know who I'm talking about, but I'm not going to call any names, because I'll be criticized for that.

I have a higher regard for fastball pitchers than for junkball pitchers. Even now, fastball pitchers are recognized more so than curveball pitchers. A good example was this fellow J. R. Richard, a few years ago. He had a stroke and they gave him all those operations. They wouldn't have given him all that consideration had he not been a fastball pitcher. Had he been a junkball pitcher, they would have given up on him when he had his stroke.

I've already mentioned Satchel and Slim Jones and how fast they were. Now, Dave Barnhill was a fast pitcher. He had a fast-ball, a curveball, and he could get it all over the plate. But Barnhill was kind of brief. What I mean by brief is, he pitched in the Negro Leagues for some time, but not as long as some of the others. Booker McDaniels, who pitched for the Kansas City Monarchs, was about as fast as Barnhill. Another boy, named Frank Bradley, pitched for the Kansas City Monarchs and might have been a little faster than Barnhill. Another fellow, named Big Red Blake, who used to pitch for the New York Cubans, might have been about as fast as Barnhill. They were the few fellows who were fast. Now, they may not have had a good curveball or good control, but they could throw hard. We had better pitchers but not faster pitchers.

I just hope that the deserving players from the Negro Leagues begin to get in the Hall of Fame with the rest of us. I don't understand why they keep passing over them every year.

# Chapter 26

## Vanishing Shadows (1981–94)

*We get together and somebody says, "Where's so-and-so?" And one of us says, "Oh, he passed." Then somebody else calls a name and another player says, "Well, he's passed, too." Then somebody calls another name and they say, "He's gone, too." Then we say, "It's time to change the subject!"*

*—Johnny Davis, Newark Eagles*

In the last ten or twelve years, it seems like we're losing a lot of players. It's been just a little over ten years since Dave Barnhill passed. I had seen him up at the Ashland reunion in 1981. And then about a year later he got sick. I knew him from the time that we played semipro ball together, right on up through the Negro Leagues and until the day he died.

I knew that Barnhill was bad sick. Barnhill was up here the summer before he died. His wife called and said that Barnhill was ailing and to come down there to his home in Greenville. So I went down there and stayed all day with him. He stayed in Greenville for about a week with his cousins and folks, and then he went back to Miami. Then I heard that a boy named Jarvis Banks,

who used to pitch around here at Rocky Mount, went down there
to see Barnhill when he was in the hospital. All of us came up
together right around here in North Carolina, and he called me
from Tarboro, North Carolina, and said Barnhill was pretty bad
sick. He had been in the hospital since June, but was out of the
hospital then and on some kind of machine, but he was in a lot
of pain.

I talked to his wife a few days before he died, and again after
I learned that he had passed. She said they were going to leave
Miami Friday morning and come into Greenville to the funeral
parlor Saturday morning at nine o'clock. And then have a graveside rite. I told her that I would meet her at the undertaker's place
Saturday about ten o'clock. I went to his cousin's house, and the
cousin said, "Monte Irvin and some of the ballplayers are here.
They're staying at the Holiday Inn." I said, "Well, I'm going to
see the fellows, and I'll meet you at the funeral home."

I left the cousin's house and went by the undertaker's house.
Then I went on to the Holiday Inn and there were about ten
ballplayers there. Monte, Parker, Israel, Harvey, Dandridge, Leon
Day, myself, and some others. We left the motel and went to the
undertaker's place to go out to the cemetery. But it was raining,
so they decided to have the ceremony in the funeral home rather
than to have a graveside rite. So the preacher preached the ceremony right in the funeral home. Then all of us went out to the
cemetery. Six of us were pallbearers, and they had the burial and
went back to the church. All of us ate at the funeral home and
had some pictures made with Barnhill's wife and daughter. Monte
was going to stay there all night and the rest of us left and went
back home.

Several other players have passed in recent years. Satchel, Judy,
and Cool Papa. And Chet Brewer and Bob Harvey. He was at the
Meadowlands about two years ago. More recently Jimmie
Crutchfield and Jimmy Hill passed, and then Roy Campanella and
Quincy Trouppe, too. Ray Dandridge died in February of 1994,
and there are more that I can't think of right now. We're all
getting older. There's not many of us left. I'm eighty-seven and I
hope I can make it to ninety.

I've always made my home here in Rocky Mount when I wasn't

off somewhere playing ball. I've seen the town change quite a bit.
Not only in size. I've seen some changes in other ways, too. I
took an interest in the civil rights movement, but not a prominent
interest. Things are better now than they were back then. At first
there was some racial unrest when they integrated the schools.
They closed the colored high school here and sent all the black
children to the white high school. And they sent most of the black
teachers over there. And the principals were the same principals
as at the white high school and not the black principals and there
were one or two black teachers that lost their job when they integrated. But they finally gave them jobs at other schools.

Now the city has even dedicated a baseball park in my name.
Buck Leonard Park is a Little League field and was dedicated
about twenty years ago, about the time I went into the Hall of
Fame in 1972.

I used to go to see baseball games as often as I could. But
since the Washington Senators have been out of the league, I
haven't been as often. Up until my stroke, I still went occasionally,
but I don't go to see games much anymore. The last regular season
game I *did* see was a minor-league game, when I went to see
Michael Jordan play at Raleigh. They've got a team in the league
and Birmingham came there to play.

I only saw him that one time, for about six or seven innings.
That's all I saw him, and I would have to see him more times
than that to have an opinion about his baseball abilities. I didn't
see him against left-handed pitchers *and* right-handed pitchers. I
don't know how he'll do in baseball. He's trying. He's got his
eye on the ball and he's hitting all right. But whether he can hit
good enough for the major leagues or not I don't know. It's too
early to say about him. Sometimes the pitchers have to see a batter
a few times before they learn how to pitch to him. He's got a
little more to learn. He might be able to make the major leagues
in a couple of years, but I don't think he's going to keep playing
baseball that long. However, ballplayers fool you nowadays. Jordan was a great basketball player and played here at the University
of North Carolina. But he gained his recognition as a basketball
player, not a baseball player.

And now they've got a girls' baseball team that completed their

first season in 1994. They're called the Silver Bullets, but I'd
never even heard about them before. I don't really think girls can
play against men at a major-league level. I know, for a while, the
Clowns had a girl playing with them just to draw a crowd, but I
never played against them then. That was while I was in Mexico.

Now I mostly watch baseball on TV. I like to watch the Braves'
games. I thought they were going to go all the way in 1994 but
that was before the strike. They may be as good as the Yankees
used to be. They've got good pitching and some pretty good left-
handed power hitters. Justice, McGriff, and Klesko were all doing
pretty good. We'll have to wait and see what happens after the
strike.

The 1994 All-Star game was played at Three Rivers Stadium
in Pittsburgh and I was the honorary captain of the National
League team. Phil Rizzuto was the honorary captain of the American League team, and my team won. I met a whole lot of ballplayers and I had a good time. I was supposed to throw out the first
pitch before the game, but they had Willie Stargell do it instead.
I don't know what happened but, for some reason, they changed it.

It was only about a month after the All-Star game that the
players went on strike. It looks like they're going to stay out. We'll
just have to see what the players do and what the management is
going to do. I don't think they're going to play any more baseball
this year. I think the management is just going to wait them out.
I want to side with the ballplayers, but they're making more
money now than we ever thought they would make. The more
they get the more they want. If I was making a million dollars a
year, I would not go on strike. I don't know what they're going
to do about it.

I don't go anywhere much anymore. I've slowed down a lot. I
didn't go to Cooperstown this year. I'm not feeling so good now.
I have some good days and I have some bad days. And I don't
know how I'm going to be feeling. From day to day.

About ten years ago, when I was semiretired, Monte Irvin
wanted me to go to Florida with him, but I told him that I had
four rabbit dogs to keep me from going. They were beagle hounds
and I raised them all from pups. They were all born right out in
my backyard, and I was still raising those beagle hounds when I

had the stroke in 1986. Before then, I stayed active. I spent my time rabbit hunting, squirrel hunting, and deep-sea fishing. That was most of my recreation then. And trying to sell a little real estate. But that's work. I don't do any of that now.

In looking back at my career, I'd say my baseball playing got me recognized as a ballplayer and got me elected to the Hall of Fame in Cooperstown. That has affected my life in some ways, not financially so particularly much, but to regard folks and for them to regard me. I found out that there are folks who will have a little more respect for you if they feel you live a clean, decent life. Whereas, had I not been elected to the Baseball Hall of Fame, a lot of people wouldn't have known me and I wouldn't have had a chance to meet a lot of folks like the commissioner and the folks from Cooperstown.

If I could have changed anything, with the way I feel now, I wouldn't have played as long as I did. I don't have anything that I could say baseball was the cause of. There's no ailment that I have now that I could put to baseball. And I don't have any bad habits now that I could say baseball was the cause of. And I don't know any baseball player I hold anything against from when I was playing baseball. I know that. If I had to pick a life again to play for fun and for money, I'd pick baseball. I enjoyed the game. The game was good to me, and I don't have any regrets about playing baseball.

There's one thing that I do regret and that is I didn't get as much formal education as I would have liked. During the winter when I was not playing baseball, I should have been going to school, getting an education. My education is limited and I regret that I didn't go farther in school than I did.

I would like to be remembered as playing the game, and playing it clean and hard. And for having the respect of the fans and letting the other ballplayers know that I regard them as ballplayers, too. And that I wasn't out there to jeopardize a fellow's living because I was also living at that time, and I think that his life and his livelihood was just as important as mine. And I would like to have seen all the ballplayers live a decent and clean life and represent baseball in a positive way.

I'm just going to live a quiet, decent life from now on. I'm going to go around a little and meet some folks and that's just about it. My back has been bothering me for a long time. I've had it X-rayed four or five times and there's nothing they can do. It's just the arthritis. But I'm eighty-seven years old and everything hurts when you get old.

I had a stroke April 4, 1986, and I was in the Regional Rehabilitation Center in Greenville, North Carolina, for a few weeks. The stroke affected my right side. I went home around the middle of the month for a few hours but went back. They said it would take about four to six weeks for rehabilitation. I went home again around the middle of May and I felt pretty good after I got back home. My right arm was out of whack and the doctor said that I would be like that for some time and then I'd be getting better. They said in the course of time, I could be okay. I expected to get better and I did improve some. Sometimes it takes three or four years. But that was seven years ago. I still can't use my right arm much and my speech is a little slurred since the stroke.

I underwent therapy and some of the use of my right hand returned, but I had to learn to write with my left hand. If you're right-handed, it's hard to write with your left hand. They said that it would get better, but it's getting worse. It has affected my short-term memory, too, and I'm having more difficulty getting around. My present wife, Jean, and I were married about three months after my stroke, on July 7, 1986. We go to the same church, but we were married at home.

When I was growing up in Rocky Mount, there was a Sunday school teacher named W. E. Gay who was especially important to me. He was a nice gentleman and a *good* person. After I got back home I started teaching a Sunday school class of boys about eight or ten or twelve years old—about the same age that I was when I was in his class. I reckon I taught the class for two or three years, until I started playing winter baseball. But when I would come back home in the fall, when I was going to stay here, I would teach them. I would rather teach them at that age.

That's the age group that I taught just about all the time. I enjoyed that. They had heard about how I played baseball, and they believed what I told them, whereas the grown-ups might not have believed what I told them. But every year, when I went away to play ball, they had to get somebody else to take my place anyway, so I just quit teaching that class.

But I still went to church, because I missed it so much when I was off playing ball. As long as I played ball, I'd get back to church when I came back to Rocky Mount in the off-season. When I played winter ball in Cuba, Puerto Rico, or South America, I sometimes went to church there. But they were singing foreign music, and I didn't know what they were saying. One winter in Havana, I went three or four times to an American church where they spoke English. But I was always glad to get back to Rocky Mount.

I went to Sunday school until I had the stroke. We had a men's class from fifty years of age on up, and I was the president or secretary of my Sunday school class for a long time. I've been at St. James Baptist Church here in Rocky Mount for about seventy years.

Even after the stroke, I used to get out and go to Sunday school and church about every other Sunday. But since the last operation, I don't go to church anymore. I'm home every day. I can't do things for myself and I don't want to be a burden. The pastor, Reverend Charles Bullock, has been an encouragement. He comes by here to visit with me.

My faith in God and in Jesus is strong. I've tried to live my life in such a way as to serve the Lord. I just felt like it was *right* to serve Him. I would tell anyone, "Be close to the Lord." My favorite Bible verse is, "Make a joyful noise unto the Lord, all ye lands. Serve the Lord with gladness. Come before his presence with singing." That's the beginning of the One-hundredth Psalm.

I don't know what the future holds for me. Well, at eighty-seven, I don't have much future. My den here at home is filled with photos and awards that I've collected over the years. I don't know what's going to happen to all of it after I'm gone. I told everybody that I didn't care what they did with all this stuff. I'm not going to worry about it—I'm going to heaven.

# Buck Leonard's Hall of Fame
# Acceptance Speech

First I'd like to thank all of the various committees and the commissioner for selecting me as a candidate for the Baseball Hall of Fame. It was something that I'd never dreamed about, something I'd never think would happen, for we in the Negro Leagues weren't eligible to even take part in the Hall of Fame ceremonies.

In our leagues we played mostly for the fun of it—and a little money. The reason why it was so far from us, first we had to get into the major leagues and also play ten years in the major leagues and qualify, that is, to receive enough votes from the committees to be eligible to be selected for the Baseball Hall of Fame. That was so far from us in the Negro Leagues until we just would read about the Hall of Fame and that's all. Sometimes we used to criticize the Hall of Fame for selecting various players for the Hall, and we made our selections for the Hall of Fame. However, we had fun and we enjoyed doing that.

The greatest moment until the present time of my life was in February in New York City. Monte Irvin, who works in the commissioner's office, called and asked would I come from North Carolina to New York to select an All-Star Negro team from the old Negro Leagues. I told him, "Yes, I would be happy to."

I arrived in New York on a Monday afternoon, called, and he

came over and said, "Stay here and I'll pick you up in the morning, we're going to the meeting." He came over on a Tuesday
morning and we went across the hall in the Americana Hotel to
the meeting and we saw the commissioner standing over there. I
asked Monte, "What's he doing over here?" He said, "Well, he
wants to sit in on the meeting." Then they opened the door and
there was all those cameras, men, lights, and I asked Monte, I
said, "What they gonna do now?" And he said, "They're going
to name Josh Gibson for the Baseball Hall of Fame."

So they were arranging the platform and after they got everything arranged, the commissioner, Campanella, Larry Doby, Irvin
on the platform, they said, "Come up here, Buck, we want you
to sit on the platform." I said, "For what?" "They're going to
ask you some questions about Josh Gibson. You played with him
nine years and you ought to know quite a few things about him."

I went up and sat on the rostrum and the commissioner began
to talk. He said—these might not be the exact words—but something like this. He said, "We have met here today to make an
announcement." He said, "The committee has seen fit to elect
Josh Gibson to the Baseball Hall of Fame.' Well, everybody
clapped. "The committee has also seen fit," and I started sweatin'.
Sweat was meetin' right under there and fallin' down on my new
suit. So then he said, "They have also seen fit to select Buck
Leonard for the Hall of Fame." I was speechless. All the cameras
started clicking and lights went on and I was already sweatin'. So
they said, "Say something." I said, "I don't have anything to
say. Somebody ask me a question. Maybe I can answer that." So
they began to ask questions. "How do you feel?" It was the
greatest moment of my life, being at that time selected for the
Baseball Hall of Fame.

Now, we in the Negro Leagues felt like we were contributing
something to baseball, too, when we were playing. We played
with a round ball and we played with a round bat. And we wore
baseball uniforms and we thought that we were making a contribu-
tion to baseball. We loved the game and we liked to play it. But
we thought that we should have and could have made the major
leagues and all of us would have desired to play in the major

leagues because we felt and we knew that that was the greatest game.

Sometimes we baseball players think our greatest thrill comes from something that we do on the baseball field. But my greatest thrill did not come from a home run that I hit nor a catch that I made or stealing a base. I ought not to have said that maybe. But anyway, my greatest thrill came from what somebody did for me. And that was select me for the Baseball Hall of Fame. I will do everything in my power to try to take care of this selection and this induction into the Baseball Hall of Fame.

Again I want to say this . . . it is nice to receive praise and honor from men, but the greatest praise and honor come from our Lord and Savior Jesus Christ. Thank you.

# Buck Leonard: Baseball Career Chronology

1921–32  Rocky Mount Elks/Rocky Mount Black Swans
        (semipro)

1933  Portsmouth Black Revels (semipro)
        Baltimore Stars (semipro)
        Brooklyn Royal Giants (independent)

1934  Homestead Grays

1935*  Homestead Grays
        (winter: Puerto Rico—Brooklyn Eagles All-Stars)

1936  Homestead Grays
        (winter: Cuba—Marianao)

1937*  Homestead Grays

1938*  Homestead Grays
        (winter: Cuba—All-Star team)

1939*  Homestead Grays
        (Winter: Cuba—All-Star team)

1940*  Homestead Grays
        (winter: Puerto Rico—Mayagüez)

1941*  Homestead Grays

1942  Homestead Grays

*Was selected to play in the Negro Leagues' East-West All-Star game.

1943* Homestead Grays
    (winter: California—Satchel Paige's All-Stars)
1944* Homestead Grays
1945* Homestead Grays
    (winter: Venezuela—All-Star team)
1946* Homestead Grays
1947  Homestead Grays
    (winter: Dan Bankhead's All-Star team)
1948* Homestead Grays
    (winter: Cuba—Marianao)
1949  Homestead Grays
    (winter: Venezuela—New York Stars)
1950  Homestead Grays
1951  Torreón (Mexican League)
    (winter: Mexico—Obregón)
1952  Torreón (Mexican League)
    (winter: Mexico—Xalapa)
1953  Torreón (Mexican League)
    Portsmouth (Piedmont League)
    (winter: Mexico—Xalapa)
1954  Durango (Mexican Central League)
1955  Durango (Mexican Central League)

# About the Author

James A. Riley author is a foremost authority on the history of baseball's Negro Leagues. His landmark reference volume, *The Biographical Encyclopedia of the Negro Baseball Leagues* (1994), is recognized as the most comprehensive work chronicling this era of baseball history. He has also written *The All-Time All-Stars of Black Baseball* (1983) and *Dandy, Day, and the Devil* (1987). His forthcoming books include the autobiography of Hall of Famer Monte Irvin.

He has contributed to many compilations, including *Insiders Baseball* (1983), *Biographical Dictionary of American Sports: Baseball* (1987), *The Ballplayers* (1990), *Baseball Chronology* (1991), and *Biographical Dictionary of American Sports: 1989–92 Supplement* (1991). He has also contributed to *The Baseball Research Journal* (1981, 1982, 1985, 1991), *Oldtyme Baseball News* (1989–94), *Negro Leagues Baseball Museum Yearbook* (1993–94), and *Athlon Baseball* (1994); has served as an editor of the Negro Leagues Section of *The Baseball Encyclopedia* (1990); continues as a regular writer for *The Diamond* (1993–94); and is the editor and publisher of the *Black Baseball Journal*. In 1990 and 1994 he was a recipient of the *SABR—Macmillan Research Award* for his scholarship on the Negro Leagues.

Counted among his forebears are frontiersman Daniel Boone, President Andrew Johnson, and an obscure Cherokee named Crow. The transplanted Tennessean has made the Sunshine State his home since graduating from college in 1961. He and his wife, Dottie, reside in Rockledge, Florida.